D0303889

Thinking
Straight

OXFORD BROOKES
UNIVERSITY
LIBRARY

00 787707 05

Thinking Straight

The Power, the Promise, and the Paradox of Heterosexuality

EDITED BY

CHRYS INGRAHAM

Routledge
New York • London

Published in 2005 by
Routledge
270 Madison Avenue
New York, NY 10016
www.routledge-ny.com

Published in Great Britain by
Routledge
2 Park Square
Milton Park, Abingdon
Oxon OX14 4RN, U.K.
www.routledge.co.uk

ACC. NO. 7 8 7 7 0 7 0 5 FUND HDCM
LOC ET CATEGORY STAN PRICE 16.99

1 2 JUL 2006

CLASS NO 306. 764 THI

OXFORD BROOKES
UNIVERSITY LIBRARY

Copyright © 2005 by Taylor and Francis Books, Inc.

Routledge is an imprint of the Taylor and Francis Group.

Printed in the United States of America on acid-free paper.

10 9 8 7 6 5 4 3 2 1

All rights reserved. No part of this book may be printed or utilized in any form or by any electronic, mechanical or other means, now known or here-after invented, including photocopying and recording, or any other information storage or retrieval system, without permission in writing from the publisher.

Library of Congress Cataloging-in-Publication Data

Thinking straight : the promise, the power, and the paradox of heterosexuality/edited by Chrys Ingraham.
     p. cm.
Includes bibliographical references and index.
ISBN 0-415-93272-6 (hardback : alk. paper) – ISBN 0-415-93273-4 (pbk. : alk. paper) 1. Heterosexuality. 2. Heterosexism. 3. Social stratification. 4. Homophobia. 5. Sexual orientation – Public opinion – United States. I. Ingraham, Chrys, 1947-
HQ76.4.T45 2004

                    2004008749

To Eileen
Muse, Mentor, Model

Contents

The Promise

Acknowledgments

This collection would not have been possible had it not been for the significant cooperation of its contributors. To all who participated, I owe a debt of gratitude. Steve Seidman, my friend and my mentor, has shown me the light on more occasions than I can count and I am forever grateful for his love and respect.

As I worked to complete this book, one person's absence in the closing days of this project became glaring. For all the years of patience, expertise, guidance, and friendship, as well as for her significant belief in the importance of this work, I will always hold Ilene Kalish in that esteemed place of Editor Extraordinaire.

And to Eileen Brownell, who through it all remains my guide, my best friend, my greatest inspiration, and my partner in crime.

Thinking Straight was a labor of commitment to a position that is frequently misunderstood. To all who helped to make this possible, contributors, editors, significant others, I thank you, from the bottom of my heart.

Introduction: Thinking Straight

CHRYS INGRAHAM

While she may have been a precocious child, Molly, at the ripe old age of 11 had figured it all out. She returned home from school one day and exclaimed to her mother, "I get it now, Mom! It's like a grid! You ask a boy to go with you and if he says yes, you're in. Then you dump him and you become more popular!" Of course, Molly's mom took her daughter very seriously and considering her age asked how she planned to go out with this boy. Molly replied, "Oh mom, you're so old-fashioned. You don't actually go out, it's just a phrase!" What this organic sociologist had discovered by sixth grade was an institution or patterned set of social behaviors and rituals we commonly understand as heterosexuality or in the contemporary vernacular, what it means to "be straight." By sixth grade, this young woman had developed her own heterosexual awareness—she had not only learned to *act straight,* she had also learned to *think straight.*

One of the most significant aspects of this story is that Molly was *learning* heterosexuality. She was discovering how the heterosexual world is constructed and how it operates. More importantly, she was discovering the path to heterosexual privilege or status. Of course, she was also learning that success in this world would mean leaving bodies in her wake but Molly was no shrinking violet when it came to mastering her social world.

In American society, we frequently refer to heterosexuality as something that is naturally occurring, overlooking the myriad ways we have *learned* how to practice heterosexuality, have given meaning to it, and allow it to organize the division of labor and distribution of wealth. To access the "natural" world in any objective way would require that we somehow step outside of meaning systems or cultural bias. In fact, we

1

have developed scientific and social scientific methodologies to enable us to bracket off these effects as best we can. Unfortunately, even with the best research methods, we are still unable to truly attain objectivity or to completely bracket off the ways we give meaning to our world. This is what makes understanding social phenomena as socially produced and as socially created—given meaning by our social world—so critical to understanding. For instance, in many of the debates about sexuality, we pose heterosexuality as the good, normal, and natural form of sexual expression and frame it in opposition to its socially constructed opposite, homosexuality, a term that was not coined until the turn of the twentieth century.[1] We even construct biological sex—whether one is male or female—in terms of opposites—"the opposite sex"—setting up the sexes to be completely different and as potentially in conflict with each other. This is a social priority, NOT something that is naturally occurring. While the sexes may be different they are not, in fact, opposite. The reality is that neither sexuality nor biological sex is made up of opposites; yet, our dominant meaning system imposes that structure. These are both examples of thinking straight—thinking in terms of opposites and polarities when none exist and naturalizing social practices and beliefs rather than seeing them as social, political, and economic creations.

Sexuality is highly variable over the life span. To manage this reality, we have created a set of identity categories and corresponding belief systems to produce the illusion that sexuality is fixed and unchanging and not highly organized and regulated—institutionalized. We use these categories to situate ourselves within a value system that is patterned hierarchically. This means we attach to these categories levels of acceptability and claim social status and legitimacy depending upon which level we occupy. In this heteronormative[2] system where heterosexuality becomes institutionalized[3] and is held up as the standard for legitimate and expected social and sexual relations, bisexuality is less valued and homosexuality the least valued. Additionally, within each of these levels, there are behaviors and identities that are not considered desirable. For example, consider the badly behaved heterosexual—unemployed or dependent husband, sexually or physically violent male partner, cross-dresser, polygamist, promiscuous wife, or marriage resister.

Constructed notions of sexual behavior and sexual identity have become primary organizing categories for many key aspects of social life including but not limited to marriage, family, politics, religion, work, and education. By giving primacy to sexual behavior in these arrangements, we make secondary all other factors in various human relations—intimate, platonic, or formal. In other words, as we socially and culturally create sexual behavior identities as organizing categories, we elevate relations of the body above all other terms for human interaction—mind, heart, soul, values, and so on. Sexuality or sexual behavior becomes the dominant category enabling and disabling a commodity culture that proclaims the primacy of sexuality. Consider, for example, the commonplace market mantra: "Sex sells!" Or, the obsession with Michael Jackson's sexual transgressions, most noticeable when the American media cut away to his arrest at the same moment President Bush and Prime Minister Blair were giving their first live speech in England regarding the war in Iraq. Sexuality or sex issues serve as the currency through which a host of exchange relations and social priorities are established.

Securing this primacy, various descriptive and hierarchical popular culture euphemisms have emerged. The "straight arrow" as the descriptor of a good and moral person who complies with society's rules for appropriate behavior—the "straight and narrow"—has evolved into the commonplace euphemism for heterosexual—someone who is "straight." To "think straight," then, is to comply with the prevailing meanings and ideological messages that organize heterosexuality.

Historically, the phrase "thinking straight" meant thinking clearly or logically. The paradox in the use of this metaphor to describe heterosexuality is that thinking straight rearranges the original meaning by embracing the logical incoherence, in this case, of institutionalized heterosexuality. In other words, to think straight as it is applied to sexuality is to operate inside the ideological contradiction that is the foundation of straightness. Consider the following examples:

- Thinking straight is understanding heterosexuality as naturally occurring and not as an extensively organized social arrangement or means for distributing power and wealth for male to female behavior.
- Thinking straight means believing that the world is only and has always been heterosexual—not historically or regionally variant or as a cultural invention.[4]
- Thinking straight is to confuse *institutionalized* heterosexuality with something that is naturally occurring.
- Thinking straight is using that famous heteronormative and biologically determinist retort that God did not create Adam and Steve, *He* created Adam and Eve. This argument denies the existence of sexual variation in behavior and the role of contradiction, history, and interpretation in *Biblical* references.
- Thinking straight is believing that heterosexuality is universal, the same in all societies as well as the animal world when there is substantial evidence to the contrary.

- One of my favorite examples of thinking straight is the notion that white weddings and diamond rings are heterosexual traditions and not just the effect of very successful marketing campaigns.[5]
- Thinking straight is embracing a sense of entitlement, social and economic, just by virtue of participating in married heterosexual life regardless of the ways that entitlement denies those who do not have access to equal opportunity and citizenship.
- Thinking straight is living in romance or the illusion of well-being that institutionalized heterosexuality promises not in its realities.
- Thinking straight is investing in the power and the promise of heterosexuality without examining and addressing its paradoxes.

This list represents only a sampling of possible manifestations of thinking straight. They can include everything from boy/girl seating at a party to global economic assumptions about the division of labor.

Until recently, even gender and sexuality scholars from across the disciplines studied heterosexuality as either a form of sexual behavior or as embedded within other institutions, such as marriage and family. They overlooked the ways in which ascribed behaviors for women and men–gender–actually organize the institution of heterosexuality. In other words, theory and research on male and female behavior participates in "thinking straight" or what I have defined in earlier writings as the *heterosexual imaginary*:

> [It is] that way of thinking that conceals the operation of heterosexuality in structuring gender and closes off any critical analysis of heterosexuality as an organizing institution. The effect of this depiction of reality is that heterosexuality circulates as taken for granted, naturally occurring, and unquestioned, while gender is understood as socially constructed and central to the organization of everyday life.[6]

By treating heterosexuality as normative or taken for granted, we participate in establishing heterosexuality—not sexual orientation or sexual behavior, but the way it is organized, secured, and ritualized—as the standard for legitimate and prescriptive socio-sexual behavior, as though it were fixed in time and space and universally occurring.

Beginning with the paradigm shift suggested by Adrienne Rich's landmark essay on compulsory heterosexuality,[7] scholars across the disciplines have worked to make visible the social, historical, and material conditions that institutionalized heterosexuality has preserved. One need only look at the current state of American society and popular culture to determine what interests are at stake in relation to the institution of heterosexuality.

The shifting landscape for institutionalized heterosexuality and its organizing institution, marriage, is providing fertile ground for this inquiry.

Historically, marriage as a heterosexual and patriarchal arrangement organizing the economic dependency of women and children relied both on the ideology and reality of the male breadwinner. Following the second wave of feminism, women generally, but especially middle-class women, entered the workforce in record numbers. The result is that women have gained a measure of economic independence from men, earning on average seventy-five cents for every dollar a man makes. The world of possibilities for women had expanded significantly. With these economic gains, women have become economically independent and less dependent upon marriage for their survival. The result of these changes means that the popularity of marriage today increasingly depends upon notions of romance and the marketing of the white wedding as the primary validation ritual. Paradoxically, this effort has resulted in not only securing a desire for weddings among self-identified heterosexuals but among other consumers as well, namely same-sex couples.

As these trends persist, other significant changes are also emerging, primary among them the increasing practice of older women marrying younger men. Frequently, this shift in age relations also indicates a shift in the sex of the breadwinner and with it, a shift in the ideological framing of this relation. Older women are more likely to have established jobs and careers and are more likely to earn more than their male partner. This shift indicates that men are more at ease doing domestic and childcare labor, formerly the exclusive domain of women. Women are entering higher education in greater numbers than men and are also pursuing and occupying more positions of power than ever in history. And, as sociologist Alan Wolfe has found, high divorce rates are increasingly a product of a highly business-oriented culture where issues of trust, loyalty, mobility, and downsizing have a significant effect on marriage.[8]

Perhaps the most powerful influence on the heterosexual imaginary in today's cultural world is the television programming that so contradictorily signals the changing landscape in U.S. heterosexual culture. Throughout 2003 and 2004, so-called "reality TV" shows have proliferated into a smorgasbord of real-life heterosexual romance dramas. Shows such as "The Bachelor," "The Bachelorette," "Joe Millionaire," "Meet My Parents," "Cupid," "For Love or Money," and "Who Wants to Marry My Dad," "Average Joe," "My Big Fat Fiance," have essentially escalated what was once the TV wedding spectacle into heterosexuality-as-spectator-sport or romance-as-reality.

Morning infotainment shows such as NBC's "Today Show" and its counterparts on CBS, ABC, and CNN now regularly provide competitions for on-air weddings. In each of these venues, the public votes for which lucky bride and groom they want to see get married and they vote on all the trappings for the newlyweds' wedding and honeymoon.

This hyper-heterosexual programming, conveying all the traditional rules of heterosexual practice with a few twists such as lie detector tests and million-dollar prize money has powerful competition from some less-than-mainstream (oppositional) programming. From highly acclaimed shows such as HBO's "Sopranos," "Six Feet Under," "Oz," and "Sex and the City" to mainstream offerings such as NBC's "Will & Grace," "Queer Eye for the Straight Guy," "Boy Meets Boy," or "Playing it Straight," each offer weekly fare that includes some version of same-sex sexuality as normative. Even the supporting television commercials and some magazine advertising have been propelled into regularly targeting same-sex couples. They have discovered the gay marketplace.

Add to this that the former "wedding pages" in a variety of local and national newspapers are now called "weddings and celebrations" or "weddings and unions." Most notable of these are the famous *Sunday New York Times* pages that include photographs and announcements of same-sex unions or commitment ceremonies. Even their distinctive narrative offering, "Vows," has included coverage of same-sex celebrations. *Bride's Magazine*, the leading wedding periodical in the world, is also doing a first-ever same-sex feature where a variety of wedding outlets are offering same-sex ceremony planning and products.

As the marketing of romance replaces the economic necessity for marriage, resulting in a $35 billion a year wedding industry, our beliefs about marriage have become increasingly grounded in another instance of thinking straight—the illusion that money buys commitment and longevity. All of these shifts suggest the distinct possibility that the patriarchal institution of heterosexuality and its marriage requirement is rapidly changing and becoming less compulsory.

In addition to internal changes within the institution of heterosexuality, other pressures are changing the way we look at heterosexual entitlement. The gay and lesbian rights movement has made enormous strides toward achieving equal standing under the law with their heterosexual counterparts. Incremental advances in the area of benefits to same-sex and different-sex domestic partners have been made, opening the possibility of litigation that addresses the inequities of entitlements available only to those who participate in state-sanctioned male/female marriage.

Substantial legal advances have also collectively increased the likelihood of gay and lesbian or same-sex equity. A sampling of those changes includes the recent Supreme Court ruling in *Lawrence v. Texas*, overturning sodomy laws in favor of one's right to privacy, long used as a form of discrimination against gays; the passage of a civil unions law in Vermont; the ruling from the Massachusetts Supreme Court that denial of marriage to same-sex couples is unconstitutional; numerous anti-discrimination laws protecting gays and lesbians on local and state levels; hate crimes laws prohibiting violence against gays and lesbians; and the decision on the part of the Canadian courts to allow the legalization of gay and lesbian marriage. The gradual codification of gay and lesbian rights and the growing awareness that benefits and rewards distributed on the basis of heterosexual marriage are inherently undemocratic has led to an erosion of heterosexual supremacist beliefs and practices.

Most recently, this deterioration became evident in the acts of civil disobedience on the part of government officials. The Mayor of San Francisco, arguing that the denial of marriage licenses to same-sex couples violates the state equal protection clause and his oath of office, allowed nearly 3,000 same-sex couples marriage licenses. In New Paltz, NY, the Mayor defied state laws and solemnized same-sex marriages, sanctioning marriage without benefit of state license. His argument was that he did not violate the law, rather the policies of the state health department were illegal. State and local officials from around the nation have joined in these efforts, claiming that denial of equal protection violates both state and national Constitutions.

In response to these activities and claiming the rise of an "activist" judiciary, President Bush proposed a Constitutional amendment that would preserve marriage as a relation between a man and a woman. With this act, the President of the United States and his administration forced the issue onto the national agenda during a Presidential election year, polarizing the American public, and forcing a national debate on the "sanctity" of marriage, claiming that a federal amendment is the only way to stop "activist" officials who "created confusion" by allowing for gay marriage. Thinking straight, Mr. Bush concluded his call for federal activism by reminding Americans that marriage "cannot be severed from its cultural, religious and natural roots" and that it is an "issue that requires clarity."

In the spirit of "straightening up," we must clarify what the boundaries of the real issues are in granting marriage licenses to same-sex couples. First and foremost, marriage is anything *but* "natural." It is a historically variant social arrangement originally established to secure ownership of women and children and thereby guarantee the inheritance of property. Its early history is linked to state control over private property. While governmental practices in relation to marriage vary significantly around the globe, state domestic relations laws in the United States also vary widely and are frequently in conflict with their own constitutions and with the U.S. Constitution.

The 14th amendment clearly states that:

> No state shall make or enforce any law which shall abridge the priv-
> ileges of citizens of the United States; nor shall any state deprive any
> person of life, liberty, or property, without due process of law; nor
> deny to *any person within its jurisdiction the equal protection of the
> laws.* (U.S. Constitution)

Evident from this amendment is the wording that prohibits states from
denying "any person" equal protection. To enact a marriage amendment
prohibiting same-sex marriage would not only violate Constitutional law
but would place this entire document in crisis by legalizing discrimination
on the basis of sex and/or marital status.

Second, the responsibility of the President and the Legislature is to uphold the laws of the land, specifically the Constitution. It is that very document and its requirement that church and state be separate that makes
Mr. Bush's position untenable. He cannot provide for laws that attend to
"religious" roots no matter how romantic or popular that may seem.

Third, let us be very clear about what is at stake here. This is not a
"moral" struggle but a civil challenge. *It is not about bodies.* It is about equality and privilege and how serious American citizens are about preserving
those rights, regardless of sex or marital status. To rely on biology as the de-
terminant of civil rights, is to revisit a host of constitutional cases related to
race and interracial marriage. Marriage is, in fact, a civil union. To imagine
it as otherwise is to confuse the issue with romance, religion, and fantasy. To
enact laws guaranteeing civil unions as a remedy for this crisis is to revisit
the "separate but equal" decision that brought down segregation.

Finally, make no mistake that religions will insert themselves into this debate. They have a long and dramatic investment in dominating private and familial relations for a variety of ideological reasons. There has been enormous
activity on the part of Christian religions in this debate over marriage. The
Vatican has launched what they are calling a "global campaign" against same-
sex marriage." The lengthy document they issued calls for politicians to resist
the momentum being made in the interests of same-sex marriage. Using language that will sound vaguely familiar, their document relies on *Biblical* text
and prejudiced assumptions in an attempt to insert themselves into the work
of the state. Consider the following quote from the Vatican document:

> [It should not be forgotten that there is always] a danger that legis-
> lation which would make homosexuality a basis for entitlements
> could actually encourage a person with a homosexual orientation to
> declare his homosexuality or even to seek a partner in order to
> exploit the provisions of the law.[9]

While this papal document is most notable for its stand against the sanctity of same-sex marriage, it is even more remarkable for its interference in the business of the state and for its glaring omission of the word *love*. Ironically, the language used in this quote mirrors the language used when the U.S. Congress was attempting to eliminate welfare benefits for poor unwed teenagers, claiming that they would get pregnant just so they could access social service benefits. Neither assertion is based in fact.

Pat Robertson and the Christian Broadcasting Network have launched "Operation Supreme Court Freedom," a national prayer campaign to alter the Supreme Court. Claiming that the Court is an example of the "tyranny of an unelected oligarchy," Robertson accuses the Justices of historically distorting the reading of the Constitution by upholding the separation of church and state and an individual's right to privacy. It is these decisions that provided women with protections from state interference in the abortion question and gays protections from state interference in consensual, private sexual behavior. In his campaign against gay rights, Robertson makes a variety of inflammatory and unfounded claims, and asks his followers to pray for the resignation of three justices who have been illness-challenged so that President Bush can appoint more religiously conservative justices. With his own considerable level of distortion Robertson asserts,

> Now, the Supreme Court has declared a constitutional right to consensual sodomy and, by the language in its decision, has opened the door to homosexual marriages, bigamy, legalized prostitution, and even incest. The framers of our Constitution never intended anything like this to take place in our land. Yet we seem to be helpless to do anything about it. Why? Because we are under the tyranny of a nonelected oligarchy. Just think, five unelected men and women who serve for life can change the moral fabric of our nation and take away the protections which our elected legislators have wisely put in place.[10]

Given that this is a democracy not a theocracy and that the law of the land separates church and state, Robertson's concerns echo the fears of many who see the shifts in the historical necessity of marriage as signifying the decreasing importance of religious institutions. This is particularly important in considering whether democracy or religion (which one?) will rule the day when it comes to attending to the challenges of a culturally diverse, advanced capitalist social order.

The Episcopal Church also entered these debates with the highly contested election of the first openly gay priest, Rev. Gene Robinson of New Hampshire, as Bishop. While threatened with the disaffection of a variety of churches throughout the world who oppose the ordination of a gay Bishop, the U.S. Episcopal Church also passed a resolution stating that each diocese can decide on the inclusion of a same-sex blessing in their liturgy. Now as Bishop Robinson has taken his place as a leader in the Episcopal Church, United States, various factions have emerged, threatening to secede from the Church claiming that Robinson's election violates the scriptures and the sanctity of heterosexuality.

The social forces circulating in these debates encourage the public to think straight. In other words, these positions and discussions create illusion and contradiction, not reality and coherence. The matter of same-sex marriage is one of civil, not religious, rights and privileges. The state cannot by law legislate or participate in religious matters—separation of church and state is the law of the land. The primary role of politics in these democratic entities is to provide for the distribution of public resources and opportunities in the context of equal rights for all citizens. Until we establish that health benefits, hospital visitation, rights of inheritance, and access to a partner's social security are a matter of personal choice or citizenship *not* marital status—gay, straight, or single—this will be an issue that will never leave us no matter how much we try to set the record straight.

Considered together, all of these institutions and cultural sites signal that dramatic changes are occurring in institutionalized heterosexuality. The stakes in this cultural shift are high with major institutions such as the state and religion working to re-secure the base they have historically relied upon for their significant power. The substantial amount of activity generated by all these social forces serves as a marker of how important institutionalized heterosexuality has been. These dramatic changes will ripple through our lives for generations to come, making the emerging area of critical heterosexual studies absolutely central to understanding the impact of these changes.

If Molly were in the sixth grade today, she would most likely reflect differently on male–female relations in this hyper-heterosexual historical moment where nearly every mainstream television channel has some version of real-life hetero-sex-in-the-city programming and the very foundation of institutionalized heterosexuality—the exclusive legitimating power of marriage—is in crisis. Thinking straight in this historical moment means responding to growing pressures on the foundation and fabric of institutionalized heterosexuality from a variety of socially significant sites. In essence, the current crisis makes visible the arbitrariness of the identity categories, beliefs, and structures of heterosexuality.

Until the late 1990s, few had pursued a critical examination of institutionalized heterosexuality, one that asks "What interests are served by the way we have organized and given meaning to heterosexuality?" This volume of essays, *Thinking Straight,* contains important and pivotal works in the emerging field of critical heterosexual studies. Written by prominent academics from across the disciplines as well as from international locations, these works interrogate the meanings and practices associated with straightness—the historical, social, political, cultural, and economic dominance of institutionalized heterosexuality. By examining the power, the promise, and the paradox associated with *thinking* straight and straightness, these essays provide insight into the operation of institutionalized heterosexuality: its history, its materiality, its meaning making systems, legitimizing practices, concealed contradictions, and the interests of power it serves.

Notes

1. Katz, 1995
2. The view that institutionalized heterosexuality constitutes the standard for legitimate and expected social and sexual relations (Ingraham 1999: 17).
3. An established social order that is rule-bound, ritualized, organized, and contains standardized behavior patterns that are also ideologically produced and maintained.
4. Katz, 1995.
5. Ingraham, Chrys. 1999. *White weddings: Romancing heterosexuality in popular culture.* New York: Routledge; Otnes, Celec and Elizabeth Pleck 2003; Cindrella dreams: The allure of the lavish wedding. Berkeley: University of California Press.
6. Ingraham, Chrys. 1994. The heterosexual imaginary: feminist sociology and theories of gender. *Sociological theory* 12(2): 203–219; Jackson, Stevi. 1999. Heterosexuality in question. London: Sage.
7. Rich, Adrienne. 1980. Compulsory heterosexuality and lesbian existence. *Signs* 5: 631–660; Katz, Jonathan. 1995. The invention of heterosexuality. New York: Penguin.
8. Wolfe, Alan. 2002. *Moral freedom: The search for virtue in a world of choice.* New York: Norton; Seidman, Steven. 2002. Beyond the Closet. New York: Routledge; Richardson, Diane. 1996. Theorising heterosexuality: Telling it Straight. Buckingham: Open University Press.
9. "Congregation for the Doctrine of the Faith, Some considerations concerning the response to legislative proposals on the non-discrimination of homosexual persons," July 24, 1992, www.vatican.ca.
10. www.patrobertson.com

1
The Power

Sexuality, Heterosexuality, and Gender Hierarchy: Getting Our Priorities Straight

STEVI JACKSON

From the beginning of second-wave feminism, sexuality was identified as a key site of patriarchal domination and women's resistance to it. Since the 1970s, despite considerable political and theoretical changes within feminism, sexuality has remained a much contested issue through the "sex wars" of the 1980s to the rise of queer theory and the resurgence of feminist debate on heterosexuality in the 1990s. Central to these debates, and the heat they have generated, is the extent to which gender and sexuality are thought of as interrelated and how that interrelationship is understood. These issues continue to be contested at the beginning of the 21st century and are still of vital importance to feminism as a theoretical and political project.

As I write this, I am very aware that biological determinism is undergoing a revival, particularly in the form of the latest version of sociobiology: evolutionary psychology. This "New Darwinism" has drawn criticism from a number of feminists,[1] but it has gained a firm hold on the popular imagination and is becoming increasingly politically influential.[2] Of particular relevance here is the way in which this approach links gender to the inevitability of heterosexuality, seeing differences between women and men as ultimately reducible to the reproductive imperative: the "need" to find a mate and pass on our genes to the next generation. Other forms of biological determinism, such as those devoted to "discovering" differences in brain structure, are also in circulation.[3] Here too, gender and sexuality have been linked, for example, through the notion that gay men have "feminized" brains.[4] Biological arguments have been taken up by reformist campaigners for lesbian and gay rights, thus representing homosexuality as the innate propensity of a small, permanent minority who pose no threat to the heterosexual majority.[5] Naturalistic accounts have also been incorporated into life narratives of gay men and, to a lesser extent, lesbians.[6] In this climate it is crucial to reassert the political relevance of social constructionist analyses of gender and sexuality and to challenge the taken-for-granted view of heterosexuality as a natural, uncontestable fact of human nature. In order to make this political point effectively, we need both to critique biologistic arguments and to offer convincing alternative formulations.

This chapter is intended as a contribution to the latter project. Rather than directly engaging with biological determinism, I will take it as axiomatic that gender and sexuality *are* social phenomena in order to explore further the processes involved in their social construction. The arguments I wish to advance derive from a materialist feminist analysis, which I have been developing over the last few years.[7] Here I am defining my position not only against naturalistic perspectives, but also against those cultural analyses that neglect the social structures and routine everyday social practices through which gender and heterosexuality are constructed, sustained, and renegotiated. My intention is not to dismiss the work of cultural theorists, many of whom have contributed a great deal to the critique of gender and heterosexuality, but rather to argue for an appreciation of the variety of social and cultural structures and practices at work in the maintenance of the current gendered and heterosexual social order. If social critique has a political purpose—and I believe it still has—it is to effect change. If we are to achieve this, we must know what we are up against.

Conceptual Ground-Clearing

Underlying many of the debates about gender, sexuality, and heterosexuality are differences in the ways these terms are defined. There are differences, too, in the ways in which the social or cultural construction of gender and sexuality are understood. Hence, before going any further, I will say a little about how I use such contested terms as "sex," "gender," "sexuality," and "heterosexuality," how I understand the relationship between them, and how I conceptualize the process of social construction. Having clarified my concepts, I will survey some influential accounts of the gender–sexuality articulation and explore their implications for the analysis of heterosexuality.

I define gender as a hierarchical social division between women and men embedded in both social institutions and social practices. Gender is thus a social structural phenomenon, part of the social order, but it is also lived out by embodied individuals who "do gender" in their daily lives, constantly (re)producing it through habitual, everyday interaction. Gender, as I understand it, is an entirely social and cultural phenomenon, in no way resting on a pre-existing biological base. So-called "biological sex differences" cannot be taken for granted as given, since the recognition of them is itself a social act.[8] It is gender that enables us to "see" biological sex: it "transforms an anatomical difference (which is itself devoid of significance) into a relevant distinction for social practice."[9] While gender is a binary division, the categories it produces are not homogeneous since we live not only in a gendered world, but also one in which class, racial, national, and other distinctions intersect with gender.

If gender is used to denote all aspects of the distinction and division between women and men (and boys and girls), then "sex" can be reserved for carnal or erotic activities. "Sexuality" is a broader term referring to all erotically significant aspects of social life and social being. This usage helps to resolve the ambiguities of everyday discourse. "Sex" and "sexual" are peculiarly imprecise terms since they can refer both to differences between women and men (the "two sexes" or "the sexual division of labor") and to specifically erotic relations and practices (to "have sex" or "sexual fantasies"). This semantic slippage is no chance effect, but the product of specific cultural assumptions. At birth we are classified as one of two "sexes" (girl or boy) on the basis of assumptions made about parts of our body designated as "sex organs"; we are then expected to grow into adults who "have sex" with the "opposite sex," thus deploying our "sex organs" in the proper way. In this way, femininity and masculinity are defined as "natural" and heterosexuality is privileged as the only "normal" and legitimate form of sexuality. Theoretically and politically, we need to challenge these assumptions, to break the chain that binds (socially defined) anatomy into gender and sexuality. Conceptually, we need to know what we are talking about: if we speak of "gender relations," we know we refer to all aspects of social life, while "sexual relations" more often means specifically physical, erotic interaction.

Sexuality and gender are empirically interrelated, but analytically distinct. Without an analytical distinction between them, we cannot effectively explore the ways in which they intersect; if we conflate them, we are in danger of deciding the form of their interrelationship in advance. If, on the other hand, we ignore the empirical linkage between them, there is a danger, evident in much current theorizing, of abstracting sexuality from the social, of analyzing it as if it were separated from other socioeconomic structures and processes, uncontaminated by material inequalities. We should recognize that sexuality, as well as gender, is fully social; sexual practices, desires, and identities are embedded within complex webs of nonsexual social relations.

Heterosexuality is the key site of intersection between gender and sexuality, and one that reveals the interconnections between sexual and nonsexual aspects of social life. As an institution, heterosexuality includes nonsexual elements implicated in ordering wider gender relations and ordered by them. As I have noted elsewhere,[10] it entails who washes the sheets as well as what goes on between them. Thus, heterosexuality is not precisely coterminous with heterosexual sexuality. While heterosexual desires, practices, and relations are socially defined as "normal" and normative, serving to marginalize other sexualities as abnormal and deviant, the coercive power of compulsory heterosexuality derives from its institutionalization as more than merely a sexual relation.

How we conceptualize the interconnections between gender, sexuality and heterosexuality depends on how we understand the process of social construction. Social constructionism is not a single perspective, but a cluster of differing approaches deriving from varied theoretical roots. First, there are different degrees of social constructionism,[11] differences in the extent to which some form of sexual drive or biological difference is presupposed, and hence differences in *what* is understood as socially constructed. Here I consider it risky to assume that any aspect of sexuality or gender is innate, since this can entail placing aspects of our gendered and sexual practices beyond critique. There are also different approaches to the question of *how* gender and sexuality are constructed. Here I conceive of social construction as a multilayered or multifaceted process, requiring attention to a number of levels of social analysis. Not all of these receive the attention they should.

It is sometimes assumed that the more radically antiessentialist positions, those that hold that there is no essential pre-given basis for either gender or sexuality, derive from postmodern theorizing. This misconception results in the erasure of earlier sociological accounts of the construction of sexuality[12] and the first feminist critiques of sex–gender distinction.[13] Newer forms of social constructionism, which take such writers as Foucault and Butler as originators, are often not very social at all. Indeed, they are often emptied of the social and are better characterized as cultural constructionism. Of course the social world includes the cultural, it includes the realms of discourse and symbolic representation, but the cultural is not all there is to the social. The distinctively social has to do with questions of social structure but also situated social practices. It is concerned with meaning, both at the level of our wider culture and as meanings emerge from or are deployed within everyday social interaction. It includes subjectivity since our sense of who we are in relation to others constantly guides our actions and interactions and, conversely, who we are is a consequence of our location within gendered, class, racial and other divisions, and the immediate social and cultural milieux we inhabit.

In my recent work I have, in keeping with this picture of the social, identified four intersecting levels or facets of social construction:[14] (1) the structural, in which gender is constructed as a hierarchical social division and hetero-sexuality is institutionalized, for example, by marriage, the law, and the state; (2) the level of meaning, encompassing the discursive construction of gender and sexuality and the meanings negotiated in everyday social inter-action; (3) the level of routine, everyday social practices through which gen-der and sexuality are constantly constituted and reconstituted within localized contexts and relationships; and (4) at the level of subjectivity through which we experience desires and emotions and make sense of our-selves as embodied gendered and sexual beings.

What cultural—as opposed to social—constructionism does is to ex-clude the first level, that of structure, altogether. It then deals with mean-ing primarily at the level of culture and discourse, but ignores the meanings emergent from and deployed within everyday social interaction. Sometimes practices are included—as in Butler's (1990) discussion of per-formativity—but rarely are these practices located in their interactional or wider social setting. Finally, subjectivity is usually theorized through psy-choanalysis, which completely abstracts it from its social context; alterna-tive perspectives linking the self and the social are rarely even considered. What I am suggesting is that an understanding of gender and sexuality as fully social, as contingent upon the material conditions of our existence, must take account of all these processes through which they are con-structed. I am not proposing here some total theory of social construction wherein all these levels are welded together as a seamless whole. Such an endeavor would be ill advised and likely to produce another form of reduc-tionism. Moreover, it is difficult, if not impossible, to focus on all these lev-els at once. We do, however, need to be aware that when we concentrate on one facet of social construction, we have only a partial view of a multifac-eted process.

I will return to this framework later in the chapter, but for now it forms the backdrop to my reading of past and current debates on gender and het-erosexuality and informs my evaluation of others' perspectives.

Past and Present Debates

In the 1970s, feminists began to lay the foundations for a radical critique of heterosexuality, which emerged at the end of the decade. This early work was informed by sociological thinking on power relations within heterosexual relations and the interconnections between sexuality and other aspects of women's subordination. At this stage, however, heterosexuality was rarely named as the object of analysis so that the critique of it remained implicit, a hidden feature of feminist accounts of male dominance in marriage and sex-ual relations.[15] The connections between different elements of heterosexual-ity were later made explicit by, among others, Adrienne Rich (1980), for whom compulsory heterosexuality both kept women *in* (within its confines) and kept them *down*, subordinated. While the link thus made between the social construction of heterosexuality and the oppression of women was productive and remains an insight that should be preserved, Rich did not offer an entirely convincing account of the construction of gender and sexuality. Although "women" can be understood in her account as a socially constituted subordinate group, traces of essentialism remain in her assumption of a common womanliness uniting us all on the "lesbian continuum." While she exposed heterosexuality as a coercive imposition, she seemed to assume that lesbianism was a propensity common to all women.

Other early accounts posed a direct link between the social construction of gender and sexuality. Catherine MacKinnon (1982), for example, saw gender as a product of men's appropriation of women's sexuality. MacKinnon's argument that sexuality should occupy the same place in feminism that labor does in Marxism overprivileges sexuality, treating it as the ultimate origin of women's oppression. As Delphy (1994) has remarked in a rather different context, men may say that women are only good for one thing, but that is no reason why we should believe them. Men gain a variety of material benefits from the subordination of women, from women's domestic labor and from privileged access to jobs in gender-segregated labor markets. Gender, then, should not be reduced to an effect of sexuality.

At the other end of the spectrum were those who dissociated the study of sexuality from the study of gender, such as Gayle Rubin (1984). Explicitly constructed against McKinnon's and others' emphasis on sexuality as a site of oppression, which she saw as "sex negative," Rubin's account focused on the oppression of sexual "minorities," their exclusion from the "charmed circle" of normative, monogamous heterosexuality. This analysis should be read against Rubin's earlier work, which did indeed tie gender too closely to reproductive sexuality through the idea that every society "has a sex/gender system—a set of arrangements through which the biological raw material of human sex and procreation is shaped by human social intervention" (1975: 165). While Rubin's move away from biological foundationalism and her analytic uncoupling of gender from sexuality represent positive shifts, she went too far in denying the empirical connections between gender and sexuality. She leaves us with no means of analyzing the hierarchical social division between women and men and the institutionalization and practice of heterosexuality, or of locating the various social minorities she champions within wider social divisions. There is a world of difference between a prostitute woman working on the streets to support her children and a millionaire pornographer profiting from the global circulation of his products.

Far more convincing accounts of gender and sexuality were produced by French materialist feminists in the late 1970s and early 1980s. These feminists saw the social division between women and men as analogous to a class relationship: just as there can be no bourgeoisie without the proletariat, conceptually and empirically there could be no "women" without the opposing category, "men." As Wittig puts it: "there are no slaves without masters" (1992: 15). Gender or "social sex" is the product of a hierarchical social relationship involving the exploitation of women's labor as well as the appropriation of their sexuality.[16] In the first issue of their journal *Questions Féministes*, the editorial collective made it clear that they saw men and women as social, not biological entities. The consequences of this are indeed radical. The political goal envisaged is not the raising of women's status, nor equality between women and men, but the abolition of sex differences themselves.

This analysis of gender divisions was explicitly related to the distinction between heterosexuality and homosexuality. In a nonpatriarchal society, "the distinction between homo- and heterosexuality will be meaningless since individuals will meet as singular individuals with their own specific history and not on the basis of their sexual identity."[17] To be male or female would no longer define our social or sexual identities. This does not mean women becoming like men "for at the same time as we destroy the idea of the generic 'Woman', we also destroy the idea of 'Man'" (1981: 215), or, as Delphy later commented, "if women were the equals of men, men would no longer equal themselves" (1993: 8).

Materialist feminists subsequently became irreconcilably divided over the issue of political lesbianism, following the publication of Wittig's *The Straight Mind* in 1980.[18] Wittig's analysis of the heterosexual contract as founding the category "woman" led her to argue that lesbians, as fugitives from that contract, "are not women" (1992: 32). Others, Delphy included, felt that no women escaped from the hierarchical order that defined them as subordinate to men. These theoretical debates took place in the context of heated exchanges on lesbianism among activists in the French movement, paralleling those going on elsewhere.

In Britain, opinions polarized around a paper produced by Leeds Revolutionary Feminists: "Political Lesbianism: The Case against Heterosexuality," in which heterosexual feminists were denounced as "collaborators" engaged in "counter-revolutionary activity" (1981: 6–7). The sense of outrage and guilty defensiveness this provoked ultimately closed off avenues for any productive debate across the battle lines. In the 1980s, on both sides of the Atlantic, the terrain of disputes over sexuality shifted to the so-called "sex wars," centered on the issues of pornography and prostitution, but also taking in questions of power, eroticism and sadomasochism. As a result, there was something of a hiatus in debates on heterosexuality itself.

It was not until the 1990s that heterosexuality and its interrelationship with gender once more became the focus of academic and feminist discussion. Much of the agenda was set by queer theory, with its critique of notions of fixed sexual and gendered identities and its emphasis on destabilizing the binary divisions between women and men and hetero- and homosexualities. At the same time, however, there was also a resurgence of feminist debate on heterosexuality.[19] This time the discussion was more productive, with the critique of institutionalized heterosexuality kept distinct from the condemnation of heterosexual feminists and greater emphasis placed on disentangling the relationship between heterosexuality as institution, practice, and identity.

While there are considerable differences within and between feminism and queer, there are also some shared concerns. Both question the ways in which male-dominated heterosexuality is routinely normalized and both assume that neither gender divisions nor the heterosexual/homosexual divide are fixed by nature. Beyond this, however, their emphases diverge. Whereas feminists have historically focused on male dominance within heterosexual relations, queer theorists have directed their attention to the ways in which "heteronormativity" renders alternatives to heterosexuality "other" and marginal. An effective critique of heterosexuality—at the levels of social structure, meaning, social practice, and subjectivity—must address both heteronormativity and male dominance. Such a critique involves more than simply a synthesis of queer and feminism: it necessarily entails an understanding of gender as a hierarchical social division since this is intrinsic to heterosexuality. Where queer theorists have tended to concentrate on texts, discourses, and cultural practices, there is clearly a need for approaches that pay attention to social structures, to the socially situated contexts of everyday sexual practice and experience, and to the material conditions under which our sexualities are lived. Such an approach is essential if we are to retain feminism's focus on heterosexuality as a hierarchical relation between men and women.

The Queer Demise of Structural Analysis

> For heterosexuality to achieve the status of the "compulsory," it must present itself as a practice governed by some internal necessity. The language and law that regulates the establishment of heterosexuality as both an identity and an institution, both a practice and a system, is the language and law of defense and protection: *heterosexuality secures its self-identity and shores up its ontological boundaries by protecting itself from what it sees* as *the continual predatory en-*

croachments of its contaminated other, homosexuality. (Fuss 1991: 2;
my emphasis)

This classically queer statement could be read as a simple reiteration of the
old sociological axiom that deviance serves to police the boundaries of
normality. But more than this, Fuss is drawing our attention to ways in
which homosexuality and heterosexuality serve to define each other,
that they are coconstructed in a reciprocal, but hierarchical, relationship.
Heterosexuality in these terms is sustained by the very presence of its marginalized other, which constantly threatens to destabilize it. In terms of
Fuss's inside/outside trope, the outsider is part of the inner workings of heterosexuality; in defining itself in relation to its "outside," it thus incorporates the outside within itself, including it in its self-definition.[20] It might be
added that heterosexuality is also sustained by a silence about itself. It dare
not speak its name, for in so doing it makes evident what it keeps hidden,
that it is only one form of sexuality. Hence, heterosexuality is named by
straights only when it is felt to be under threat. "Homosexuality" (or its
more pejorative synonyms) is often mentioned in everyday straight talk,
whereas the term heterosexuality is sometimes not even understood.
Heterosexuals often do not know what they are; they do not need a name
for themselves—they are simply "normal."

Heterosexuality is not, however, sustained only by particular patterns of
speaking and silence, nor just by keeping outsiders penned within their deviant enclosures. Fuss draws a parallel with gender, and I am sure she is well
aware that both heterosexuality and homosexuality depend for their definition on gender. What she does not say—and this is indicative of Queer's
preoccupation with heteronormativity alone—is that what is fundamental
to heterosexuality, to what sustains it, in her words, "as an identity and an
institution, both a practice and a system," is gender hierarchy. Its "inside"
workings are not simply about guarding against the homosexual other, but
about maintaining male domination—and these two sides of heterosexuality are inextricably intertwined.

Other accounts effectively do away with gender inequality. In her discussion of queer desire and subjectivity, Elizabeth Grosz (1995) deals with the
blurring of the distinction between sex and gender in recent feminist theory by declaring the concept of gender redundant, replacing it with "sex,"
and focusing on its intersection with sexuality. She then defines "sex" as referring to "the domain of sexual difference, to questions of the morphologies
of bodies" (1995: 213; her emphasis) and sexuality as "sexual impulses, desires, wishes, hopes, bodies, pleasures, behaviors and practices." Gender, she
says, is redundant because "all its effects, the field that it designates, are cov-
ered by the integration of and sometimes the discord between sexuality and
sex" (1995: 213). All the differences between women and men are reduced

to "morphologies of bodies" and relations between them to the sexual. Almost the entire field of gender, as I would understand it, is erased. Who is doing the housework and raising children? Are wage differentials between women and men to be reduced to bodily morphologies?

Where gender is placed center stage in discussions of heterosexuality, this does not necessarily mean that it is understood as fully social. Judith Butler, for example, does take gender seriously, but it figures in her work more as a cultural difference than a social hierarchy. While she effectively demonstrates that gender is a construction with no necessary relationship to particular bodies or sexualities (1990) and has insisted that gender is no ephemeral, voluntaristic performance (1993), she seems unable to relate it to the social contexts of its construction. In *Bodies That Matter*, she discusses the enforced "materialization" of "sexed" bodies as coercive and constraining, but conceptualizes these processes and effects almost entirely in terms of norms—with no sense of where these norms come from, why they are effective, or how they are constituted (Ramazanoglu 1995)—and with no discussion of how they impact upon everyday social relations and practices. The social is thus reduced to the normative and what is normative goes unexplained.

More recently, Butler (1997) has questioned whether issues of gender and sexuality are "merely cultural," invoking a form of Marxism in order to explain heterosexual hegemony. In so doing she returns to Lévi Strauss's notion of the exchange of women, which, she claims, breaks down distinctions between the cultural, economic, and the social, demonstrating their interrelationship. Butler distances herself from Lévi Strauss's universalism, suggesting that queer studies might be a means of returning to critiques of the family "based on 'mobilizing an insight *into a socially contingent and socially transformable account of kinship*" (p. 276, Butler's emphasis). And what is the current structuring of gender and sexuality contingent on? Apparently, the functions that the heterosexual family performs for capitalism! Butler retreats to a functionalist and reductionist form of Marxism and tacks it on to Lévi Strauss's cultural explanation for gender division—an explanation, moreover, that presupposes what it is taken to explain, since women would have to be already defined as other and subordinate to become real or symbolic objects of exchange.

Nowhere does Butler consider the possibility that gender and heterosexuality might be structurally related to male dominance, despite her early reliance on the work of Monique Wittig for whom the heterosexual contract is fundamental to the maintenance of the patriarchal order (Wittig 1992). Whereas Wittig sees heterosexuality as founded upon the appropriation of women's bodies and labor, Butler ignores the latter and thus uproots Wittig's argument from its materialist foundation. In so doing she fails to address heterosexuality itself and the gender hierarchy internal to it; instead she seems to find heterosexuality and gender interesting only as norms against which the destabilizing possibilities of gender and sexual transgression can be asserted.[21] There seems to be an enormous gulf in her theorizing between heterosexuality's functions (for capitalism), the norms that enforce it (asserted but never fully explicated), and the performativity through which gender is produced in everyday life.

A Question of Priorities: Gender, Sexuality, and Heterosexuality

From my earliest to most recent work, I have argued for the logical priority of gender over sexuality in shaping their interrelationship. There are a number of reasons for this. First, I wished to challenge the undue emphasis given to sexuality by feminists and nonfeminists alike within Western culture. I have thus contested psychoanalytic arguments that reduce gender divisions to the direction of sexual desire as well as accounts of male domination that reduce it to men's appropriation of women's sexuality. Such accounts miss the many nonsexual ways in which gender division is sustained, such as divisions of paid and unpaid labor. Here and elsewhere I have also suggested that the existence of gender categories is what makes it possible to categorize sexual desires and identities in terms of same-gender or other-gender relationships, to distinguish between heterosexuality, male homosexuality, and lesbianism. Two qualifications are needed here. First, in according priority to gender, I nonetheless see gender and sexuality as *inter*-related, thus accepting that sexuality has effects on and implications for gender as well as vice versa. Second, the picture becomes less clear-cut when it comes to considering the relationship between gender and heterosexuality, precisely because heterosexuality encompasses more than erotic sexuality.

Part of the problem we have in thinking through the connections between gender, sexuality in general, and heterosexuality in particular is that we do not all mean the same thing by these terms and are often talking about different objects at different levels of analysis. The term "heterosexuality" can be used in relation to the erotic or to denote an institution involving a much wider social relation between women and men. "Sexuality" itself is sometimes understood primarily in terms of the hetero/homo binary, or the straight, gay or lesbian identities deriving from it, while others take it to encompass a fuller range of desires, practices, and identities. "Gender" can mean the division or distinction between women or men, whether this is seen as primarily a bodily difference or a social hierarchy, but also refers to the content of these categories, to what we understand as femininity or masculinity.

I would always opt for the broader senses of these terms because to narrow them down risks losing sight of significant portions of social life. It is on these grounds that I have been critical of such theorists as Elizabeth Grosz and Judith Butler. As I use the term gender, then, it covers both the division itself and the social, subjective, and embodied differences that give it every-day substance. Sexuality is not just a question of the maintenance of the het-erosexual/homosexual binary, but of the multitude of desires and practices that exist on both sides of that divide. Heterosexuality is not a monolithic entity, but a complex of institution, ideology, practice, and experience, all of which intersect with gender. Moreover, heterosexuality is not only a means of ordering our sexual lives but also of structuring domestic and extrado-mestic divisions of labor and resources. Hence, the intersections between gender and heterosexuality are exceedingly complex.

If sexuality as a field of inquiry entails more than the homo–hetero bi-nary, then it is crucial to retain a means of analyzing the ways in which all sexualities are gendered. If all aspects of social life are also gendered, then we need to be able to think about how this gendering process is related to heterosexuality without deciding the issue in advance. If heterosexuality as an institution is not merely about specifically sexual relations, we should consider whether the term is best confined to the actualities of social rela-tions between heterosexual couples (in and out of marital and monoga-mous relations) or might be extended to cover wider aspects of social life. For example, are gendered labor markets and wage differentials themselves heterosexual or are they simply related to the social organization of hetero-sexual life?

These issues and questions are crucial in evaluating the arguments of those who dispute the prioritization of gender from perspectives that do in-corporate broad definitions of both gender and heterosexuality.[22] I will con-centrate here on Chrys Ingraham's (1994) thesis that heterosexuality should displace gender as the central category of feminist analysis, since this is the most persuasive and consistent challenge to the primacy of gender that I have encountered. Ingraham is working within a sociological and material-ist feminist framework very similar to my own. She shares my skepticism about the sex–gender distinction and defines heterosexuality as an institu-tion that regulates far more than our erotic lives. The object of her analysis is the "heterosexual imaginary," which masks the ways in which gender has consistently been defined from a heteronormative perspective. Drawing at-tention to the construction of "women" and "men" as mutually attracted "opposite sexes," she argues that sociologists (including feminists) have failed to see the heterosexual ends to which this gender divide is directed.

As Ingraham points out, the definitions of gender employed by feminist sociologists indicate that it is a binary "organizing relations *between* the sexes." She goes on to suggest that heterosexuality "serves as the organizing institution and ideology... for gender" (1994) and is implicated in the operation of all social institutions at all levels of society, from family to workplace to the state. She asks:

> Without institutionalized heterosexuality—that is, the ideological and organizational regulation of relations between men and women—would gender even exist? If we make sense of gender and sex as historically and institutionally bound to heterosexuality, then we shift gender studies from localized examinations of individual behaviors and group practices to critical analyses of heterosexuality as an organizing institution. (1994)

Ingraham's question cannot be conclusively answered, but I do find it possible to imagine a male-dominated society that is not ordered around the heterosexual contract, while it is inconceivable that heterosexuality could exist without gender. Aside from this, I take Ingraham's point that heterosexuality is *an* organizing principle of many aspects of social structure and social life, and an important one; this has, for example, emerged from recent studies of workplace cultures,[23] but I still have my doubts about according it primacy. Defining heterosexuality so broadly that it encompasses all aspects of gendered relations, and then collapsing heterosexuality and gender into one term—heterogender—does not, for me, represent an adequate solution to the problem of conceptualizing their interrelationship. While gender and heterosexuality are so closely entwined that it is not easy to unravel their intersections, we should retain the capacity to tease out the tangled web of connections between them. Hence it seems necessary to maintain an analytical distinction between gender, as the hierarchical relation between women and men, and heterosexuality, as a specific institutionalized form of that relation.

Accepting the need to challenge the "heterosexual imaginary" and subject heterosexuality to rigorous feminist and sociological inquiry, why, given our shared theoretical perspective, do Ingraham and I come to differing conclusions? One clue resides in the quotation above, in Ingraham's characterization of gender studies as being concerned with "individual behaviors and group practices." This may be an accurate depiction of gender studies in the United States, but it would not apply to the ways in which feminist sociologists have operationalized the concept of gender on the other side of the Atlantic. Here, studies of gender have sometimes focused on localized settings, but there is a strong tradition of materialist sociological work concerned with the structuring of gender within major institutions and at the level of the social totality. When British and French feminist sociologists talk of gender in terms of relations between women and men, we do not generally mean only localized, personal, or face to face relations, but wider, structural, social relations analogous to class relations.[24] In the end, the differences between Ingraham and myself may come down to a difference of emphasis attributable to our differing national and sexual locations. Whatever the significance of these differences, I can certainly endorse Ingraham's call for a critique of institutionalized heterosexuality as a formal area of inquiry within sociology. Moreover, as my discussion of her work should indicate, while I remain convinced that gender is logically prior to sexuality (erotically significant desires, practices, relationships, and identities), I am far more uncertain about how much weight it should be given in relation to institutionalized heterosexuality.

Rethinking the Intersections

How, then, might we begin to explore in more detail the complex of intersections between gender and heterosexuality? I will sketch out possible approaches to this question by returning to the four interconnected levels of social construction identified earlier in this chapter. Given limitations of space, I can offer here only a bare outline of how such an analysis might proceed and my ideas are offered here in the spirit of work in progress rather than a finished analysis. In trying to work through these ideas, it has become increasingly apparent that the ways in which these intersections operate probably differs from one aspect of social construction to another and varies even within each level, so that the linkages between heterosexuality and gender are stronger at some points than others and not always unidirectional.

Ingraham's analysis of heterosexuality is exceptional in that she confronts what most other theorists in the field ignore: the impact of social structures in shaping our gendered and sexual being. This has been so neglected that social structures and institutions are very rarely thought of as contributing to the process of social construction at all. Yet it should be self-evident that structural inequalities and institutions are fundamental to the everyday conditions of our existence. Gender is itself a structural phenomenon, founded on a hierarchy between men and women:[24] it is because heterosexuality is rooted in the very structural fabric of social order that it is so effectively normative. Moreover, heterosexuality as an institution is by definition gendered and the heterosexual contract is a powerful mechanism whereby gender hierarchy is guaranteed. Here there is clearly a strong link between gender and heterosexuality but, as I have already argued, I would want to keep the two analytically distinct in order to facilitate further exploration of the ways in which they sustain each other.

We also need the conceptual space to think about the ways in which sexual (erotic) practices, identities, and desires are enmeshed with nonsexual aspects of social structure. For example, attention has been drawn to the ways in which a normatively heterosexual society accommodates queer practices as lifestyle choices within commodity capitalism[25] and to the ways in which heterosexual sex is also commodified as style.[26] The structural enabling of sexual lifestyle choices is certainly not equally available to all; access to them is facilitated or limited by location within class, racial, and gendered hierarchies. Here it is evident that structural factors impact on other facets of social construction, on meanings, practices, and subjectively constructed identities.

Where questions of sexual and gendered meanings are concerned, there are a variety of complex intersections to be teased out. At the level of society and culture as a whole, gender and sexuality are constituted as objects of discourse and through the specific discourses in circulation at any historical moment; these discourses serve to distinguish male from female, to define what is sexual, to differentiate the "perverse" from the "normal" and masculinity from femininity. While the concept of discourse is usually held to be antithetical to ideology, I would argue that discourse is frequently ideological in its effects, for example in naturalizing gender and sexuality and thus concealing their social foundations. Meaning is also deployed within, and emergent from, the routine, everyday social interaction through which each of us makes sense of our own and others' gendered and sexual lives. Here we can see how certain discourses available within our culture become hegemonic, informing the "natural attitude"[27] whereby most of the population, most of the time, takes the existence of "men" and "women" as given categories of people who "naturally" form sexual liaisons with members of the "opposite" gender for granted. Here we are constantly "doing gender" in the sense of attributing it to others, rarely noticing the variety of cultural competences and complex interpretational processes this entails. Thus gender and normative heterosexuality are constantly reaffirmed, but it is also here that their meanings can be unsettled or renegotiated—although we need to be aware of how easily such challenges can be neutralized.

At the level of meaning we can see how gender and sexuality constantly intersect, where the construction of gender difference is bound up with the assumption of gender complementarity, the idea that women and men are "made for each other." Hence, the boundaries of gender division and normative heterosexuality are mutually reinforced. However, as Kessler and McKenna (1978) suggest, the attribution of gender is the primary one, at least at the level of everyday interaction. That is to say, we "do" gender first: we recognize someone as male or female before we make any assumptions about their sexuality. Moreover, as I have repeatedly asserted, it makes no sense to classify sexualities in gendered terms—as desiring the same or the other gender—without the prior existence of gender categories.

Because gender and sexuality are reflexively given meaning in our everyday lives, we come to embody them as we go about our mundane routines. They are thus continually produced and reproduced at the third level of so-

cial construction, that of everyday practices. Here too, there are obvious intersections. Women are constantly located in terms of their sexual availability to
men and their presumed "place" within heterosexual relationships as wives
and mothers—this is evident in everything from sexualization of women's
labor[28] to men's resistance to equal opportunities policies.[29] Hence, gendered
assumptions here seem to be informed by heterosexual ones. But let us not
forget (as we still all too easily do) to look at the dominant gender: men. The
sexualization and heterosexualization of women is a means by which men ha-
bitually establish women as "other" and position themselves as "just people."
Not that men always represent themselves as ungendered, but where manli-
ness is specifically called for it does not have to be demonstrated in relation to
heterosexuality. Although this is one way in which it is routinely demonstrated, and a gay man may find his claims to masculinity imperiled by his
sexuality, there are a host of other ways in which a man can be a man—by
virtue of physical or mental prowess, courage, leadership abilities, and so
on—whereas womanliness is almost always equated with (hetero)sexual attractiveness and (heterosexual) domesticity. When thinking specifically about
how heterosexual sex confirms femininity and masculinity, there is again a
marked gender asymmetry. As Janet Holland and her colleagues found in investigating the experience of first heterosex, having sex may make a boy a
man, but it does not make a girl a woman (1996). What confirms masculinity is being (hetero)sexually *active*; what confirms femininity is being sexually
attractive to men. Moreover, gendered meanings are also encoded into the
sexual practices of lesbians and gay men—eschewing heterosex does entail
having ungendered sex, but negotiating different ways of eroticizing gender.
The connections between the everyday meanings of gender, sexuality, and
heterosexuality seem too complex and variable to permit any simple explanation of causal priority.

In our everyday social and sexual lives, gender and sexuality are constantly being socially constructed and reconstructed, enacted and reenacted
within specific social contexts and relationships. Since heterosexuality entails more than just sexuality, as it is lived it constantly entails nonsexual
gendered practices. Each heterosexual couple "does" heterosexuality as
much through divisions of labor and distributions of household resources
as through specifically sexual and reproductive practices. This is another
point at which the social threads binding gender and heterosexuality are
more closely knotted together, particularly evident in the ways in which
particular gender inequities cross between the sexual and nonsexual aspects
of a typical heterosexual couple's life. The wife who cooks meals to suit her
husband's tastes and work routines and who has sex how and when he
wants it is putting his needs before hers in both contexts; she is bolstering
his ego whether she is pretending interest in his work and hobbies or faking

orgasms. Such mundane activities are central to the ways in which gender and heterosexuality are coconstructed in everyday life. And the wife who says no—to sex or housework—is unsettling this everyday order.

This raises the question of how we come to be the embodied gendered and sexual individuals who enact these practices, but who nonetheless have the capacity to renegotiate gender divisions and resist dominant constructions of sexuality. This brings me to the social construction of subjectivity, the complex social and cultural process by which we acquire sexual and gendered desires and identities.

The dominance of psychoanalytic approaches to the construction of subjectivity has produced accounts in which gender and sexuality are inextricably conflated: "sexed" (gendered) subjects are produced through the highly charged sexual–emotional relationships of infancy and becoming one "sex" entails desire for the "other sex." I am proposing a rather different approach, based on the concept of the social self, initially developed by G.H. Mead (1934) and underpinning the account of the social construction of sexuality later produced by Gagnon and Simon (1974).

The idea of a reflexive, social self is sometimes resisted on the grounds that it presupposes a presocial, or prediscursive "I" that does the work of reflexivity. However, if we take this idea back to its origins in Mead's work, it does not assume an essential, inner "I," but an "I" that is only ever the fleeting mobilization of a socially constituted self. This self is not a fixed structure but is always "in process" by virtue of its constant reflexivity. One way in which this reflexive self-construction has been analyzed recently is through the idea of narratives of self, an idea that has roots in both the sociological tradition of interactionism and in more recent discourse analysis.[30] Such a perspective allows us to think of subjectivity as a product of individual, socially located, biographies—but not in the same sense as the old idea of socialization. Here, it is not only the past that shapes the present, but the present significantly reshapes the past in the sense that we are constantly reconstructing our memories, our sense of who and what we are through the stories we tell ourselves and others. Remembered experience is constantly worked over, interpreted, and theorized through the narrative forms and devices available to us. These cultural resources are of course historically specific, enabling us to understand the ways in which particular modes of self-construction become available at different historical moments in specific social locations. This is what makes this approach potentially congruent with materialism, in that it allows us to think of the self as fully social, but also permits—and is premised on—a capacity for agency, although that agency is always constrained by the social order we inhabit.

How might we apply this to gender and sexuality? Here too, there are grounds for arguing for the primacy of gender attribution in that the moment we are born we are ascribed a gender.[31] While heterosexual assumptions may play a part, as is evident with those born intersexed, it is the difference itself that seems to matter here. It is this difference, one of the first social categories a child learns, that forms the foundation for the ways in which we locate ourselves within a gendered sexual order and male sense of ourselves as embodied, gendered, and sexual beings. At the level of our individual subjectivities, I have argued that gender is temporally prior to sexuality since we acquire a sense of ourselves as gendered long before we become reflexively aware of ourselves as sexual.[32] As soon as we turn to heterosexuality, however, the picture becomes more complicated, because children come to understand nonsexual aspects of heterosexuality—families, mothers and fathers, for example—way before they gain access to specifically sexual discourses. There is clearly more work to be done to work through the implications of these ideas both conceptually and empirically, but in my view this approach offers a viable, and preferable, alternative to psychoanalysis. It also permits us to investigate the ways in which our individual sexual, gendered selves continue to be reflexively renegotiated or reconfirmed throughout our lives, and how they continue to interconnect as we go about our daily lives within a gendered, heterosexually ordered social world.

Subversion and Transformation

I will conclude by reflecting on the political consequences of the theoretical issues I have been discussing. In particular, I want to question some of the claims made about the subversive potential of dissident sexualities and gender transformations emanating from queer, bisexual, and transgender theorists, specifically Butler (1990), Daümer (1992), and Bornstein (1994). If, as I have suggested, heterosexuality and gender are constituted and sustained not only at the institutional level, but also through our everyday sexual and social practices, their perpetuation requires our continual reaffirmation. Most people "do" heterosexuality and gender every day without reflecting critically on that doing. This is accomplished through talk and action, through the embodied practices of dress and demeanor, through active participation in formal institutional settings, and through the mundane activities through which our everyday lives are ordered. This idea of gender and sexuality as a constantly reiterated performance does not derive, as some think, from Judith Butler, but has much older sociological roots in the work of writers such as Garfinkel and Goffman; and it is their vocabulary I have consciously chosen here.

If we "do heterosexuality" and "do gender" in our everyday lives, to what extent can we "undo" them? Those who live their lives outside compulsory heterosexuality are, of course, not complicit in its maintenance to the same extent as heterosexuals, and some are politically committed to undoing, or at least unsettling, it. Yet despite the emphasis in recent theory on destabilizing gender and heterosexuality, there is a reluctance to think about the possibility of thoroughly undoing them: doing away with them. The currently fashionable ideas of performative subversions of gender and sexual binaries, deriving from the work of Judith Butler, are not so much undoing gender as doing it in new ways, as in Butler's reflections on a lesbian femme's claim that she likes her "boys to be girls" (1990: 122). Formulations such as these do reveal the artificiality of gender, but the destabilizing effects of such transgressive performances are limited. If Butler and her followers have a utopian vision, it is a world of multiple genders and sexualities, not a world without gender or heterosexuality.

Beneath the postmodern posturing of Queer lies the old assumption that the whole of human potential equals the sum of its gendered parts,[33] but reformulated in a new way. Where androgynists hoped to weld the two incomplete "halves" of masculinity and femininity into a complete whole, queer theorists seek to destabilize both and create more "genders" by jumping between them or recombining their elements in innovative or parodic forms. They still, therefore, have a stake in "doing gender," which is radical only to the extent that the performance, the act of "doing," is made visible. If we can free ourselves from assuming the inevitability of some form of gender, then combinations of femininity and masculinity—and of same-gender or other-gender desire—do not represent the only human possibilities. If men and women are products of a hierarchical relation, in the absence of that relation very different subjectivities and desires might emerge.

Much of what passes as radical in these "postmodern" times, then, does not envisage the end of gender hierarchy or the collapse of institutionalized heterosexuality, but simply a multiplying of genders and sexualities or movement between them. It might be argued that this would ultimately have the effect of rendering the difference between women and men as simply part of a fluid continuum of differences and of divesting heterosexuality of its privileged location. But seeking to undo binary divisions by rendering their boundaries more permeable and adding more categories to them ignores the hierarchical social relations on which the original binaries were founded. We cannot hope to abolish hierarchies by creating finer gradations or more movement within them. All that this can achieve is a concealment and mystification of the material inequalities through which heterosexuality and gender are sustained at the macrolevel of structures and institutions as well as the microlevel of our everyday social practices.

Sexual lifestyles and practices are shaped by the commodification of sexuality within late capitalism, and what today is radically oppositional soon becomes commercially chic. Moreover, opportunities to engage in and with queer parodic practices are constrained by our location within social structures, by patterns of material privilege and disadvantage.[34] If our capacity to undo gender and heterosexuality is constrained by the structural inequalities that sustain them, then our ability to conceptualize their undoing is limited to the extent that our sense of ourselves has been constructed within a heterosexual, patriarchal, late capitalist social order. It may be that this accounts for the lack of vision underpinning much queer writing, the failure to imagine a world without gender, without heterosexuality—and without other systematic inequalities deriving from the global reach of transnational capitalism.

In much feminist writing, concern with material inequalities has given way to a preoccupation with difference as something to be valued and affirmed. But we should be cautious of valorizing differences—such as those of class, race, or gender—which are products of systematic inequalities. I do not want heterosexuality to be treated as simply one difference among many, nor masculinity and femininity "appreciated" as differences that could be rendered harmless if only we valued them equally, permitted fluid movement between them, or admitted the possibility of other genders. Why not think instead of the end of gender, the end of the hetero/homosexual division? This idea is often interpreted as making everyone the same. But why should it? Might it not open up the possibility that differences other than the ones we know today might flourish, differences that are not founded on hierarchy?

Radical intellectuals have abandoned those metanarratives, such as Marxism, which once promised a better future in favor of Foucault's view that power is inescapable. We can resist, subvert, and destabilize, but nothing much will change; or, if it does, there will be new deployments of power to be resisted, subverted, and destabilized. This is a politics of resistance and transgression, but not a politics of radical change. Some of my colleagues, those infatuated with queer possibilities, tell me that my ideas are not only passé, but also hopelessly utopian. Yet, despite this long-term pessimism, the queer celebration of gender and sexual transgression seems to be naively overoptimistic about what is achievable in the shorter term. It assumes an unbounded potential for the subversion of gender and sexuality without realization that the opportunities for such transgression are confined to the privileged few and are, in any case, easily recuperated as niche markets for commodity capitalism. Many queer theorists seem blissfully unaware of their lack of impact on the taken-for-granted assumptions of most of the population, who are far more eager to buy into "scientific" arguments about the inevitability and fixity of gender divisions and normative heterosexuality than to engage in subverting them. My own perspective inverts the queer view: I am more pessimistic about the short term, but believe it essential to retain some degree of optimism about the longer term potential for social transformation. If we cannot even imagine social relations being radically other than they are, we will lose the impetus and capacity to think critically about gender, heterosexuality, and every other social institution that orders our daily lives.

References

Adkins, Lisa. 1995. *Gendered work: Sexuality, family and the labor market*. Milton Keynes: Open University Press.

Bornstein, K. 1994. *Gender outlaw*. New York: Routledge.

Butler, Judith. 1990. *Gender trouble: Feminism and the subversion of identity*. New York: Routledge.

———. 1993. *Bodies that matter*. New York: Routledge.

———. 1997. Merely cultural, *Social text*, 15(3/4): 265–278.

Cameron, D. 1997/1998. Back to nature, *Trouble and strife*, 36: 6–15.

Cockburn, C. 1993. *In the way of women*. London: Macmillan.

Daümer, E. 1992. Queer ethics: or, the challenge of bisexuality to lesbian ethics, *Hypatia*, 7(4): 91–105.

Delphy, Christine. 1984. *Close to home: A materialist analysis of women's oppression*. London: Hutchinson.

———. 1993. Rethinking sex and gender, *Women's studies international forum*, 16(1): 1–9.

———. 1994. Changing women in a changing Europe: is difference the future for feminism? *Women's studies international forum*: 27(2): 187–201.

Evans, D. 1993. *Sexual citizenship: The material construction of sexualities*. London: Routledge.

Fausto-Sterling, Anne. 2000. *Sexing the body*, second edition. New York: Basic Books.

Fuss, D. 1991. *Inside/out: Lesbian theories, gay theories*. New York: Routledge.

Gagnon, John and William Simon. 1974. *Sexual conduct*. London: Hutchinson.

Grosz, E. 1995. Experimental desire: re-thinking queer subjectivity, in *Space, time and perversion*. New York: Routledge.

Guillaumin, C. 1995. *Racism, sexism, power and ideology*. London: Routledge.

Hennessy, R. 1993. *Materialist feminism and the politics of discourse*. New York and London: Routledge.

———. 1995. Queer visibility in commodity culture, in L. Nicholson and S. Seidman (eds.) *Social postmodernism*. Cambridge: Cambridge University Press.

———. 2000. *Profit and pleasure*. New York: Routledge.

Holland, J., C. Ramazanoglu, S. Sharpe and R. Thomson. 1996. In the same boat? The gendered (in)experience of first heterosex, in D. Richardson (ed.) *Theorising heterosexuality: Telling it straight*. Buckingham: Open University Press.

Ingraham, C. 1994. The heterosexual imaginary: feminist sociology and theories of gender. *Sociological theory*.

———. 1996. The heterosexual imaginary, in S. Seidman (ed.) *Queer theory/sociology*. Oxford: Blackwell.

———. 1999. *White weddings: Romancing heterosexuality in popular culture*. New York: Routledge.

Jackson, S. (1995) Gender and heterosexuality: a materialist feminist analysis, in M. Maynard and J. Purvis (eds.) *(Hetero)sexual politics*. London: Taylor & Francis.

———. 1996a. *Christine Delphy*. London: Sage.

———. 1996b. Heterosexuality and feminist theory, in D. Richardson (ed.) *Theorising heterosexuality: Telling it straight*. Buckingham: Open University Press.

———. 1998. Telling stories: memory, narrative and experience in feminist theory and research, in K. Henwood, C. Griffin and A. Phoenix (eds.) *Standpoints and differences*. London: Sage.

———. 1999a. *Heterosexuality in question*. London: Sage.

———. 1999b. Feminist sociology and sociological feminism: Recovering the social in feminist thought, *Sociological research online*, 4(3), http://www.socresonline.org.uk/socresonline/4/3/jackson.html

———. 2000. For a sociological feminism, in J. Eldridge, J. MacInnes, S. Scott, C. Warhurst and A. Witz (eds.) *For sociology*. Durham: Sociology Press.

———. 2001. Why a materialist feminism is still possible (and necessary), *Women's studies international forum*, 24(2–3).

Jackson, S. and S. Scott. 1997. Gut reactions to matters of the heart: reflections on rationality, irrationality and sexuality, *Sociological review*, 45(4): 551–575.

———. 2000. Risk anxiety and the social construction of childhood, in D. Lupton (ed.) *Risk and sociocultural theory*. Cambridge: Cambridge University Press.

Kessler, S.J. 1998. *Lessons from the intersexed*. New Brunswick: Rutgers University Press.

Kessler, S.J. and W. McKenna. 1978. *Gender: An ethnomethodological approach*. New York: Wiley

Leonard, Diana and Lisa Adkins. 1995. *Sex in question: French materialist feminism*. London: Taylor and Francis.

LeVay, S. 1993. *The sexual brain*. Cambridge, MA: MIT Press.

McIntosh, M. 1968. The homosexual role, *Social problems*, 16(2): 182–192.

MacKinnon, Catherine. 1982. Feminism, marxism, method and the state: an agenda for theory, *Signs*, 7(2): 515–544.

Mead, G.H. 1934. *Mind self and society*. Chicago: University of Chicago Press.

Plummer, K. 1995. *Telling sexual stories: Power, change and social worlds*. London: Routledge.

Questions Féministes Collective. 1981. Variations on a common theme, in E. Marks and I. de Courtivron (eds.) *New french feminisms*. Brighton: Harvester.

Rahman, M. 2000. *Sexuality and democracy*. Edinburgh: Edinburgh University Press.

Rahman, M. and S. Jackson. 1998. Liberty, equality and sexuality: essentialism and the discourse of rights, *Journal of gender studies*, 6(2): 117–29.

Ramazanoglu, Caroline. 1995. Back to basics: heterosexuality, biology and why men stay on top, in M. Maynard and J. Purvis (eds.) *(Hetero)sexual politics*. London: Taylor & Francis.

Rees, A. 2000. Higamous, hogamous, woman monogamous, *Feminist theory* 1(3): 365–370.

Rich, Adrienne. 1980. Compulsory heterosexuality and lesbian existence, *Signs*, 5(4): 631–660.

Richardson, Diane. 1996. *Theorizing heterosexuality: Telling it straight*. Buckingham: Open University Press.

Rubin, Gayle. 1975. The traffic in women: notes on the "political economy" of sex, in R. Reiter (ed.) *Toward an anthropology of women*. New York: Monthly Review Press.

———. 1984. Thinking sex: notes for a radical theory of the politics of sexuality, in C. Vance (ed.) *Pleasure and danger*. London: Routledge.

Segal, L. 1999. *Why feminism?* Cambridge: Polity.

Stanley, L. 1984. Should "sex" really be "gender" or "gender" really be "sex"?, in R. Anderson and W. Sharrock (eds.) *Applied sociology*. London: Allen & Unwin.

Vance, C.S. 1989. Social construction theory: problems in the history of sexuality, in D. Altman et al. (eds.) *Which homosexuality?* London: Gay Men's Press.

Whisman, Vera. 1996. *Queer by choice*. New York: Routledge.

Wilkinson, Sue and Celia Kitzinger (eds.) 1993. *Heterosexuality: A feminism and psychology reader*. London: Sage.

Wilton, T. 1996. Which one's the man? The heterosexualization of lesbian sex, in D. Richardson (ed.) *Theorizing heterosexuality: Telling it straight*. Buckingham: Open University Press.

Wittig, M. 1981. One is not born a woman, *Feminist issues*, 1(2): 47–54.

———. 1992. *The straight mind and other essays*. Hemel Hempstead: Harvester Wheatsheaf.

Notes

1. Cameron, 1997/1998; Segal, 1999; Rees, 2000
2. See Cameron, 1997/1998
3. See Fausto-Sterling, 2000
4. LeVay, 1993
5. See Rahman and Jackson, 1997; Rahman, 2000
6. Whisman, 1996
7. See Jackson, 1996b, 1999, 2000, 2001
8. Kessler and McKenna, 1978; Delphy, 1993
9. Delphy, 1984: 144
10. Jackson, 1996a, b, 1999a, b
11. Vance, 1989
12. For example, McIntosh, 1968; Gagnon and Simon, 1974

13. See Kessler and McKenna, 1978; Delphy, 1984; Stanley, 1984. Elsewhere I have attributed this to the "cultural turn" in feminist and social theory (Jackson 1999b, 2000), which has also had the effect of diminishing the scope of social constructionist accounts.
14. Jackson, 1999a, b, 2000
15. Jackson, 1996b, 1999a, b
16. The works cited here are all collections including work that dates back to the late 1970s and are the best English language sources on this group of theorists. Earlier English translations of these writings are of variable quality; some were published in sources that are now not easy to find and do not always represent the most significant of these authors' contributions. Note also that Delphy was alone among the original materialist feminists to use the term "gender"—the others talked of "sex" because they did not accept the sex–gender distinction, or the importation of an Anglophone concept. Delphy prefers "gender" since it marks out a social rather than a natural category (see Delphy 1993). The term "genre", in the sense of "gender", is now, however, becoming more common in France, especially among sociologists. See, for example, Delphy, 1984; Wittig, 1992; Guillaumin, 1995; Leonard and Adkins, 1996.
17. *Qf Collective*, [1977] 1981: 215
18. See Wittig, 1992; Jackson, 1995, 1996a
19. Kitzinger and Wilkinson, 1993; Ingraham, 1994; Richardson, 1996
20. Fuss, 1991: 3
21. Jackson, 1995, 1999a, b
22. For example, Ingraham, 1994; Wilton, 1996
23. Adkins, 1995
24. Delphy, 1993
25. Evans, 1993; Hennessy, 2000
26. Jackson and Scott, 1997
27. Kessler and McKenna, 1978
28. Adkins, 1995
29. Cockburn, 1993
30. Jackson, 1998; Plummer, 1995; Whisman, 1996
31. Kessler and McKenna, 1978
32. I am not suggesting that children are intrinsically asexual (or intrinsically sexual either). Rather, the distribution of sexual knowledge within our society and the definition of children as asexual innocents means that their access to crucial elements of adult sexual knowledge is restricted. While children now become sexually knowing earlier than in the recent past, the pattern remains and shapes the ways in which children become sexual and also contributes to the social construction of childhood (see Jackson, 1998., 1999; Jackson and Scott 2000).
33. See Delphy, 1993
34. Hennessy, 2000

CHAPTER 2

From the Polluted Homosexual to the Normal Gay: Changing Patterns of Sexual Regulation in America

STEVEN SEIDMAN

The idea of heterosexuality as an institution initially appeared in the writings of gay liberationists and lesbian feminists in the late 1960s and early 1970s.[1] Previously, accounts of a homosexual's unique subordinate status were explained by referring to either individual acts of harassment or legal disenfranchisement. Understanding gay life in relation to an "institution" of heterosexuality shifts the analytical and political focus to the ways that social institutions and culture enforce heterosexuality as the right and preferred way to organize personal and social life.

Over the last several decades, an archive of research and theorizing has accumulated that analyzes the institution of heterosexuality. Carl Wittman's (1992) classic "A Gay Manifesto" expressed the gay liberationist view that homosexual oppression is sustained by a society-wide mobilization of the state, the criminal justice system, the mass media, and scientific–medical discourses. Drawing on a rich history of lesbian feminism, Adrienne Rich's "Compulsive Heterosexuality and Lesbian Existence" argues that "heterosexuality as an institution has been organized and maintained through the female wage scale, the enforcement of middle class women's leisure, the glamorization of so-called sexual liberation, the withholding of education from women, the imagery of 'high art,' and popular culture, the mystification of the 'personal' sphere, and much else."[2] Queer theory and politics in the 1990s continued to place the notion of heterosexuality as an institution at the center of sexual theory.[3]

The idea of heterosexuality as an institution has often been used without regard to history and changes in its social organization. For example, Rich assumes both that a system of compulsive heterosexuality is universal and that it operates everywhere by means of social repression (1983: 197). Similarly, Sedgwick (1990) and Fuss (1991: 4) maintain that since the late 19th century, the institution of heterosexuality has functioned uniformly across nations to create the closet as a defining reality of modern homosexuality. Recent historical research however suggests that the concept of the closet may have unique sociohistorical preconditions.[4] Instead of assuming the universality of the institution of heterosexuality and its uniform social logic, I underscore its historically emergent and changing character.

Analysts of heterosexuality as an institution have, moreover, focused exclusively on its role in regulating homosexuality. While queer approaches have theorized that homosexuality gains coherence in relation to heterosexuality, the impact of regimes of normative heterosexuality on heterosexuality has largely been ignored.[5] I will argue that normative heterosexuality not only establishes a heterosexual/homosexual hierarchy but also creates hierarchies among heterosexualities. Analyzing the way in which regimes of normative heterosexuality create hegemonic and subordinate forms of heterosexuality should be central to critical sexuality studies.

Using commercial Hollywood films between 1960 and 2000, I trace changing patterns of normative heterosexuality in the United States.[6] The first section examines the enforcement of normative heterosexuality by means of a homophobic pollution logic. The second section traces a shift in the operation of normative heterosexuality to a normalizing logic. Normalization allows for the open integration of gay men and lesbians while not threatening the normative status of heterosexuality. In the final section, I argue that gay normalization creates a division not only between the respectable and disreputable homosexual but also between the bad and good heterosexual. Indeed, gay normalization fashions a binary of the good and bad sexual citizen that locates the "normal gay" in the category of the good citizen. Curiously, in films that champion the normal gay, I detect an intensification of sexual regulation for the good citizen, straight and gay.

The Polluted Homosexual

The Children's Hour (1961) and *Advise and Consent* (1962) were among the very few star-studded Hollywood films of the early 1960s that featured an explicitly homosexual character. These films tell a story of homosexual calamity as a social tragedy. For example, in *The Children's Hour*, Shirley MacLaine (Martha) plays a lesbian whose sexual identity is revealed, but only after she is labeled by others. Despite her status as a good citizen (she's a devoted teacher, competent administrator, compassionate friend, and law-abiding citizen), she and everyone associated with her are stigmatized and shunned after she is exposed as a lesbian. Ruin and misery are depicted as the product of social intolerance: Martha commits suicide; Joe (James Garner) loses his job and then his fiancée (Audrey Hepburn); and the school for young girls that Martha owns and manages is shut down. The message of the film seems clear: the problem of homosexuality today is not that there are homosexuals but social prejudice.

The meaning and place of homosexuality in the heartland of America was still somewhat unsettled in the 1950s. While a film such as *The Children's Hour* criticized intolerance toward homosexuals, as did Kinsey's famous studies, the government was aggressively engaged in the persecution of homosexuals. For the most part, the politics of homosexuality was not a major focus of public attention. The figure of the homosexual scarcely registered a presence in popular culture.

By the early 1970s, however, lesbians and gay men had established a national public presence. In contrast to the quiet, barely noticeable political activities of the homosexual movement in the 1950s and early 1960s, lesbian-feminism and gay liberationism championed gay pride and visibility; these movements challenged a homophobic culture and the network of state-enforced laws and practices sustaining the closet. Gays began to come out—in their families, at work, and in the political arena. Popular culture discovered the homosexual. The idea of an exclusively heterosexual public sphere was challenged.

Hollywood, like the rest of America, had no choice but to respond to the new public visibility of the homosexual. Mainstream films of the 1970s and 1980s were almost uniformly condemning. These films reveal something of America's anxiety toward "the new homosexual"—proud and assertive.

Hollywood overwhelmingly framed "the homosexual problem" as a personal tragedy, as a tale of individual sickness and deviance. The social drama in these films revolves around the danger that the homosexual presents to the children, families, moral values, and the very national integrity of America.

As the homosexual stepped into public life in the 1970s, Hollywood fashioned images of this figure as an outsider and social threat. If the homosexual's public presence could not be denied or effectively suppressed, this figure could at least be portrayed in ways that clearly reinforced the norm and ideal status of heterosexuality. *The homosexual became the impure other to the pure heterosexual.*

Consider some of the films in the 1970s and 1980s that featured gay characters.

In a comedy about black working men, *Car Wash* (1976) presented an openly homosexual character—Lindy (Antonio Fargas). Excepting Lindy, all of the other characters were not just assumed to be heterosexual but were often emphatically presented as heterosexual. For example, the men were either married, had girlfriends, dated women, hired prostitutes, or flirted with women customers. Lindy's polluted status is dramatized by stereotyping him as a "queen"—swishy, limp-wristed, and exhibiting an exaggerated, affected feminine style. This film presents the male homosexual as a gender invert—a feminized male preoccupied with his looks and obsessed with sex. Lindy is tolerated as part of the public world, but only because he reinforces the purity of heterosexuality by representing the impure, inferior homosexual. He is positioned as outside the circle of the respectable heterosexual, gender-conventional citizen.

Viewing the homosexual as a freakish, cartoon-like figure was a way to minimize his/her threat to a social order that made heterosexuality into the only acceptable way to be a good citizen. However, many Americans viewed the new homosexual, who demanded respect and challenged heterosexual privilege, as dangerous. This menacing figure was translated on celluloid into posing a real physical and moral threat to the heterosexual citizen. In films of the 1970s and 1980s, the homosexual was often portrayed as a sociopath—an aggressive, violent, evil figure.

In *Sudden Impact* (1983), the fourth of the "Dirty Harry" films, Harry (Clint Eastwood) is a police detective who wages a war against a corrupt world. Harry believes that crime, incivility, and immorality are ruining America. He dedicates himself to purifying America—by any means necessary.

Harry is investigating a series of murders. The perpetrator is Jennifer (Sandra Locke) whose killing spree is revenge for her and her sister's rape. One of the rapists is Ray—a white lesbian in her twenties. Reflecting the new social reality of gay visibility, Ray is portrayed as part of the public world. The film proceeds though to characterize her as the very antithesis of the respectable heterosexual citizen.

We first meet Ray in a bar. Flagging the lesbian's suspect moral character, the bar is crowded with deviant social types. Ray is the only woman in the bar. She has short hair, wears blue jeans and a jean jacket with the sleeves cut off. She smokes, curses, and talks in an aggressively masculine style. Ray is the stereotypical butch, a mannish woman who is also violent and dangerous. Ray is a moral and physical threat. She participated in the rape and plans to kill Jennifer. However, Jennifer kills Ray first. The presentation of the lesbian as a psychopathic killer who is murdered perhaps expressed America's unconscious fear of the homosexual's new public assertiveness and a desire to expel her from civic life.

Films such as *Car Wash* or *Sudden Impact* construct a sharp opposition between the pure heterosexual and the polluted homosexual. The latter figure appears as a gender freak, moral degenerate, sociopath, or psychopathic killer. There are however films in the 1970s and 1980s that are more complex, without challenging the inferior status of the homosexual.

Looking for Mr. Goodbar (1977) depicts a world shaped by the sexual and gender liberationist ideas of the 1960s. Teresa (Diane Keaton) grew up in a repressed Irish Catholic family in Brooklyn. She moves to Manhattan to find herself. Teresa's journey of self-exploration involves a certain blurring of the line between good and bad or polluted sexual desires and acts. For example, the film exposes the dark side of a heterosexual marital norm by showing the repressive and violent aspects of her parents' marriage. And through Teresa, the film explores, in a morally ambiguous way, a world of sexual experimentation—from one-night stands and group sex to commercial and rough sex.

In the course of her sexual coming-of-age story, we encounter homosexuals. In one scene, Teresa finds herself in a gay bar. Men are dancing and laughing. At first, the viewer might think this is a positive portrayal of gay men; the intermingling of heterosexuals and homosexuals might even suggest the film's advocacy of social tolerance. This generous impulse, however, is quickly contradicted.

The bar scene focuses on two men. Gary (Tom Berenger), a muscular, handsome man in his twenties, dressed in clone-style jean pants, a teeshirt, and jean jacket, approaches a much older, wealthy-looking man. They kiss in a way suggesting an intimate bond.

The two men reappear in a New Year's Eve scene sometime later. They are celebrating in Times Square. The older man is dressed as a clown and Gary is in drag, complete with wig, high heels, and makeup. Abruptly, the scene turns dangerous; chaos descends as crowds of drunken men are fighting and destroying property. Gary and his friend run to escape the violence.

> Older Man: Did they hurt you?
> Gary: No, don't ever ask me to wear this crap again. I'm no nellie. You ought to know that. Christ, look at us. We're a couple of freaks.
> Older Man: [crying hysterically] I'm sorry.
> Gary: I've had it with you…and your fancy shirts, shoes….
> Older Man: [desperately holding Gary] Please don't go. [Gary hits him].
> Older Man: Please don't go…I'll wait for you at the apartment. You need some money.
> Gary: You're the nellie, not me. I'm a pitcher not a catcher and don't you ever forget that.

Gary expresses one of the pillar fears about gay men: they are not real men, but sissies or nellies. They are men who can be fucked, just like women. The film also offers a portrait of homosexual relationships that is damning.

In contrast to the heterosexual ideal of a love-based companionate intimacy, a homosexual relationship is presented as an exploitative and corrupting exchange of youthful beauty for material comfort. The older man is wealthy, closeted, and effeminate; Gary is an ex-con who trades on his masculine sexual attractiveness for material comfort. Gary's true sexual identity is however unclear. If he is in fact a homosexual, perhaps breaking with his benefactor will lead him to an affirmative gay identity.

Gary's status is clarified in the final scene when he meets Teresa for the first time in a bar. Enjoying each other, they decide to go to her apartment. Gary is unable to fuck. He is upset. "In my neighborhood if you didn't fight you were a fruit. In prison if you didn't fight you spread ass." Gary again tries to fuck but cannot. Teresa asks: "What are you trying to prove?" Gary says: "You think I'm some kind of flaming faggot." Gary will prove his manhood at any cost: he violently rapes her. However, he can only enter her from behind, as if he was having sex with a man. Humiliated by this implicit acknowledgement of his homosexuality, and his failed manhood, Gary stabs Teresa repeatedly and kills her.

The older man may be a pathetic and pathological figure who confuses desire with love and purchases the affections of young, handsome men, but Gary is a psychopath. Filled with rage and self-hatred, he murders to cleanse himself of his homosexual feelings. Both figures are presented as social threats. The older man represents the power of the homosexual to seduce and corrupt innocent vulnerable youth. Gary presents a mortal danger to Americans. Like *Sudden Impact*, this film reveals the American's wish to purge homosexuals from public life. In its portrayal of gays, the film enacts the social death of the homosexual by rendering this figure into a virtual subhuman species (psychopath) who should not be part of civic life.

Hollywood films of the 1970s and 1980s acknowledge the reality of homosexuals, but represent them as either harmless but freakish and pathetic figures (e.g., *Car Wash, Next Stop Greenwich Village, St. Elmo's Fire*), or as serious physical, moral, and social threats (e.g., *Sudden Harry, Looking for Mr. Goodbar, Cruising, Deliverance*). These films view heterosexuality and homosexuality as mutually exclusive social identities. America is imagined as divided into a heterosexual majority and a homosexual minority. This is a moral division: the heterosexual represents a pure and good human status in contrast to the impure and dangerous homosexual. The link between homosexual pollution and social repression is established through the notion of moral contagion. Heterosexual exposure to homosexuals threatens their seduction and corruption. Accordingly, homosexuals must be excluded from the public world of visible, open communication by means of repressive strategies such as censorship, civic disenfranchisement, and sequestration. In short, these films construct a social world in which heterosexual privilege is reinforced by purifying the heterosexual while vilifying and positioning the homosexual outside of normal, respectable American civic life.

The Normal Gay

Stereotypes that scandalize homosexuals are hardly a thing of the past. But, images of the polluted homosexual are now often publicly criticized as a form of bigotry; tolerance of public homophobic expressions can no longer be taken for granted. A shift in the cultural status of the homosexual is clear in films of the 1990s. Polluting stereotypes are giving way to another representation: the normal gay.

The normal gay is presented as fully human, as the psychological and moral equal of the heterosexual. Accordingly, gays should be integrated into America as rights-bearing, respected citizens.

However, the normal gay also serves as a narrow social norm. This figure is associated with specific personal and social behaviors. For example, the normal gay is expected to be gender conventional, link sex to love and a marriage-like relationship, defend family values, personify economic individualism, and display national pride. Although normalization makes it possible for individuals to conduct lives of integrity, it also establishes a moral and social division among gays. Only normal gays who conform to dominant social norms deserve respect and integration. Lesbians and gay men who are gender benders or choose alternative intimate lives will likely remain outsiders. And, as we will see, the normal gay implies a political logic of tolerance and minority rights that does not challenge heterosexual dominance.

Philadelphia (1993) was in many ways a breakthrough movie. As a big studio production starring Tom Hanks and Denzel Washington, Hollywood brought AIDS and homosexuality to middle America. This was one of the first big-budget, star-studded Hollywood productions to present the gay individual as a normal, good citizen.

The movie tells the story of Andy (Tom Hanks), a rising star in a prestigious law firm who is fired for having AIDS. Represented by Joe (Denzel Washington), Andy files an AIDS discrimination suit and wins. The film simultaneously tells a larger story of the changing moral status of gay Americans.

Andy's experience in his law firm pointedly depicts a society that fears and discriminates against gays. The culture of the firm is aggressively masculine and heterosexual. Andy's good standing at the law firm is maintained by concealing his homosexuality. This decision is a response to homophobic comments (fag jokes) made by the senior law partners. Andy's dismissal from the firm is related less to his having AIDS than to his being homosexual, although AIDS is shown to be the ultimate fear of homosexual pollution and contagion come to literal life. In a telling scene, the law firm's senior partner (Jason Robards) advises against settling the lawsuit by invoking the image of the homosexual defiling the firm. "Andy brought AIDS into our office, into our men's room, brought AIDS to our annual family gatherings." Just as AIDS can literally spread by contact, so might Andy's homosexuality. In short, the film's portrayal of the law firm depicts a social order in which gay people are either forced to pass or suffer considerable personal harm.

If the focus of the film was Andy's decision to pass and his firing for homophobic reasons, it would describe the world of the closet. Rather, the main drama of *Philadelphia* centers on Andy's decision to fight antigay prejudice and his triumph in the American criminal justice system. Instead of surrendering to the power of prejudice and intolerance, Andy fights back by suing the law firm. His legal victory suggests that America is changing and that gays will not and should not accept the closet as a condition of social integration. *Philadelphia* advocates a view of gays as normal human beings who deserve equal rights and respect.

While the film depicts the fight against homosexual pollution as an institutional drama, it powerfully dramatizes this struggle through the character of Joe.

Joe, as in your average Joe, represents the typical American. Newly married, hard working, he is a "guy's guy." Predictably then, his homophobia is established early in the film. After being turned down by many lawyers, Andy approaches Joe, a gritty streetwise lawyer. As they are shaking hands, Andy tells Joe that he is seeking counsel for an AIDS discrimination suit. Joe abruptly withdraws his hand, takes several backward steps away from Andy, looks at Andy with apparent fear and loathing, watches everything that Andy touches in his office, and refuses to take the case for personal reasons, which he subsequently discloses as a hatred of homosexuals. This scene reveals the logic of homosexual pollution: Joe's behavior establishes a division between the pure heterosexual and the impure homosexual. Andy's polluted status is illustrated by Joe's fear of contamination, his refusal to represent Andy, and his frank expression of disgust towards homosexuals.

Philadelphia is not a coming-out film, at least in the classic sense. Andy does not struggle with self-acceptance. From the very first scene, Andy is out and reveals no moral anguish over being gay. He lives with Miguel (Antonio Banderas) and is integrated into a dense network of kin and friends. Instead, it is Joe's personal struggle with his own homophobia, and ultimately with America's intolerance toward gays, that is the moral focus of the film.

Anticipating the end of his trial, and his death, Andy and Miguel have a party. At one point, Andy and Miguel are intimately embraced as they dance. Similarly intimate with his wife, Joe glances at, and then fixes on, Andy and Miguel. Andy notices and smiles, as if he is signaling that his love for Miguel is equivalent to Joe's love for his wife. Joe is beginning to recognize Andy as fully human. His realization comes later that evening. After the guests leave, Joe and Andy are supposed to review Andy's testimony. Instead, in a poignant scene, Andy relates to Joe the story of a Maria Callas opera that is playing in the background. It is a sad tale of love, injustice, and tragic death. As Andy is absorbed in the operatic narrative, Joe is fixed intently on Andy. Tears begin to well up. No words are spoken, but the meaning seems clear. For the first time, Joe is seeing Andy as someone who, like him, feels joy and sadness, love and loss, justice and oppression. By the end of the film, Andy has ceased to be polluted for Joe. As Andy is dying in the hospital, he signals for Joe to sit next to him. This is a dramatic moment as their physical and emotional closeness marks the end of Andy's polluted status. Joe sits on the bed and touches Andy's face as he adjusts his breathing apparatus. This act symbolizes Joe's acknowledgement of the moral equivalence of the heterosexual and the homosexual.

The film's moral standpoint is clear: it asserts the normality of homosexuality and the bigoted status of homophobia. As a typical Hollywood story of good vs. evil, *Philadelphia* depicts the antigay behavior of the law firm and the "early" Joe as evil, while Andy and the "latter" Joe become symbols of goodness.

Philadelphia abandons polluting stereotypes and condemns social intolerance. Still, the normal gay remains a distinct social minority to be tolerated but not considered the equal to the straight majority. Heterosexual domination is not threatened.

First, homosexuality is not presented as an emotional and sexual orientation that is diffusely distributed across a population but is an identity of a small minority. The majority of citizens is either assumed to be or acts as heterosexual, for example, are married or display a sexual interest in the opposite gender. Indeed, the heterosexuality of all of the main characters, except Andy and Miguel, is unambiguously conveyed. For example, in the opening scene of the movie, Joe is in a hospital celebrating the birth of his first child. Andy's parents and their adult children are all married. Andy's law partners are married or otherwise signal their heterosexuality by their homophobic comments or their interest in the opposite sex. The film does not challenge the dominant and privileged status of heterosexuality.

Second, gays, or some gays may be normal and good citizens, but heterosexuality is still the ideal. The figure of Andy as the normal gay is surrounded by idealized images of the straight American. For example, Andy's parents live in a white picket-fenced colonial home in a small town where, we are led to believe, they have lived happily—as they celebrate their 50th wedding anniversary—for their entire adult lives. Andy's family is an extended heterosexual kin unit, presented as lovingly bonded and intact.

The film projects an almost 1950s family ideal—the white colonial home in small-town America, the extended loving family, the parents who live and love together for life, and the conventional gender division between men and women. So, while the film assigns a normal status to being gay, it endorses the norm and ideal of heterosexuality.

Third, Andy exhibits personal traits and behaviors that many Americans would consider "normal" or ideal in every way other than his sexual identity. He is conventionally masculine, is in a quasimarital relationship, is part of an extended close-knit family, is hard working and economically independent, and is a champion of the rule of law—a core part of the American creed. This characterization of Andy does not challenge a social order that assumes that the division and complementarity of men and women is natural and right, and it does not question the ideal of heterosexual marriage and family; it only creates a space of social tolerance for gays, or, more correctly, for normal gays.

Finally, in the ideal society imagined in *Philadelphia*, discrimination toward gays would be uncivil—that is the message of Andy's legal victory. However, the culture and institutions of America would remain organized around heterosexual privilege. Thus, the law firm that fired Andy may no longer be able to discriminate but it remains organized around a binary gender order that sustains men's domination; the men in the firm are still the senior partners, the women are still the receptionists, secretaries, or junior partners; and all of the men, including Andy, are conventionally masculine and the women conventionally feminine. A gender order that divides men and women into different identities and roles underpins a system of compulsory heterosexuality. Moreover, the culture of the law firm remains organized around the ideal of heterosexuality in its public rituals of sexual play, dating, romance, weddings, marriages, and family celebrations. The film's sexual politics do not go beyond claiming a minority but continued subordinate status for the homosexual.

If *Philadelphia* represents Hollywood's film debut of the normal gay, *In and Out* (1997) suggests that middle America is ready and willing to accept gays as full citizens. This is a coming-out story, but less the classic closet tale of an individual's struggling for self-acceptance in a hostile society. Rather, this film narrates a moral drama of a nation that comes of age through recognition of the gay individual as one of its own.

In and Out tells the story of the coming out of Howard (Kevin Kline). As he is unintentionally "outed" by a former student turned actor, Cameron Drake (Matt Dillon), Howard's family and friends are forced to deal with the issue of homosexuality. The film rehearses a conventional coming-out story. Initially in denial, Howard gradually acknowledges and accepts that he is gay.

Coming out is not however the chief story of the film. Howard's coming out is almost painless. For example, after Cameron's outing of Howard, his parents are immediately comforting: "Howard, we want you to know that we love you—gay (or) straight. It's not a bad thing." Another coming-out scene similarly conveys its routine character. As the outing of Howard becomes national news, a television reporter, Peter Malloy (Tom Selleck), is assigned to cover the story. Peter matter of factly tells Howard that he is gay. Howard asks Peter how others have reacted to his revelation.

> Peter: I came out to everyone, my folks, my boss, my dog. One day I snapped. I couldn't take lying to the people I love.
> Howard: What happened?
> Peter: My mom cried for exactly ten seconds. My boss said who cares. My dad said 'but you're so tall.'

By portraying people's response to Howard's and Peter's coming out in a matter of fact and accepting way, the film suggests that not only do gay people approach being gay as a normal identity but much of straight America does as well.

In this regard, it is not coincidental that the movie takes place in a small town in the Midwest (Greenleaf, Indiana). If the film is announcing America's growing acceptance of the normal status of being gay, where else should it take place than in the national heartland? Greenleaf is pure Americana—white picket-fenced homes, a Gemeinschaft-like community, marriages that are permanent, and men who work as farmers (Howard's father) and women who are housewives and mothers (Howard's mother). If Greenleaf citizens can accept the gay citizen, the film seems to be saying, all Americans can and should.

Howard comes out on the day of his wedding, but it is anticlimactic because he has already been accepted by his parents. The most dramatic scene is graduation day at the high school. Howard has been fired by the Principal and was not expected to attend. Encouraged by his father, Howard shows up just in time to hear Cameron Drake—who returns to his hometown to set things right—ridiculing the homophobia of the school administration. Drake asks the Principal why Howard is no longer a teacher.

> Principal: The community felt that it was a question of influence. It's all right to be this way at home but Mr. Bracket is a teacher.
> Drake: So you're thinking about the students. What your saying is that because Mr. Bracket is gay he's going to send out some kind of gay microwaves to make everyone else gay. Well kids you've had Mr. Bracket, is that the way it worked?

Mocking the belief in the contagious polluted status of homosexuality, a student says: "I had Mr. Bracket and I must be gay." After other students similarly ridicule this homophobic logic, the Principal declares that the community has made its decision. At that point, Howard's father declares:

"I'm his father and I'm gay." And Howard's mother chimes in: "I'm his mother and I'm a lesbian." Soon the entire community joins in what I would describe as a public ritual of gay normalization. Greenleaf citizens are announcing the end of the polluted status of the homosexual. By publicly identifying with Howard, they are declaring that the gay individual is a normal human being, one of their own.

The film's defense of the normality of being gay does not however mean that it challenges the norm of heterosexuality. As in *Philadelphia*, the homosexual is presented as making up a very small social minority. The social world of Greenleaf is overwhelmingly heterosexual. Aside from Howard and Peter, whose sexual identity is known only by Howard and his fiancée, Greenleaf citizens are assumed to be heterosexual. And, the film celebrates the institutions of heterosexual marriage and family. In an uncanny parallel with *Philadelphia*, Howard's parents' marriage is portrayed in ideal and nostalgic terms. They are small-town folks who grew up and still live in Greenleaf; and they are so happily married that they celebrate their 50th wedding anniversary with renewed wedding vows. In short, the film champions the normal gay self, but America—as symbolized by Greenleaf—is a nation where almost all of its citizens are heterosexual and the institutions that sustain heterosexual dominance such as binary gender roles, weddings, marriage, and the nuclear family remain unchallenged.

In a further striking parallel to *Philadelphia*, Howard (like Andy) represents what many Americans would consider to be a "normal," indeed an ideal American citizen in every way other than his homosexuality. In fact, Howard betrays a kind of wistful longing for an America that is long gone, if it ever was a reality. With a Midwestern, small-town backdrop, Howard could have stepped out of a 1950s television sitcom such as *The Andy Griffith Show* or *Leave it to Beaver*. His character exemplifies small-town respectability. He is a devoted, popular high-school teacher who wears a bow tie and seersucker suit and peddles his bike to work. He has been engaged for three years to a hometown girl whose femininity is thoroughly conventional, including her virginal status. Howard personifies middle American virtues: he is honest, hard working, trustworthy, devoted to family, and respectful of tradition. So, while the film declares the normality of being gay, it also champions conventional gender roles, sex linked to love and marriage, family values, and a Protestant work ethic. In short, the film simultaneously tolerates the homosexual as a part of America and leaves in place the ideal of a nation anchored by heterosexual marriage and the family.

Philadelphia and *In and Out* substitute an image of the normal gay for the polluted homosexual. However, the norm of heterosexuality remains institutionally secure. Both films evoke idealized images of an America that are strikingly nostalgic and conservative. The gay citizen, it seems, can be tolerated only if a norm and ideal of America is defended that asserts the good, right, normal, or pure status of dichotomous gender roles, heterosexual love, marriage, and the family.

In some films of the 1990s, admittedly exceptional, the normal gay citizen is portrayed in a way that is troubling to an exclusive norm of heterosexuality. *Boys on the Side* (1995) is one such film. It is about the lives of Jane (Whoopi Goldberg), Holly (Drew Barrymore), and Robin (Mary Louise Parker). At one level, it is a story of a generation of women who have the freedom to define their own lives. Each woman has her own personality and story. Jane is a freewheeling, black lesbian. Holly is a somewhat naïve, sexually active straight white woman whose life is defined by her relations with men. Robin is a career-oriented, conventionally feminine straight white woman who, because of a one-time lapse, is HIV positive. The relationship between Jane and Holly is the emotional center of the film.

This is not a coming-out film. Jane does not anguish over her homosexuality. She does not exhibit any shame or ambivalence. Moreover, others do not fret over Jane's sexual identity. When Holly matter of factly tells Robin about Jane's sexual identity, she is surprised but accepting. And when Robin tells her mother about Jane's sexual identity, she is initially upset but soon comes to care deeply about Jane. The fact that Holly and Robin live with Jane underscores the film's moral conviction of the normal status of gays.

However, *Boys on the Side* projects an image of the "good gay" without her thoroughgoing normalization. Whereas Andy and Howard reinforce dominant social norms in every way but their homosexuality, Jane is nonconventional in many respects. For example, her economic values are less middle American than countercultural and working class. She is a struggling musician who survives by driving a taxi in New York. Moreover, Jane is not conventionally feminine. Her self-presentation (e.g., grooming, dress, and talk) is much more masculine than Holly or Robin. However, she is not a stereotypical "mannish lesbian," and her gender nonconformity is not associated with individual pathology or social deviance. Jane retains conventional markers of black femininity (e.g., braids), and psychologically she exhibits stereotypical feminine traits such as being empathetic and nurturing. Finally, Jane is neither settled in a quasimarital relationship (like Andy) nor desexualized (like Howard); she is depicted as a sexually assertive woman who eventually finds another woman.

The way Jane is portrayed challenges an exclusive norm of heterosexuality. For example, her androgynous gender identity contradicts the norm of a binary heterogender order. Similarly, against norms of feminine sexuality that link sexual desire to nurturing and love, Jane is erotically adventurous but not predatory. More to the point, Jane presents a credible lesbian alternative to heterosexuality. Her lesbian sexual desire lacks any trace of shame or guilt. And, the film cautiously legitimates lesbian relationships as an alternative to marriage by suggesting in a final scene that Jane and Anna will live together as lovers. Indeed, the film legitimates the idea of multiple types of family—not just gay families (Jane and Anna) but the chosen family of Jane, Holly, and Robin. As Robin is dying, she decides to live with Jane and Holly, not with her family of origin.

Boys on the Side is also one of the few commercially successful films of the 1990s that features a lesbian. Of the 20 odd films produced in the 1990s that I looked at, only *Boys* featured a normalized lesbian character—although less mainstream films such as *Chasing Amy* (1997) and *Set It Off* (1996) also present affirmative lesbian characters.

The politics of gender is crucial to explaining the relative absence of respectable lesbians compared to gay men in recent popular culture. While both gay men and lesbians threaten the norm of heterosexuality, the lesbian also challenges men's dominance. Lesbians are women who live independently of men or without being economically, socially, and sexually or emotionally dependent on them. Lesbians claim masculine privilege—in the choice of socioeconomic independence, in the pursuit of women as sex and love partners, and, at least for some lesbians, in the integration of masculine styles of self-presentation as a way to flag their sexual identity and to claim social respect and power. The lesbian, moreover, may be understood as a threat to the heterosexual family as she signals to all women the possibility of roles outside of wife and mother. As a perceived threat to men's dominance, to a conventional dichotomous gender order, and to a norm of the heterosexual family that has relied on the domestic labor of women, the lesbian is a truly menacing figure. It is hardly surprising then that American culture remains reluctant to legitimate the figure of the normal lesbian.

As a movie such as *Basic Instinct* (1992) illustrates, the perceived lesbian threat has been responded to by projecting a stereotypical, polluting image of her as a menacing predator and seducer. However, as polluting representations are less tolerated, another strategy is prominent: the homosexuality of women is, if not denied, then depicted as not stable or fundamental. The lesbian is imagined as a transitional status—an immature phase or a case of gender maladjustment.

The idea that homosexuality is somehow transitory or less stable for women is in evidence in two movies. In *Silkwood* (1983), Cher plays a "lesbian" (Dolly). She lives with a heterosexual couple (Meryl Streep and Kurt Russell) that accepts her. Yet, her self-presentation as a plain, depressed, and isolated individual conveys a rather dreary, if not polluted, sense of self. Moreover, Dolly never publicly comes out as a lesbian, leaving her identity somewhat ambiguous. Dolly's sexual identity is suggested when Angela

(Diana Scarwid) enters her life. Dolly and Angela are shown as an ordinary, loving couple. They decide to live together and share a house with Karen and Drew. However, Angela soon leaves Dolly to return to her husband. It turns out that Angela's lesbian experience was a response to being badly treated by her husband. And, after Angela leaves, Dolly returns to her former lifeless and ambiguously identified self. The movie trades on a sense of the unstable, ambiguous status of lesbianism.

A similar ambiguity surrounds the presentation of lesbianism in John Singleton's *Higher Learning* (1995). Kristen, a naïve, attractive, and initially straight-acting college student, becomes romantically involved with a somewhat older woman student. Tellingly, Kristen's lesbianism is introduced only after a man rapes her. As her emotional scars heal, Kristen rediscovers her true heterosexual nature. Her psychological healing parallels her involvement with a man. Her lesbianism, it seems, was a temporary response to a traumatic event. Interestingly, the older woman is presented as a politically active feminist, leaving the audience to wonder whether her lesbianism is more about gender politics than a core self-identity.

If the lesbian is not polluted in these films, her literal reality is denied or doubted. She is viewed as a straight women who is confused, manipulated, or acting out. Sometimes, lesbianism is denied by interpreting it as a type of intense bonding between women. This has been a prominent pattern in recent films such as *The Color Purple* (1985), *Thelma and Louise* (1991), and *Fried Green Tomatoes* (1991). *Boys on the Side* trades on the ambiguous meaning surrounding the intimate bonding between women. For example, in a courtroom scene in which Robin is explaining the kinship status of the three friends, she says:

> I don't know what it is but there's something that goes on between women.... I'm just saying like speaks to like. Love or whatever doesn't always keep, (but) you find out what does, if you're lucky.

Robin's statement blurs the line between women bonding and lesbianism and allows Jane's "lesbianism" to be read as an instance of the former.

Jane's ambiguous sexual status is suggested by her overriding identity as an eccentric person. Jane is a black woman with no apparent ties to a black community; her dearest friends are white women. She is a musician with little or no integration into a network of musicians. And, to really mark her as an outsider, Jane has apparently no kin ties. Jane is presented as a free-floating, marginal individual whose identity, sexual and otherwise, seems fluid and ambiguous.

While the film does not explicitly deny Jane's lesbianism, its political significance is considerably diminished by her isolation from any sense of a lesbian or gay community. Her closest social bonds are with straight women. Her journey of self-discovery takes place entirely in the straight world. And Jane's self-presentation and behavior are free of any lesbian subcultural markings. Accordingly, whatever challenge Jane might present to men's dominance or to heterosexual domination might easily be read as a merely personal, idiosyncratic statement rather than an expression of a community or social movement.

Hollywood films of the 1990s evidence a cultural shift: the polluted homosexual gives way to the normal gay. The status of "normality" makes possible a life outside the closet, but it also restricts social integration to individuals who display the traits or behaviors that are associated with normality. Only gays who are gender conventional, connect sex to romantic, quasimarital, and family values are considered "normal." Individuals who do not conform to these social norms may be considered deviant or inferior and will not necessarily merit respect and integration. And, to the extent that the normal gay is typically imagined as male, white, or middle class, individuals who do not possess these traits will not be recognized in the public image of the normal gay. Finally, the very behaviors that have the status of "normal" (e.g., gender binary) reinforce a heterosexual norm and ideal.

Regulating Heterosexuality: The Good/Bad Sexual Citizen

Many scholars believe that the meanings that collect around the term gay are not simply a reflection of the nature of real gay people. Rather, the meaning of being gay is in part fixed by its role as a point of contrast or opposition to the idea of being straight. For example, the association of homosexuality with hedonism and promiscuity is in part explained by a contrasting ideal that links heterosexuality to being loving and monogamous. From this perspective, stigmatizing representations of homosexuality affect both homosexuals and heterosexuals. Behaviors associated with homosexuality such as promiscuity are defined as bad for both homosexuals and heterosexuals. If public meanings surrounding being gay change, we would expect changes in norms of heterosexual behavior.

In one respect, though, the meaning of homosexuality has apparently had no influence on general sexual norms. Whether films pollute or normalize homosexuality, all the films I previewed hold to an ideal that values sex as a medium of love, relationship-building, and family-making. Accordingly, these films operate with a global division between the good and bad sexual citizen. The bad sexual citizen weakens or uncouples body-and-pleasure-centered sex from intimate bonding. In the shift from polluting to normalizing representations, there is however a change in the role of homosexuality in shaping the image of the bad sexual citizen. In films of the 1960s through the 1980s that pollute homosexuality, the homosexual is the exemplar of the bad sexual citizen. In films that promote gay normalization, the homosexual, at least the normal gay, is no longer associated with the bad sexual citizen. Indeed, the division between the good and bad sexual citizen is less closely tied to the division between the heterosexual and the homosexual.

A public culture that pollutes homosexuality took shape in the 1960s and 1970s. No doubt, this was a response to the rise of a national gay movement. However, it is not coincidental that the figure of the homosexual gained cultural authority during a period of social turmoil in America. Rebellions by youth, women, gays, and sexual liberationists challenged dominant social norms that linked sex to intimacy, love, marriage, and the family. These sex rebels championed a culture of sexual variation. They defended the idea that sex has multiple meanings. Sex was valued not only as a way to establish intimacy or a family but as a type of pleasure, self-expression, and communication apart from love or relationship-building. Some rebels championed a minimalist ethic: as long as sex was between consenting adults, it should be considered legitimate and deregulated.

Stigmatizing the homosexual was in part a reaction to these efforts to renegotiate sexual norms to permit more choice. The polluted homosexual restricted the field of legitimate sexuality to heterosexuality. Moreover, to the extent that American culture associated homosexuality with a cluster of sexual meanings such as multiple sex partners, public sex, and recreational sex, polluting homosexuality also discredited these practices. Heterosexuals who engaged in these behaviors experienced something of the defiled status of homosexuals. Polluting the homosexual then functioned to defend both heterosexual privilege and a specific heterosexual and gender order.

Midnight Cowboy (1969) expressed something of the rebellious spirit of the time. For example, the figure of Joe Buck (Jon Voight) gave expression to a culture that valued individuals who fashioned lives independently of social roles and conventions.

Joe is a small-town, handsome, working-class Texan who sets out to make his fortune in New York by hustling women. Through the character of Joe, the film explores and cautiously endorses a culture of sexual variation. For example, scenes of commercial sex are depicted in a morally neutral way. Indeed, the women he has sex with are presented as sexually autonomous; they make sexual choices based on need and desire. Joe seems to flourish in the giving and receiving of sexual pleasure, as do the women.

Although the film is tolerant towards sexual variation, homosexuality is off limits. Both Ratso (Dustin Hoffman) and Joe view the homosexual as a despicable human type. Ratso, the lowest of street hustlers, is aggressively hostile toward homosexuals. He refers to them as "faggots," a term signaling their defiled moral status. And Joe, who turns to men after he proves inept in hustling women, is repulsed by homosexuals. In one scene, an older, closeted man purchases Joe's sexual favors. However, this man is unable to go through with the arrangement for reasons that apparently have to do with his religious convictions. Despite being paid, Joe assaults the man because, we are led to believe, the mere anticipation of homosexual sex is so disgusting and repulsive. Joe avoids any taint of being homosexual by both his homophobic actions and repeated flashbacks to a past girlfriend.

As this film explores an underground world of street people, hustlers, and sexual rebels, it is not merely coincidental that the figure of the polluted homosexual appears time and again. Gay "queens" and closet types, along with countercultural figures whose gender presentation and erotic fluidity might suggest homosexuality, are a striking presence. At one level, the polluted homosexual serves to establish a clear, absolute moral boundary for legitimate sexual variation. Heterosexuality is the exclusive field of legitimate sexuality. But the haunting presence of the polluted homosexual suggests that this figure performs a further boundary-defining role. The continuous juxtaposition of homosexuality and "deviant" sexualities (e.g., commercial sex, public sex, casual sex) suggests the dangers of an eroticism loosened from its solid mooring in love, intimacy, marriage, and the family. In other words, the figure of the polluted homosexual is a cultural response to a sense of danger and disorder surrounding the relaxation of sexual controls.

In *Five Easy Pieces* (1970), Bobby (Jack Nicholson) steps forward as a sexual rebel. Although he lives with his girlfriend, Bobby has sex with many women, sometimes at the same time and sometimes with prostitutes. The movie portrays Bobby's sexual behavior as meaningful, and valuable, not only as a medium of intimate love but also as a form of pleasure and self-expression. In the spirit of the 1960s, the film seems open toward Bobby's ethic of self- and sexual experimentation. His freewheeling, guiltless eroticism is presented as an almost pure realm of self-expression and freedom.

Bobby's pursuit of sexual variation, however, does not extend to homosexuality. Despite exploring a wide range of nonconventional sexual behaviors, Bobby has no homosexual encounters. Indeed, his masculine swagger and (hetero) sexual bravado establishes Bobby's unequivocal heterosexual identity.

Bobby's sexual experimentation is tolerated because it is confined to the field of heterosexuality. If his sexual adventures included homosexuality, he would have likely forfeited a normal and respectable status. To the extent however that he values erotic play more than marriage and family values, Bobby's character looks more and more like the cultural stereotype of the irresponsible, sex-driven, dangerous homosexual.

In the course of the film, Bobby's self-control weakens. Desire threatens to take over his life. His passion ceases to be playful; it becomes menacing. Thus, Bobby not only cheats on his girlfriend, but he has an affair with his brother's fiancée. And, in a final scene in which Bobby must decide between marriage and sexual freedom, Bobby chooses the latter even though it means abandoning his pregnant girlfriend. As the quest for erotic pleasure and expressiveness becomes his chief sexual value, the film presents him as a social danger. Bobby's "liberated" sexuality threatens the institutions of marriage and the family—and ultimately endangers society by projecting a world of fatherless children. The fear of an eroticism that in its boundless quest for pleasure and excitement tears apart the fabric of moral order is a threat that has been closely associated with the homosexual.

Looking for Mr. Goodbar is, as we have seen, a coming-of-age story narrated as a journey of sexual self-exploration. Teresa grew up in a sexually repressed family. Having polio as a child reinforced feelings of shame around her body. Sexual liberation is her chosen path to adulthood. Teresa tries it all—one-night stands, paid sex, group sex, affairs with married men, and rough sex. Her sexual adventurousness is part of a struggle to be free of shame and guilt; it is her chosen path to freedom.

Teresa's sexual experimentation occurs exclusively in the field of heterosexuality. In a scene depicting group sex, a woman invites Teresa to participate. She declines.

In the course of the film, a sense of danger surrounds Teresa's erotic openness. As her experimentation takes her further away from norms of sexual romanticism, marriage, and family-making, it comes to signify a world of risk—to herself and society. For example, in one scene Teresa gets involved with a man (Richard Gere) whose free-spirited sexuality passes into sexual violence. And, in the end, Teresa's sexual adventurousness results in her brutal murder by, tellingly, a homosexual—the very symbol of a desire free from social convention.

In the course of the 1960s and 1970s, sexual norms were being renegotiated to permit more individual choice. Reflecting the times, these films explore the moral meaning of a culture of sexual variation. Homosexuality is used to establish moral boundaries. The exclusive legitimacy of heterosexuality is established by polluting homosexuality. Moreover, to the extent that homosexuality was associated with specific behaviors such as multiple-partner sex, recreational sex, a body- and pleasure-centered sexuality, or public sex, its defiled status also meant the pollution of these behaviors. To the extent that characters such as Bobby, Teresa, and Joe champion an eroticism that uncouples the pleasurable and expressive qualities of sex from love, marriage, and the family, they evoke the very same fears of social disorder associated with the homosexual. Introducing the figure of the polluted homosexual regulates sexuality by restricting legitimate sexual variation to heterosexuality and to a narrow heterosexual pattern. The homosexual circulates, so to speak, as a free-floating signifier of a dangerous desire.

Turning our attention to films that portray gays as normal, I found, unexpectedly, a tightening of heterosexual regulation. These films retreat from a culture that values expanded sexual choice and variation. Heterosexual practices that deviate from a narrow romantic-companionate norm are morally suspect. Indeed, *gay normalization, at least in the films of the 1990s, is accompanied by a sexual ethic that legitimates sex—for both heterosexuals and homosexuals—exclusively in intimate, preferably love-based, monogamous, preferably marital-type relationships.* In other words, these films establish a division between the good and bad sexual citizen that is uncoupled from the hetero-/homosexual binary. The narrowing of the range of legitimate sexual variation is a response to fears of moral and social disorder raised by gay normalization. The social integration of gays creates an anxiety that other "deviant" sexualities (sex workers, sadomasochists, pedophiles, and polygamists) will make similar claims to normality and also demand respectability. Bringing homosexuality into the American heartland evokes fears of unleashing an unbridled eroticism that will bring chaos and decline.

In and Out uses humor and parody to mock homosexual pollution. Gays are viewed as normal Americans. But, as we have seen, the ideal of heterosexuality is not threatened. Heterosexual marriage and the family are celebrated. After Howard's coming-out scene, the movie ends, tellingly, with a renewal of his parents' wedding vows after 50 years of marriage. The idealization of marriage not only serves to reinforce the norm of heterosexuality but to enforce a particular heterosexual norm—lifetime marriage based on love and family obligations.

The narrowing of legitimate heterosexual behavior to a romantic intimate norm is dramatized in the character of Cameron Drake (Matt Dillon). Cameron, the Oscar-winning movie star, lives a "Hollywood lifestyle." He is surrounded by beautiful women and lives lavishly. Cameron returns to Greenleaf, where he grew up, to help Howard. Unexpectedly, he falls in love with Howard's ex-fiancée who, in contrast to his beautiful, bimbo-type girlfriend, is a plain-looking, overweight, clumsy, small-town high-school teacher. The film creates a good/bad moral division between the hedonistic, narcissistic sexual values associated with Hollywood and the romantic, marital, and family values of Greenleaf.

In and Out was a huge commercial success in part because it trades on a nostalgic image of America. It champions an America where individuals marry as virgins for love, where marriage inevitably leads to family, and where men and women occupy different and complementary social and sexual roles. The real threat to America is not the normal gay who is a variation of the ideal national citizen, but hedonistic, narcissistic, and consumerist sexual and social values that are dramatically symbolized by Hollywood culture.

Ironically, then, as films of the 1990s champion a notion of the normal gay, they also narrow the range of legitimate sexual-intimate choices, for gays and straights. As the normal gay assumes the status of a respectable citizen, it is the "bad" sexual citizen defined by his/her violation of a romantic, monogamous intimate norm that is polluted. The division between the good and bad sexual citizen may make it possible for the normal lesbian and gay man to become a full American citizen, but one effect is a tightening of sexual controls for all citizens.

Conclusion

Between 1960 and 2000, Hollywood films gradually, even if unevenly, exchanged polluting for normalizing images of lesbians and gay men. Politically speaking, the logic of gay normalization involves tolerance and integration, but only for normal or good gays. The good gay expresses a narrow social norm; she must be gender conventional, committed to romantic-companionate and family values, uncritically patriotic, and be detached from a subculture. The normal gay just wants to blend in, to be an ordinary American. Individuals who deviate from this norm, for example, gays who are gender benders, who like sex apart from love or intimacy, or gays who want to change society, may not gain entry into the magical circle of normality and respectability. The normal gay does not challenge or threaten the norm of heterosexuality.

Unexpectedly, I found that in films that normalize gays there is a tightening of heterosexual regulation. Films such as *Philadelphia* and *In and Out* appeal to strikingly nostalgic images of an America of small towns, of men who work and women who mother, of virgin courtship and marriages that last a lifetime, and of *Gemeinshaft*-like communities. This is an America that is intolerant of sexual variation—of sexually active youth, of children born outside of marriage, of cohabitation, of multiple sex partners, and of an eroticism loosened from the grip of romantic love and intimacy. Only individuals whose behavior conforms to norms of the good sexual citizen can claim the full privileges of heterosexuality.

The link between gay normalization and the tightening of social control is more then coincidental. Assigning a fully human, normal status to gay individuals fuels a fear of disorder because of the association of homosexuality with a freewheeling, promiscuous desire. It also creates a fear that other sexual outsiders will demand inclusion, further fueling anxieties of impending disorder. It is then to be expected that every step toward gay integration will likely prompt some opposition that will appeal to fears of children being confused and abused, of families and marriages being weakened, and of a nation tumbling down the path toward moral chaos.

As gays are viewed as normal, they are no longer necessarily associated with the bad sexual citizen. Of course, the homosexual was never the only bad sexual citizen; there was the prostitute, the sex offender, pornographer, or the sexual libertine. Still, in the early postwar years the homosexual emerged as the personification of the menacing sexual citizen. The homosexual became a kind of symbol of a perverse, dangerous eroticism that was detached from romantic, marital, and family values. Accordingly, the hetero-/homosexual division came to serve as an important regulatory force. This has changed somewhat as gays are viewed as normal; the good/bad sexual citizen is less dependent on sexual identity. The bad citizen is today someone who violates romantic, intimate, familial norms, regardless of his/her sexual identity. The bad sexual citizen, not the homosexual, at least not the normal gay, is becoming a chief focus of social control.

References

Adams, Mary Louise. 1997. *The trouble with normal: Postwar youth and the making of heterosexuality*. Toronto: University of Toronto Press.
Atkinson, Ti-Grace. 1974. *Amazon odyssey*. New York: Links Books.
Bunch, Charlotte. 1975. Lesbians in revolt, in C. Bunch (ed.) *Lesbianism and the women's movement*, pp. 29–38. Baltimore, MD: Diana Press.
Butler, Judith. 1990. *Gender trouble: Feminism and the subversion of identity*. New York: Routledge.
Chauncey, George. 1994. *Gay New York: Gender, urban culture, and the making of the gay male world 1890–1940*. New York: Basic.
Corber, Robert. 1997. *Homosexuality in cold war America: resistance and the crisis of masculinity*. Durham: Duke University Press.
D'Emilio, John. 1983. *Sexual politics, sexual communities: The making of a homosexual minority in the United States, 1940–1970*. Chicago: University of Chicago Press.
Doty, Alexander. 1993. *Making things perfectly queer: Interpreting mass culture*. Minneapolis: University of Minnesota Press.
Dubinsky, Karen. 1993. *Improper advances: Rape and heterosexual conflict in Ontario, 1880–1929*. Chicago: University of Chicago Press.
Dyer, Richard. 1986. *Heavenly bodies: Film stars and society*. New York: St. Martin's Press.
Epstein, Debbie and Richard Johnson. 1998. *Schooling sexualities*. Buckingham: Open University Press.
Fuss, Diana (ed.) 1991. Introduction. *Inside/out: Lesbian theories, gay theories*, pp.1 – 10. New York: Routledge.
Herman, Didi. 1997. *The antigay agenda: Orthodox vision and the christian right*. Chicago: University of Chicago Press.
Ingraham, Chrys. 1999. *White weddings: Romancing heterosexuality in popular culture*. New York: Routledge.
Katz, Jonathan. 1995. *The invention of heterosexuality*. New York: Penguin.
Kennedy, Elizabeth. 1996. But we would never talk about It: the structures of lesbian discretion in South Dakota, 1928–1933, in Ellen Lewin (ed.) *Inventing lesbian cultures in America*. Boston: Beacon.
Marotta, Toby. 1981. *The politics of homosexuality*. New York: Houghton Mifflin.
Rich, Adrienne. 1983. Compulsory heterosexuality and lesbian existence, in Ann Snitow et al. (eds.) *Powers of desire: The politics of sexuality*, pp. 177–205. New York: Monthly Review Press.
Russo, Vito. 1987. *The celluloid closet: homosexuality in the movies*, revised edition. New York: Harper and Row.
Sedgwick, Eve Kosofsky. 1990. *Epistemology of the closet*. Berkeley: University of California Press.
Seidman, Steven. 2002. *Beyond the closet*. New York: Routledge.
Steinberg, D., D. Epstein, and R. Johnson (eds.) 1997. *Border patrols: Policing the boundaries of heterosexuality*. London: Cassell.
Straayer, Chris. 1996. *Deviant eyes, deviant bodies: sexual orientation in film and video*. New York: Columbia University Press.

Vaid, Urvashi. 1995. *Virtual equality: The mainstreaming of gay and lesbian liberation*. New York: Doubleday.

Warner, Michael. 1993. Introduction, in M. Warner (ed.) *Fear of a queer planet*. Minneapolis: University of Minnesota Press.

Wittman, Carl. 1972. A gay manifesto, in K. Jay and A. Young (eds.) *Out of the closets: Voices of gay liberation*, pp. 330–341. New York: New York University Press.

Notes

1. Katz, 1995; Seidman, 2002
2. Rich, 1983: 201; cf. Atkinson, 1974; Bunch, 1975
3. Butler, 1990; Ingraham, 1999; Warner, 1993
4. Chauncey, 1994; Kennedy, 1996; Seidman, 2002
5. For exceptions, see Adams, 1997; Dubinsky, 1993; Steinberg et al., 1997.
6. To research these themes, I studied films. In 1998, I analyzed 47 films. Several criteria guided this research. First, reflecting the focus of the study, only films produced in the U.S. were included. Second, I considered primarily "mainstream" films. These were defined as commercially successful films as measured by box office sales (Appendix). I have assumed that commercial success lends plausibility to the claim that the sexual meanings in these films are indicative of the beliefs and values of a substantial segment of America. I do not assume though that normalizing representations in films are necessarily indicative of trends in all institutional spheres. For example, research on the social organization of public schools documents that normative heterosexuality continues to be enforced by means of polluting homosexuality (e.g., Epstein and Johnson 1998). At the same time, normalizing trends in television, academic disciplines, in law, and in business and governmental policy make plausible the claim that normalization is one defining social trend in contemporary America. Finally, while normalizing representations may be indicative of empirical trends, they also function as normative social forces defining the preferred social meaning and social role of homosexuality. Third, I considered only films with explicit gay characters. I disregarded films where homosexuality was implied. While queer cultural analysis has often brilliantly analyzed symbolically coded forms of homosexuality as a way to show the presence of homosexuality in shaping heterosexuality (e.g., Doty 1993; Corber 1997; Straayer 1996), my aim is less to do a queer reading of film than to trace logics of normative heterosexuality.

   This research strategy still posed methodological problems. There are well over 1,000 movies that meet the above criteria. I decided against a random sample, in part because film collections are spotty and archival access presented impossible demands. I wanted moreover to make sure that "breakthrough" films (e.g., *The Children's Hour*) or commercial hits (e.g., *Philadelphia, My Best Friend's Wedding*) were included. Finally, films were selected that included segments of the gay population such as lesbians or persons of color who are underrepresented in media culture.

CHAPTER 3

Claiming Citizenship? Sexuality, Citizenship, and Lesbian Feminist Theory

DIANE RICHARDSON

In recent years, citizenship has re-emerged as a key concept in social theory, albeit one that is widely contested both in respect of its meaning and potential utility. This has been reflected in the proliferation of academic works on the theme of citizenship across a variety of disciplines. An important aspect of this emergent literature has been critiques of traditional discourses, which have privileged analyses of the relationship between social class and citizenship, for their "gender-blind" approach. Feminist analyses, in particular, have examined the relationship between concepts of citizenship and gender pointing out how, despite claims to universality, a particular version of the normal citizen/subject is encoded in dominant discourses of citizenship.[1] Historically, citizenship has been constructed in "the male image." Indeed, in ancient Greece, where concepts of civil and political citizenship have their origins, women, along with children and slaves, were excluded from the status of citizenship and, it is argued, have continued to be marginalized in contemporary accounts where the paradigmatic citizen is male.[2] Traditional accounts of citizenship have also been much criticized for neglecting to consider the relationship of citizenship with race. Thus, for example, writers such as Anthias and Yuval-Davis (1992) and Alexander (1994) have demonstrated how ideas of citizenship are racialized, as well as gendered.

A further challenge to understandings of citizenship is the emergence, over the last few years, of a new body of work concerned with sexuality and citizenship. Much of this work, although it has an interdisciplinary flavor, has come from within sociology,[3] political theory,[4] and legal theory.[5] With all of its disciplinary diversity it is, perhaps unsurprisingly, a literature that has been developed largely by lesbian/feminist, gay, and queer theorists. Since the 1980s, social movements concerned with "sexual politics" have increasingly couched their demands in terms of the attainment of rights, particularly "lesbian and gay" movements. This has been most evident in the United States, but is increasingly dominant elsewhere. The increasing use of the language of citizenship, in contrast to the language of liberation spoken by social movements of an earlier generation, has in a sense, therefore, prompted this examination of the ways in which sexuality intersects with the status of citizenship in modern democracies.

These developments led me to start asking a number of questions about how this work related to lesbian/feminism. My starting point I suppose was how, as feminists, do we respond to this growing interest in and use of the term *sexual citizenship*? How is it being defined? Is it a concept that is being used in a gender-neutral or, some might want to argue, a gender-blind way? Do we need to develop gendered understandings of the concept of sexual citizenship? What are the implications of not doing so? And, insofar as citizenship is defined in terms of rights and duties, what do we mean by sexual rights and obligations? What do such analyses tell us about the limitations placed upon our rights as citizens; in particular, women's role as citizens, especially as lesbians?

Within the limits of this chapter, I can do no more than begin to address some of these questions through an examination of how the concept of "sexual citizenship" is currently in the process of being defined. The aim is not to provide an exhaustive review of the literature, but rather to identify common themes and issues, as well as vocabularies used, in discussions of sexuality and citizenship.

It might be claimed, given its relative newness as a field of study, that it is too soon to attempt to map the shifts in understanding of citizenship that we are witnessing through an expansion of the concept to include "private" and intimate practices and identities associated with sexuality. However, I would argue that it is possible to begin to identify a number of distinct, albeit overlapping, strands emerging within the literature, which draw on different epistemological concerns: (1) the sexualized nature of concepts of citizenship; (2) notions of sexual or intimate citizenship; and (3) the claims of different communities to "sexual justice" and the principles and models of citizenship upon which such claims are founded. I will briefly sketch out these three interrelated strands before going on, in the remainder of this chapter, to critically examine such developments from a lesbian/feminist perspective. In particular, I want to explore the concept of lesbian citizenship and some of the theoretical and political issues that this raises.

Is the Concept of Citizenship Sexualized?

A number of writers have addressed the question of how ideas of citizenship are based upon certain assumptions about sexuality, in particular, hegemonic heterosexuality. The main focus of such work is to demonstrate how citizens are normatively constructed as (hetero)sexual subjects and, related to this, offer a way of analyzing the resultant inequalities faced by "excluded" citizens in terms of the institutionalization of heterosexuality.

This is a common theme in lesbian/feminist work that has engaged with questions of sexuality and citizenship. Indeed, Shane Phelan (1994) claims that one of the strengths of feminist analyses is that they have exposed both the assumed maleness and heterosexuality of the "normal citizen." In my own work,[6] I have addressed this issue through an examination of definitions of citizenship as a set of civil, political, and social rights,[7] as social membership both of a nation-state and social membership conceptualized more broadly,[8] as cultural rights,[9] and in terms of consumerism.[10] In each of these different approaches to understanding citizenship, I have argued that it is possible to show that heterosexuality is constructed as a necessary if not sufficient basis for full citizenship. Crucially, what this demonstrates is that what we have conventionally understood as "citizenship" is itself a hegemonic form of sexual citizenship. In a similar vein, other writers, albeit at differing levels of specificity, have contended that citizenship is constituted through heterosexual norms and practices.[11]

Texts such as these draw either implicitly or explicitly on a more thoroughgoing critique of heterosexuality, most closely associated with radical feminism, which aims to denaturalize what Adrienne Rich (1980) in her groundbreaking article referred to as "compulsory heterosexuality." The notion of the normative category citizen as heterosexual is not, however, limited to lesbian/feminist analysis. Some queer/gay male writers have also acknowledged the relationship between citizenship and the institutionalization of heterosexuality.[12] This is, perhaps, hardly surprising given that the concept of "heteronormativity" has been central to queer theory, which, in common with feminist approaches, has problematized the heterosexual/homosexual binary.[13] Having said this, the importance of earlier feminist work on developing critical analyses of heterosexuality, laying the foundations for later work, is not always acknowledged by queer theorists.

What do we Mean by Sexual or Intimate Citizenship?

The second theme I have identified can be understood in terms of a more general trend toward the expansion of the idea of citizenship, as is evidenced in the diversity of arenas in which citizenship is being contested.[14] It is a concern shared by a number of writers who seek to theorize a new version of citizenship: sexual or intimate citizenship in which both universalistic notions of "the sexual citizen" and differing versions of sexual citizenship, based on diverse forms of sexuality, are conceptual possibilities.

Much of this work has been by gay/male writers and is predominantly informed by sociological thinking. For example, one of the first to claim to address citizenship and its relation to sexuality was David Evans in his book *Sexual Citizenship* (1993). Evans provides examples of what he delineates as different forms of sexual citizenship, including the experience of male homosexuals, bisexuals, transvestites, transsexuals, and children. Of the latter, he asks: "Can children be legitimately regarded in any sense as sexual citizens? Do they have sexual rights? Do they consume, or are they merely consumed sexual commodities?"[15] In posing such questions, Evans highlights the right of consent to sexual behaviors as basic to sexuality as citizenship status, alongside a notion of the citizen as a consumer. For Evans, sexual citizenship is primarily constructed as membership of sexual communities, with rights and privileges determined by individuals' relative moral worth and status as consumers.

Evans' work is useful in developing a framework for understanding how formalized degrees of citizenship are accorded to categories of sexual difference and, also, what might be termed "sexual rights." However, a distinction can be made between his approach and that taken by other writers whose interests are to rethink citizenship more generally. This broader concern with sexuality and citizenship includes the work of writers such as Giddens (1992), Weeks (1995), and Plummer (1995), who seek to rethink citizenship through notions of "the intimate." Plummer, for example, proposes that a "fourth notion of citizenship" be added to those based on the traditional Marshallian model of civic, political, and social rights (Marshall, 1950): the idea of "intimate citizenship." By his own admission, Plummer offers a very "loose definition" of what he means by intimate citizenship. It is about: "a cluster of emerging concerns over the rights to choose what we do with our bodies, our feelings, our identities, our relationships, our genders, our eroticisms, and our representations."[16]

A different conception of sexual citizenship can be found in the work of those who are critical both of a "rights-based" reading of the term and of the emphasis upon intimacy. For some, there is a concern that these kinds of formulations emphasize love, domestic partnerships, and friendship but not sex. Thus, for example, writers such as David Bell and Jon Binnie are concerned to "bring in the erotic and embodied dimensions excluded in many discussions of citizenship."[17] Another important aspect of such critiques is a contestation of the locus of sexual citizenship. The issue of the

relationship between intimacy and privacy is a complex one[18] and, although some theorists insist on a necessary relationship between the two, no such simple reading can be made from Plummer's vision of intimate citizenship. Nevertheless, it can be argued that one of the effects of discussions of sexual citizenship, which focus on the "private space" of intimate relations, and of accounts of the rights and freedoms granted to particular categories of sexual citizen, which are frequently based upon privacy-based rights claims, is a (re)privatization of sexual citizenship. Following this argument, and against a construction of sexual citizenship as located in the private, there has been an attempt by various writers to focus on the meaning of sexual citizenship in the *public* sphere, which, in some instances, incorporates a concern to "put back the sex in sexual citizenship." For example, David Bell (1995) has written about public sex in the context of developing notions of sexual citizenship.

This discussion touches on a tension in bringing together the two terms sexuality and citizenship. On the one hand, we can understand Plummer's expansion of the concept of citizenship to include intimate citizenship as a radical move, since such issues have previously been excluded from discourses of citizenship on the grounds of their being "private" rather than public matters. On the other hand, the recognition of citizenship claims in relation to sexuality on the basis of a "right to privacy" represents a form of sexual politics, which has a long history both in Europe and the United States. Moreover, it is primarily through utilizing such discourses of citizenship that rights movements have been successful in gaining specific rights and freedoms, much more so than more radical campaigns.[19] This, as it is often termed, integrationist or assimilationist approach to sexual citizenship is regarded as reformist rather than radical, especially by lesbian/feminist and queer movements where the focus is upon critiquing and destabilizing the public/private binary. Thus, in the context of discourses of sexuality rather than citizenship, the construction of the private as central to sexual citizenship can be read as problematic, leading some writers to claim that a more radical focus is to rethink citizenship through a resistance to privacy and an examination of democratic sexual citizenship enacted in public spaces.[20]

These discussions highlight that one of the challenges of the discourse of sexual/intimate citizenship is that it problematizes the public/private binary. Concepts of the "public" and the "private" have, of course, been extremely important within feminist theorizing. Related to this, some feminists writers such as Ribbens McCarthy and Edwards (1999) have expressed concern that the recent focus on democracy within "intimate relationships" might threaten to marginalize some crucial feminist issues, especially around caring for children and domestic activities, in transforming the meaning of "the private" to refer primarily to sexual intimacy.

What Rights and Demands are the Concern of Sexual or Intimate Citizenship and What are the Principles and Models of Citizenship Underlying Such Claims?

Work relevant to this third theme has examined claims for "sexual rights" and the justifications advanced for them, as well as the arguments offered by those who oppose such claims. One of the main ways in which sexual citizenship has been addressed in terms of analyses of the rights claims of various "sexual constituencies" is through an examination of the relationship of lesbian and gay rights with the state. This is perhaps hardly surprising, since lesbian and gay communities have been among the most vocal in demanding various rights claims. (The implications of regarding lesbian and gay communities as a single constituency will be discussed later.) For example, Davina Cooper (1993, 1994, 1995), in her discussion of local government initiatives for lesbian and gay rights in the U.K. in the 1980s, looks at the discourses of citizenship that were utilized. Didi Herman (1994) likewise has analyzed the arguments of lesbian and gay rights movements and their opponents in Canada.

Analyses of campaigns for specific rights in relation to sexuality, such as those mounted by lesbian and gay political movements, have not only been concerned with identifying the type of demands and arguments that are expressed within the discourse of sexual rights. A further concern has been to explore the political and policy implications of different models of citizenship in relation to forms of inclusion and exclusion that are related to sexual status. The focus here is on examining how useful various frameworks of citizenship may or may not be in furthering "sexual justice."[21]

In my recent work, I have approached the question of theorizing "sexual rights" from a somewhat different perspective,[22] emphasizing how this is a contested concept both in terms of meaning, given competing claims over what are defined as "sexual rights," and in terms of differing views over its political utility. For feminists, claims to rights in relation to sexuality have largely been about safety, bodily control, sexual self-definition, agency, and pleasure. Lesbian and gay movements have emphasized the extension of specific sexual rights, including an equal age of consent, as well as more broadly the right to freely choose adult sexual partners and the right to socially and legally recognized lesbian, bisexual, or gay identities and lifestyles. Recently, there have also been attempts to place sexual rights on the agenda of disability movements, especially in relation to disabled people's rights to sexual expression.[23] Some writers also include in their discussion of sexual citizenship the right to consume "sexual commodities," which can be defined as services and goods related to sexual practices and identities.[24]

What is lacking is a clear framework of how differing interpretations of the term "sexual rights" relate to one another, especially from a sociological

and feminist perspective. To this end, I have outlined a framework for understanding sexual citizenship as a system of rights, which tries to make sense of the different ways of interpreting "sexual rights" in terms of three main substreams that are apparent within "sexual rights" discourse: conduct-based, identity-based, and relationship-based rights claims. This is not to imply an uncritical acceptance of the concept of "sexual rights," however this may be defined. On the contrary, it is to attempt to clarify similarities and differences between both individual writers and social groups campaigning for social change in relation to sexuality in order that we may have a more detailed understanding of the limitations and potential of the notion of sexual citizenship.

In the remainder of this chapter, I will draw upon all three of these strands in assessing the possible significance of contemporary debates about sexuality and citizenship for lesbian/feminist theory and practice.

Feminist Politics and the Language of Rights

Historically, in Britain, lesbian/feminism has been closely associated with radical and revolutionary feminist perspectives, although not exclusively so.[25] Struggles have been far less about the pursuit of "formal equality" and rights of citizenship and much more about critiquing and seeking to transform the heteropatriarchal nature of society.[26] In this sense, we can identify common ground with the first theme, which I have characterized as focusing on how claims to citizenship status are closely associated with the institutionalization of heterosexual, as well as male, privilege.

Although lesbian/feminism has developed powerful critiques of heterosexuality, marriage, and the family, in contrast to the increasingly dominant and U.S.-influenced "equal rights" approach to political change, which seeks to integrate lesbians and gays into such social institutions and practices, it has not entirely eschewed the language of sexual citizenship. Indeed, the concept of sexual (and reproductive) rights has a long history within feminism. Examples of this can be identified in demands for the right to sexual pleasure, which were an aspect of feminist politics in the first part of the 20th century and, much more centrally, in the early years of "second wave" feminism during the 1970s, as well as claims expressed in terms of the right to sexual self-determination, bodily control, and safety—often characterized as "the right to say no."[27]

Lesbian/feminist analyses have made an important contribution to these and related debates within feminism over what are defined as sexual rights, or lack of rights. More specifically, lesbians have insisted on the right to *be* lesbian and the freedom (for all women) to be able to choose to have relationships with other women. Some of the most contested debates within lesbian/feminism, however, have been over claims to "rights" that center on forms of sexual practice such as, for example, the use of pornography and, recently, relationship-based claims, in particular the right to marry.[28]

I am not, of course, suggesting that we should understand lesbian/feminist demands as calls for "rights" in the "equal rights" sense of the term. Indeed, rather than seeking inclusion and equal treatment, lesbian/feminists have critiqued the rights and privileges accorded heterosexuals. Moreover, lesbian/feminist demands have not been premised on the idea of lesbians as a "minority group" entitled to certain rights that have previously been denied. They have been based on a more complex argument for the rights of all women to have sexual relationships with other women, and for conditions that enable women to exercise sexual autonomy more generally.

With these important provisos in mind, I want to suggest that, although perhaps not immediately apparent, it is possible to rearticulate issues and debates within lesbian/feminist theory in the present context of analyzing the construction of a notion of sexual citizenship (the second theme) and theorizing "sexual rights" claims (the third theme). This is one way we may begin to critically assess the interrelationships between this new body of work and lesbian/feminism. As a first step in this process, I would argue that we need to ask how and in what ways "lesbian citizenship" is being defined?

The Lesbian Citizen?
Over the last fifteen to twenty years, many of the major debates within feminism have been concerned, in one way or other, with the question of differences between women and, related to this, the meaning and political utility of the category "woman." In part, this reflects the influence of poststructural and postmodern perspectives on feminist theory, which challenge the idea of "woman" as a fixed, natural category, regarding it instead as a "constantly shifting signifier of multiple meanings."[29] Another important reason for this problematization of the category "woman," which is often given insufficient recognition relative to the attention paid to the influence of postmodernism and deconstructionism, has been the response of women who felt excluded from such a "unitary" category. Black and lesbian feminists, in particular, have critiqued the way in which the use of the category "woman" within feminism has often served to conceal racial and sexual difference.

These apparent tensions between theorizing difference and diversity and using an analytical category that might be seen as a universalistic (e.g., "woman," "patriarchy," and "citizen") have also been apparent within the discourse on citizenship. Within feminist perspectives, this can be characterized as a concern with the terms upon which women's claims to citizenship are articulated.

> Typically, women have been faced with a choice between a universalistic claim based on the principle of their equality with men or a particularistic claim based on their difference from men. These represent on the one hand a gender-neutral and on the other a gender differentiated model of citizenship.[30]

It is against this background of debate within current discourses about gender and citizenship that I want to try to decipher some of the possible implications of the newly articulated concerns with sexuality and citizenship, previously outlined, for how we think about and experience lesbian relationships.

The immediate parallel to be drawn, it seems to me, is the question of whether we are encouraged to theorize sexual or intimate citizenship in terms of universalistic notions of "the sexual citizen" or to embrace a gendered and sexually differentiated model that would allow for a specific notion of "lesbian citizenship." Jeffrey Weeks (1998), for example, has described the "sexual citizen" (or would-be sexual citizen) in the following very broad terms, which might be taken as implying the former undifferentiated approach.

> The sexual citizen, I want to argue, could be male or female, young or old, black or white, rich or poor, straight or gay: could be anyone, in fact, but for one key characteristic. The sexual citizen exists—or, perhaps better, wants to come into being—because of the new primacy given to sexual subjectivity in the contemporary world.[31]

Here, Weeks does not deal directly with the question of the tension between universality and difference; however, despite this very inclusive and, some might claim, universal definition of "the sexual citizen," his work clearly suggests a desire to embrace a "differentiated universalism" rather than the either/or positions presented above. For example, he talks of the importance of "balancing the claims of different communities with constructing new common purposes" and of "learning to live with diversity at the same time as building our common humanity."[32] There are parallels here with some feminist work on citizenship, which has been critical of binary characterizations and has attempted to "ride the tension between the universal and the particular."[33]

Another influential writer who has addressed the theme of sexual relations and citizenship—what he often refers to as emotional democracy—in very broad-based terms is the sociologist Anthony Giddens (1992). In exploring the values of the intimate sphere, Giddens argues that sexual relationships built on a sense of equal vulnerability and mutual trust, respect and care, free from coercion or violence, are democratic. He uses the term "pure relationship," defined as "a relationship of sexual and emotional equality" (Giddens 1992: 2), to refer to the democratic restructuring of intimacy. Moreover, he claims that it is through such a "transformation of intimacy," which so far women are deemed to have played the major part, that there exists the possibility of a radical transformation of the personal sphere.

What is important in the context of this discussion is the fact that Giddens regards lesbians, whom he variously refers to as "lesbian women" and "gay women," as brand leaders in the practice of emotional democracy; more likely to be in relationships that are based on the principles of the "pure relationship" than those who are involved in heterosexual relationships.

> ... it is the gays who are the pioneers in this respect—the prime everyday experimenters. They have for some while experienced what is becoming more and more commonplace for heterosexual couples.[34]

Whether one agrees with this statement or not—balancing concerns over what, to me at least, seems an overgeneralization and, perhaps, a tendency toward romanticizing lesbian relationships on Giddens part, with the fact that there is some evidence that is supportive of what he says[35]—the point I want to make is that access to citizenship is perceived here as a sexualized process. However, contrary to understanding this as a part and parcel of the institutionalization of heterosexuality that characterized the first theme that I outlined, within this conceptualization it is lesbians *and* gay men who are regarded as "privileged" insofar as it is assumed that, at present, lesbian and gay relationships provide a context in which more equal and intimate relationships can be achieved. Thus, although Giddens does not talk about specific categories of sexual or intimate citizenship, such as "the lesbian citizen," but rather focuses on an inclusive notion or ideal of the "pure relationship," he nevertheless implies a link between the historical attainment of forms of sexual or intimate democracy and different sexualities.

As I indicated in the first part of this chapter, a distinction can be drawn between this kind of broad approach and that of writers who seek to acknowledge difference through the articulation of concepts of citizenship that refer to forms of participation (or forms of exclusion) of specific sexual constituencies such that we might talk of the lesbian citizen, the queer citizen, and so on. An obvious example is David Evans (1993), referred to earlier, who discusses female sexual citizenship, male homosexual citizenship, as well as the experience of bisexuals, transvestites, and transsexuals as examples of differing forms of sexual citizenship. The experience of lesbian citizenship is barely mentioned, however, neither under the heading of homosexual, nor under female sexual citizenship. This absence of "the lesbian citizen" is interesting for a number of reasons, not least because it prompts the question of how useful it is to use discrete categories of sexual citizenship in the manner that Evans does. In addition, it highlights how the question of the interrelationship between gender and sexuality, crucial to much feminist theory, is not adequately addressed.

While Evans can be criticized for ignoring lesbians, other authors have been accused of neglect of a different kind. The dominant trend in analyses, which conceptualize sexual citizenship in terms of varying degrees of access to specific sets of rights, has been to focus upon "lesbian and gay" struggles for equality, rather than specifically analyzing lesbian citizenship per se, thus failing to differentiate lesbians from other "queers" or "gay men." What we then have are "lesbian and gay" citizens or queer citizenry, which embraces lesbian, gay, bisexual, and transgender citizens. This is particularly salient given that, in many countries, such rights movements are associated historically with demands, mainly by gay men, for the decriminalization of "male homosexual" offenses, in particular, age of consent and sodomy laws.[36] Thus, in making no distinction between lesbians and gays, the concern is not simply that possible differences in the experience of social inclusion/ exclusion are being ignored, but that lesbians are at risk of being subsumed under the category "gay." As Phelan (1994: xi) points out, "the 1990s paradigm of 'lesbian and gay' too often heralds a return to male-dominated politics."

It is in the context of such critiques—that lesbians have either been ignored altogether or made invisible, to varying extents, through being subsumed under a universal notion of the "sexual citizen" or a sexually differentiated but not gender-specific category such as "queer citizen" or "lesbian and gay citizen"—that we need to understand the development of analyses of lesbian citizenship. In addition, it is important to recognize that such debates highlight the extent to which gendered understandings of the concept sexual or intimate citizenship are being used in contrast to "gender-neutral" definitions.

The majority of attempts at fleshing out what the term "the lesbian citizen" might mean have come, not surprisingly, from lesbian/feminist writers, especially within sociology, political, and legal theory. There are several approaches to this question, and I will explore these by examining the three main ways in which lesbian citizenship has been conceptualized.

The first of these is concerned with lesbian citizenship as a partial or "unjust" citizenship. This includes accounts of how and in what ways lesbians are penalized within legal and welfare systems, which are founded upon and support normative assumptions about heterosexuality and "the family." Wilton (1995), for example, examines the effects of the law and the welfare state in Britain on "the lesbian citizen," while Carabine (1996) provides a theoretical analysis of the ways in which social policy regulates non-heterosexual sexualities. Then, there are accounts that describe political responses to such injustices, in terms both of examining the specific campaigns for "lesbian rights" and the justifications advanced for them. The collection edited by Rosenbloom (1996), for instance, documents "human rights violations" against lesbians in 30 countries around the world and discusses the strategies and arguments that lesbian movements have used to challenge such discriminatory social practices. More commonly, however, these questions are addressed, even by lesbian/feminist writers, through an analysis of the demands for equality for lesbian *and* gay citizens.[37]

Within such political struggles for full citizenship, the lesbian citizen is cast as the legitimate citizen who has been wrongly excluded from certain rights such as, for example, the right to be legally married or the right to adopt or foster, because of her different (relative to heterosexuals) sexual status. The focus, in what is often referred to as an assimilationist or integrationist model of citizenship, is on reforming current frameworks of citizenship in order that lesbians may have access to the same rights as those currently granted to heterosexuals. What is often missing in analyses of "equal rights" claims, however, is a critical examination of the ways in which access to rights to, say, pensions is influenced by gender or, much more fundamentally, a problematizing of the notion of "lesbian and gay" equality itself. To whom do gay men want to be equal, heterosexual women or heterosexual men? And is the same answer likely to be forthcoming from lesbians? Clearly, these are complex questions, but we need to ask them if we are to recognize the possible gendered meanings of sexual citizenship.

A different approach to this is one that, despite an awareness that lesbians are denied certain rights and protections by the state, is critical of attempts that seek to change the citizenship status of lesbians within present systems that are understood to be founded on heterosexual and gendered norms. This second approach is sometimes characterized as a "separatist" approach. Perhaps one of the most well-known proponents of this position is Ruthann Robson (1992), an American feminist who argues for the development of *lesbian* legal theory. Robson's work covers a range of issues, but of importance here is her view of the lesbian citizen as an (out)law. That is, rather than seeking rights *in* law, Robson argues that lesbians should be without and create their own approach to the law. Instead of conceptualizing a universal system of citizenship, which can and should be modified to include the demands of lesbians, lesbians are seen as a socially distinct group with their own specific interests, who need to develop a uniquely lesbian approach to legal reasoning. In distinguishing lesbian experience from that of both gay men and heterosexual women, Robson's is both a gendered and sexually differentiated notion of sexual citizenship. Within this kind of framework, we can think about lesbian citizenship not as a set of equal rights demands, but rather in terms of the elaboration of a "lesbian-specific" system of rules of justice governing claims to citizenship.

One of the major criticisms leveled at such an approach is that it presupposes that we know who we "lesbians" are and that there are clear and identifiable shared common "lesbian interests," which may be expressed as demands.[38] Since the 1980s, it has become increasingly clear that the term "lesbian," far from defining a unitary and homogeneous category, encompasses a complex and diverse population of women who hold multiple social identities and different political positions. The contested terrain among lesbians further evidences the problematic nature of these suppositions over many "rights claims" such as, for instance, lesbian marriage, motherhood, and various forms of sexual practice. Furthermore, the influence of postmodernism on lesbian/feminist thinking, with its valorization of difference and sexual plurality, has brought new understandings of lesbian identities as fluid and shifting, rather than as fixed and stable.[39] In the light of such criticisms, writers such as, for example, lesbian political theorist Shane Phelan (1994, 1995) have put forward a "third way" of thinking about lesbians and sexual citizenship. Phelan argues that lesbians should claim "the space of citizenship," understood here as a claim to political participation and public recognition. However, she dismisses the idea that within this space of citizenship, we can predetermine what will be a "lesbian issue." She still talks of specific citizenships, of which "lesbian citizens" are an example, and of forging bonds "between specificities." What Phelan is trying to achieve is recognition that there may be concerns specific to lesbians, although not all lesbians may share in these, and that other groups may have similar concerns. The demand is for lesbians to be recognized as citizens "not 'in spite' of our lesbianism but simply regardless of it," as equal members in a "radical democracy" where the privilege of hegemonic identity is eliminated.[40]

The Limits of Claiming Citizenship

In this chapter, I have examined a new and rapidly expanding body of work on the relationship between sexuality and citizenship, looking at how lesbian and gay theorists have engaged with the concept of sexual citizenship and lesbian citizenship in particular. In an age when the politics of citizenship increasingly define "sexual politics," it is important to engage constructively with such developments rather than to simply ignore or dismiss them.

That said, the theoretical and political shift toward citizenship is extremely problematic from a lesbian/feminist perspective. What is required, therefore, is the development of lesbian feminist critiques of sexual/citizenship. In this final section, I want to highlight some of the directions that future critiques might take.

At a fundamental level, we need to consider the political utility of developing a concept of sexual citizenship. Should we support claims for sexual rights and, if so, what claims and why? These are extremely complex and sensitive questions. In the context of resistance by certain religious and right wing movements to rights demands by lesbians and gay men, and the existence of social and legal discrimination on the basis of (nonheterosexual) sexual status, it can be difficult to contest moves to claim sexual/citizenship without being accused of being reactionary or "unjust." As a consequence, this may both limit the development of lesbian/feminist critiques and be used strategically to undermine the theoretical arguments contained within them. (There are parallels here with the conflation of radical feminist and right wing arguments against pornography.)

In addition, we need to recognize that although radical/lesbian/feminists have regarded liberal citizenship as problematic, in practice such feminisms have been influential in the formation of liberal citizenship to some extent. For example, feminist organizations such as Rights of Women have campaigned for the rights of lesbian mothers with respect to loss of custody of their children and to barriers to accessing assisted conception. Similarly, feminists have campaigned for access to free contraception and abortion, changes in the law concerning rape and divorce, and many other issues connected with what one might regard as aspects of sexual citizenship.

Despite the fact that feminists have campaigned around the legal and social rights of lesbians, the focus on individual "rights" has not been a dominant emphasis within lesbian/feminist political discourse. On the contrary, such an approach to political change has been subject to fierce criticism. As Stevi Jackson comments:

> The fact that women have gained many such rights without attaining social equality should demonstrate the limitations of a politics of rights which ignores the structural bases of social inequality.[41]

Furthermore, a major aspect of lesbian/feminist theory has been the development of critical perspectives on the social construction of gender and sexuality. In particular, such analyses have addressed the ways in which heterosexuality, as a system of privileged, institutionalized norms and practices, is central to the oppression of women *and* lesbians and gays. Within such a theoretical framework, in which sexuality is seen as a key mechanism of patriarchal control,[42] the expansion of a concept of sexual citizenship is far from unproblematic. Why should we attempt to further rights within a system whose very operation depends on logic that defines lesbians as "deviant outsiders in order to confirm the 'normality' of heterosexuality."[43] These dilemmas are thrown into sharper relief by the fact that many of the recent campaigns for "equal rights" for lesbians and gay men represent demands that, far from taking a similar critical stance on heterosexuality, uphold heterosexual institutions and their interlinkage with gender hierarchies as the normative framework of sexual citizenship (see Richardson, 2004).

A further fundamental difference is that the claims to such rights are frequently premised on assumptions about sexuality as an essential characteristic of individuals, defined as a person's "sexual orientation." Such is the perceived persuasive power of biological determinism, that even where activists are unconvinced by "born that way" arguments, they may nevertheless adopt a position of "strategic essentialism" to defend lesbian and gay rights.[44] In contrast to this, lesbian/feminist analyses of sexuality have been central to the development of social constructionist models, which see the current social organization of sexuality and gender as socially and historically produced rather than naturally given. Furthermore, they have not sought to counter the criticisms that if sexuality is a "choice," then there are no grounds for giving lesbians and gay men "equal rights," through a theoretical about-turn. On the contrary, in addition to pointing out that both "choice" and essentialist arguments can be used against lesbians and gay men, feminists have been extremely critical of essentialist arguments that reaffirm culturally dominant assumptions about sexuality, in particular, the idea of heterosexuality, in a particular gendered form, as both natural and normal.[45]

These debates over claims over citizenships also represent, then, struggles over the meaning of sexuality. It is not simply a case of whether we are able to reach agreement on particular rights claims or not, although such debates can be just as contentious, but whether the models of citizenship operating, and the theoretical arguments put forward for them, are compatible with the kind of frameworks that have been used by lesbian/feminists in developing a politics of gender and sexuality. To further illustrate this point, we might consider the recent shift toward a focus on relationship-based rights claims by lesbian and gay movements and campaigning groups, both in the United States and Europe. As a number of feminist writers such as, for example, Christine Delphy (1996) have argued, this kind of model of citizenship reinforces both the desirability and necessity of sexual coupledom, privileged over other forms of relationships, as a basis for many kinds of rights entitlements. Moreover, it represents the integration of lesbian and gay men into a couple-based system of rights originally founded on heterosexual and gendered norms.

As I have outlined in previous sections, despite these tensions, not all lesbian/feminist writers have rejected completely the concept of sexual/lesbian/citizenship, choosing instead to ask questions about how it is being used and defined and, in some cases, offering alternative models and meanings. Here, I have touched on some of these questions briefly in my attempt to sketch out the emerging intellectual terrain. First, I have pointed to the need to ask how the concept of sexual citizenship is being defined and used. I would argue that our theoretical understanding of sexual citizenship needs to be critically informed by a gendered analysis. Second, at both a theoretical and political level, we need to seriously consider whether the forms of citizenship that are being articulated are ones that embrace lesbian/feminist perspectives? We can address this question on a number of different levels. At a general level, it demands that we consider what models of citizenship are being proposed. In the previous section, I outlined how different versions of lesbian citizenship have been suggested. However, this question also touches on another set of dilemmas in debates over sexuality and citizenship: the problems arising from the interpretation of "sexual rights." As I have already stated, there are competing claims for what are defined as sexual rights both from within and outside feminism. This is nothing new to lesbian/feminists, of course. Questions related to conduct-based rights claims have been some of the most controversial and divisive within lesbian/feminism debates. For example, one objection to feminist critiques of sexual practices such as, for example, sado/masochism by writers such as Sheila Jeffreys (1990, 1994) is that they contravene the feminist assertion of a woman's right to a self-defined sexuality, one of the early demands of the women's liberation movement in the 1970s. Similar arguments have been used in the "political lesbianism" debates and those over the production and consumption of pornography by lesbian/feminists. This combination of "sexual rights" as a contested concept, and the increasing usage of the language of citizenship in relation to sexuality, underlines the need for a critical analysis of its meaning and value as a concept.

Paralleling debates on citizenship more generally, the dominant emphasis in debates about sexual citizenship is on "rights" rather than "obligations." However, just as I have argued that it is necessary to question the meaning of the term "sexual rights," I also believe that it is important to analyze what we might understand to be the obligations and duties of sexual citizens. In a different theoretical context, feminists have drawn attention to women's "sex-duties," challenging these as well as demanding "sex-rights." For example, feminist campaigns for changes in policy and practice concerning sexual violence have highlighted how in many countries the law decrees that rape in marriage is not a crime. (A view that was only overturned a few years ago in England with the introduction of the Rape in Marriage

Act in 1991.) Under such laws, a man's right of sexual access to his wife's body is privileged over her right to consent; this is part of a man's "conjugal rights" and a woman's "sexual responsibilities" as married citizens.

The question of obligation is also implicit in Anna-Marie Smith's (1995) analysis of discourses of what she calls the "good" homosexual citizen, who is socially and legally constructed as "dutifully" occupying the private sphere. Both these examples illustrate how sexual duties and obligations are very often implicit in concepts of citizen and citizenship. However, what is not clear is how we should interpret the language of obligations, as well as rights, in the case of lesbians. Can we assume that the good (and bad) lesbian citizen is the same as the good (and bad) homosexual citizen? Are lesbians subject to similar obligations as sexual citizens as heterosexual women? To the extent that lesbians do not fulfill the demands of citizenship as it has been constructed for women, that is, primarily through their reproductive and domestic role within the heterosexual, nuclear family, they do not meet the requirements of "responsible" female citizenship.[46]

There is another level at which we need to consider this question of obligation and duty as a defining feature of sexual citizenship, and this is in terms of "the new deal" of negotiating for equal rights for lesbians and gay men. Previously, as Smith (1995) recognizes, the "deal" was that in return for certain rights of toleration, the obligation of the "homosexual citizen" was to remain within socially and legally defined boundaries of the private, that is, to remain closeted. Now, when demands are centered upon *public* recognition of lesbian and gay relationships and identities, the question that arises is what are the kinds of obligations that are concomitant on the recognition of such rights? Who or what, in this political context, will be representative of good and bad lesbian citizenship?

In the context of the increasingly dominant emphasis within contemporary social/sexual movements on pursuing a politics of citizenship, it becomes all the more important to raise these kinds of questions. Globally, we are witnessing that large sections of gay and lesbian (and sometimes bi/sometimes transgender) communities demand "equal rights" with heterosexuals. Alongside and as a part of this, we can observe a symbolic "representation" of lesbians and gay men in ways that warrant their inclusion as equal citizens. We are described as "virtually normal" (Sullivan 1995), living lives that, in all other respects besides "sexual orientation," exhibit appropriate civic qualities such as, for example, respect for "marriage" and "family values." The pursuit of citizenship at both these levels, the material and the symbolic, represents an expression of the "normalization" of lesbians and gay men, which is antithetical to the radical challenge of lesbian/feminist theory. Furthermore, and related to my earlier question about "obligations," in the process of demanding and gaining access to new forms of citizenship status, lesbians are being constituted as "good" and "bad" citizens in ways that are likely to further marginalize those who are critical of the gendered heterosexual norms underpinning citizenship.

In conclusion, I want to make it clear that I am not suggesting we should not be concerned with issues such as pension and employment rights or the unequal age of consent for same-sex relationships between men. It is important to analyze the ways in which various forms of polities—nation-states, organized religions, supra-states—exclude and discriminate against lesbians and gay men. However, rather than uncritically accepting the discourse of citizenship, I have argued that we need to acknowledge that such discourses have reproduced a particular version of the responsible/good citizen focused on the values and norms associated with the heterosexual, nuclear family. We also need, at the same time, to recognize the increasing power of the language of citizenship and consider what the implications of this are for "alternative languages." What are we giving up if we collapse theoretical analyses of and demands for political change in the social organization of gender and sexuality into that of claiming citizenship?

References

Alexander, M. J. 1994. Not just (any) body can be a citizen: the politics of law, sexuality and post-coloniality in Trinidad and Tobago and the Bahamas, *Feminist review*, 48: 5–23.

Anthias, N. and N. Yuval-Davis, 1992. *Racialized boundaries: Race, nation, gender, color and class, and the anti-racist struggle.* London: Routledge.

Bamforth, N. 1997. *Sexuality, morals and justice: A theory of lesbian and gay rights law.* London: Cassell.

Bell, D. 1995. Perverse dynamics, sexual citizenship and the transformation of intimacy, in D. Bell and G. Valentine (eds.) *Mapping desire. Geographies of sexualities*, pp. 304–317. London: Routledge.

Bell, D. and J. Binnie, 2000. *The Sexual Citizen: Queer Politics and Beyond.* Cambridge: Polity.

Binnie, J. 1995. Trading places: consumption, sexuality and the production of queer space, in D. Bell and G. Valentine (eds.) *Mapping desire. Geographies of sexualities*, pp. 182–199. London: Routledge.

Campbell, B. 1980. A feminist sexual politics: now you see it, now you don't, *Feminist review*, 5: 1–18.

Carabine, J. 1996. Heterosexuality and social policy, in D. Richardson (ed.) *Theorizing heterosexuality: Telling it straight*, pp. 55–74. Buckingham: Open University Press.

Cooper, D. 1993. An engaged state: sexuality, governance and the potential for change, in J. Bristow and A. R. Wilson (eds.) *Activating theory: Lesbian, gay and bisexual politics*, pp. 190–218. London: Lawrence and Wishart.

———. 1994. *Sexing the City: Lesbian and Gay Politics Within the Activist State.* London: Rivers Oram Press.

———. 1995. *Power in struggle: Feminism, sexuality and the state.* Buckingham: Open University Press.

Delphy, C. 1996. The private as a deprivation of rights for women and children, paper presented at the International Conference on Violence, Abuse and Women's Citizenship, Brighton, November, 10–15.

Doan, L. (ed.) 1994. *The lesbian postmodern.* New York: Columbia University Press.

Duggan, L. 1995. *Sex wars: Sexual dissent and political culture.* New York: Routledge.

Dunne, G. 1997. *Lesbian lifestyles: Women's work and the politics of sexuality.* Basingstoke: Macmillan.

Epstein, S. 1987. Gay politics, ethnic identity: the limits of social constructionism, *Socialist review*, 93/94: 9–54.

Evans, D. 1993. *Sexual citizenship. The material construction of sexualities.* London: Routledge.

Giddens, A. 1992. *The transformation of intimacy: Sexuality, love and eroticism in modern societies.* Cambridge: Polity Press.

Hall, S. and Held, D. 1989. Citizens and citizenship, in S. Hall and M. Jacques (eds.) *New times: The changing face of politics in the 1990s.* Buckingham: Open University Press.

Herman, D. 1994. *Rights of passage: Struggles for lesbian and gay equality.* Toronto: University of Toronto Press.

Herman, D. 1995. A jurisprudence of one's own? Ruthann Robson's lesbian legal theory, in A.R. Wilson (ed.) *A simple matter of justice?: Theorizing lesbian and gay politics*, pp. 176–92. London: Cassell.

Ingram, G. B., A. Bouthlitte and Y. Retter, (eds.) 1997. *Queers in space: Communities/public places/sites of resistance.* Seattle: Bay Press.

Jackson S. 1996/1997. Taking liberties, *Trouble and strife*, 34: 36–43.

Jackson, S. and S. Scott, 1996. Sexual skirmishes and feminist factions: twenty-five years of debate on women and Sexuality, in S. Jackson and S. Scott (eds.) *Feminism and Sexuality: A Reader*, pp. 1–31. Edinburgh University Press.

Jamieson, L. 1998. *Intimacy: Personal relationships in modern societies.* Cambridge: Polity Press.

Jeffreys, S. 1990. *Anticlimax: A feminist perspective on the sexual revolution.* London: The Women's Press.

———. 1994. *The lesbian heresy: A feminist perspective on the lesbian sexual revolution.* London: The Women's Press.

Kaplan, M. B. 1997. *Sexual justice. Democratic citizenship and the politics of desire.* New York: Routledge.

Lister, R. 1990. Women, economic dependency and citizenship, *Journal of social policy*, 19(4): 445–468.

———. 1996. Citizenship engendered, in D. Taylor (ed.) *Critical social policy. A reader*, pp.168–London: Sage.

———. 1997. *Citizenship: Feminist perspectives.* London: Macmillan.

Marshall, T. H. 1950. *Citizenship and social class.* Cambridge: Cambridge University Press.

McIntosh, M. 1993. Queer theory and the war of the sexes, in J. Bristow and A.R. Wilson (eds.) *Activating theory: Lesbian, gay, bisexual politics*, pp. 30–52. London: Lawrence & Wishart.

Pakulski, J. 1997. Cultural citizenship, *Citizenship studies*, 1(1): 73–86.

Palmer, A. 1995. Lesbian and gay rights campaigning: a report from the coalface, in A.R. Wilson (ed.) *A simple matter of justice? Theorizing lesbian and gay politics*, pp. 32–50. London: Cassell.

Phelan, S. 1994. *Getting specific: Postmodern lesbian politics.* Minneapolis: University of Minnesota Press.

———. 1995. The space of justice: Lesbians and democratic politics, in A. R. Wilson (ed.) *A simple matter of justice? Theorizing lesbian and gay politics*, pp. 193–220. London: Cassell.

Phillips, A. 1991. Citizenship and feminist theory, in G. Andrews (ed.) *Citizenship.* London: Lawrence and Wishart.

Plummer, K. 1995. *Telling sexual stories: Power, change and social worlds.* London: Routledge.

Rankine, J. 1997. For better or for worse?, *Trouble and strife*, 34: 5–11.

Ribbens McCarthy, J. and R. Edwards, 1999. Gendered lives, gendered concepts? The Significance of children for theorizing "public" and "private," paper presented to the Annual Conference of the British Sociological Association, Glasgow, April 6–9.

Rich, A. 1980. Compulsory heterosexuality and lesbian existence, *Signs*, 5(4): 631–660.

Richardson, D. 1996. Heterosexuality and social theory, in D. Richardson (ed.) *Theorizing heterosexuality: Telling it straight*, pp. 1–20. Buckingham: Open University Press.

———. 1997. Sexuality and feminism, in V. Robinson and D. Richardson (eds) *Introducing women's studies: Feminist theory and practice,* 2nd edition, pp. 152–174. Basingstoke: Macmillan.

———. 1998. Sexuality and Citizenship, *Sociology*, 32, 1:83–100.

———. 2000. Constructing sexual citizenship: Theorizing sexual rights, *Critical social policy*, 20(1): 105–35.

————. 2004. Locating Sexualities: From Here to Normality, Sexualities, 7(4): 6–22.

Rights of Women. 1984. *Lesbian mothers on trial.* London: Community Press.

Robson, R. 1992. *Lesbian (out)law: Survival under the rule of law.* Ithaca: Firebrand.

Rosenbloom, R. (ed.) 1996. *Unspoken rules: Sexual orientation and women's human rights.* London: Cassell.

Segal, L. 1987. *Is the future female? Troubled thoughts on contemporary feminism.* London: Virago.

Shakespeare, T., K. Gillespie-Sells and D. Davies, 1996. *The sexual politics of disability: Untold desires.* London: Cassell.

Smith, A. M. 1995. *New right discourse on race and sexuality: Britain, 1968–90.* Cambridge: Cambridge University Press.

Stacey, J. 1991. Promoting Normality: Section 28 and the regulation of sexuality, in S. Franklin, C. Lury and J. Stacey (eds.), *Off centre: Feminism and cultural studies.* London: Unwin Hyman.

————. 1997. Feminist theory: capital F, capital T, in V. Robinson and D. Richardson (eds.) *Introducing women's studies: Feminist theory and practice,* 2nd edition, pp. 54–76. Basingstoke: Macmillan.

Stevenson, N. (ed.) 2001. *Culture and Citizenship.* London: Sage.

Stychin, C. 2000. *Granting rights: the politics of rights, sexuality and European Union,* Northern Ireland Legal Quarterly, 51: 281–302.

Sullivan, A. 1995. *Virtually normal.* New York: Alfred A. Knopf.

Squires, J. 1994. Ordering the city: public spaces and political participation, in J.Weeks (ed.) *The lesser evil and the greater good: The theory and politics of social diversity,* pp. 79–99. London: Rivers Oram.

Turner, B. S. 1993. Contemporary problems in the theory of citizenship, in B.S. Turner (ed.) *Citizenship and social theory,* pp. 1–18. London: Sage.

Walby, S. 1990. *Theorizing patriarchy.* Oxford: Blackwell.

————. 1994. Is citizenship gendered? *Sociology,* 28: 379–95.

————. 1997. *Gender transformations.* London: Routledge.

Warner, M. (ed.) 1993. *Fear of a queer planet: Queer politics and social theory.* Minneapolis: University of Minnesota Press.

Weeks, J. 1995. *Invented moralities: Sexual values in an age of uncertainty.* Oxford: Polity Press.

————. 1998. The sexual citizen, *Theory, culture and society,* 15(3–4): 35–52.

Wilson, A. 1993. Which equality? Toleration, difference or respect, in J. Bristow and A.R. Wilson (eds.) *Activating theory: Lesbian, gay, bisexual politics,* pp. 171–189. London: Lawrence & Wishart.

————. 1995. Their justice: heterosexism in a theory of justice, in A.R. Wilson (ed.) *A simple matter of justice? : Theorizing lesbian and gay politics,* pp. 146–175. London: Cassell.

Wilton, T. 1995. *Lesbian studies: Setting an agenda.* London: Routledge.

Notes

1. Lister, 1990, 1996; Phillips, 1991; Walby, 1994
2. Wilton, 1995
3. See, for example, Evans, 1993; Plummer, 1995; Richardson, 1998; Weeks, 1998.
4. See, for example, Phelan, 1994; Wilson, 1995.
5. See, for example, Herman, 1994; Robson, 1992.
6. See, for example, Richardson, 1996, 1998.
7. Marshall, 1950
8. Turner, 1993
9. Stevenson, 2001
10. Evans, 1993
11. See, for example, Wilson 1993; Herman 1994; Cooper 1995; Duggan 1995.
12. See, for example Kaplan, 1997.
13. Warner, 1993
14. Hall and Held, 1989; Pakulski, 1997
15. Evans, 1993: 209
16. Plummer, 1995: 17

17. Bell and Binnie, 2000: 20
18. Squires, 1994
19. Cooper, 1993
20. See, for example, Ingram et al., 1997.
21. See, for instance, Cooper, 1993; Phelan, 1994; Bamforth, 1997; Kaplan, 1997.
22. Richardson, 2000
23. Shakespeare et al., 1996
24. Binnie, 1995
25. See, for example, the work of Campbell (1980) and McIntosh (1993) as examples of socialist feminist approaches.
26. Wilton, 1995
27. Segal, 1987; Jackson and Scott, 1996
28. Rankine, 1997
29. Stacey, 1997: 55
30. Lister, 1997: 197
31. Weeks, 1998: 35
32. Weeks, 1998: 49
33. Lister, 1997: 200
34. Giddens: 1992: 135
35. e.g., Dunne, 1997; Jamieson, 1998
36. Herman, 1994
37. See, for example, Cooper, 1993; Herman, 1994; Palmer, 1995.
38. Phelan, 1994; Herman, 1995
39. Doan, 1994
40. Phelan, 1995: 206
41. Jackson, 1996/1997: 43
42. See Walby, 1990; Richardson, 1997
43. Jackson: 1996/1997: 37
44. Epstein, 1987
45. These kind of theoretical and strategic differences were particularly apparent in Britain during the campaigns against Section 28 of the 1998 Local Government Act. See Stacey, 1991.
46. Stychin, 2000

CHAPTER 4

The Transformation of Heterosexism and its Paradoxes

CHRIS BRICKELL

> My God, my God, this bloody country's got it all wrong, I mean
> they've got more rights than we have…don't get me wrong, live and
> let live, that's what I say, but when normal people have less rights
> than…. I mean does it make sense to you, because nothing makes
> sense to me any more…. (Mr. Rattigan, "This Life," TV4, June 1,
> 1998, pauses in original).

This fictional character from the British television series *This Life* expresses in his statement some key elements of the heterosexist *Zeitgeist*. He files for divorce when his wife has an affair with a woman, and when he finds that does not "count" as adultery he flies into a rage at his (unbeknown to him) gay male lawyer.

It is unspoken but implicit in this discourse that "normal people" have "less (sic) rights" than "them." "They" are lesbians and gay men, and "they" are supposed to know their place. In this discourse, the normative status of heterosexuality is under threat in a country that has allegedly "got it all wrong." The homosexual can be tolerated ("live and let live") provided that he or she does not usurp the place reserved for "normal people." Yet, according to this television character, "this bloody country" (England in this case) has granted lesbians and gay men "more rights than" heterosexuals.

This text encapsulates a shift in forms of heterosexism. Heterosexuals are positioned as "normal people," a construction that relies upon lesbians and gay men being positioned as the abnormal. The category of the abnormal belongs to older forms of heterosexism, which are exemplified by medical and conservative Christian discourses. Those positions can be termed *ontological heterosexism*, because in such forms the lesbian or the gay man is considered to have a disordered being. According to conservative Christian discourses, the homosexual subject suffers from a flaw of the moral self; he or she was traditionally "sinful" and in need of moral regulation. As homosexuality was medicalized, the homosexual subject came to be seen as mentally or physically disordered and requiring medical intervention. Traces of this ontological inferiority live on in recent categorizations of the homosexual as the abnormal Other, "outside" of the universe of fully adjusted, mature, and fulfilling heterosexuality.

While aspects of ontological heterosexism continue within some discourses about homosexuality, the primacy of notions of homosexuals as sinful, sick, or in some other way innately deficient has been recently giving way to other forms of heterosexism. These newer forms can be described as *cultural heterosexism*. In the logics of cultural heterosexism, heterosexuality is understood to be under sustained political threat from "politicized" lesbians and/or gay men. The shift in forms of heterosexism, then, is a shift in focus from the inner deficiencies of the homosexual subject to his or her relationships to a wider culture. On one level, this culture is presented as neutral and as treating all equally, yet on another it is constructed as heterosexual and is defended on this basis. The homosexual "outside" is presented as threatening to enter the heterosexual "inside" and to overtake, subdue, and even dismember it. While not explicitly articulated, the fear is that ultimately heterosexuality will become "undone" and lose its normative status within the social order.[1]

Heterosexism can be understood as an interlinking of discourses. I do not mean to rely on an understanding in which discourse is so vaguely defined and yet so reified that it "does all the doing" in society. Sometimes, the concept of discourse is so pervasive that it envelops all within it like a fog, and yet it is so imprecise that it is hard to see what is meant by it in any specific sense. Instead, I regard discourse as the textual and symbolic means of transmitting and reproducing understandings of the social world. Discourse is intimately bound up with the expression and reproduction of power relations, where power is understood as both constitutive of selves, identities, and relationships in a Foucauldian sense as well as a force enabling relationships of domination between selves that are socially located in particular ways. Power constitutes social institutions as well as working through these in ways that secure forms of domination. The form of domination at issue here is that between heterosexuality and homosexuality. The deployment of particular, power-laden discourses about heterosexuality and homosexuality is one means by which domination is reproduced.

This chapter traverses four fundamental areas of discussion. First, I examine the notion of cultural heterosexism, using cultural racism as a template. I outline cultural racism here because it was the starting point for my inquiry about changes in forms of heterosexism in New Zealand, despite the fact that much of the racism literature was British. I move from a discussion of racism to an examination of heterosexism. Second, I examine four ideological positions that inform cultural heterosexism: libertarianism, liberalism, authoritarian conservatism and neoconservatism. Third, I summarize some specific discursive themes that appeared in discourses of cultural heterosexism—the 'taxpayer', totalitarians and defenders, the "ordinary person", and marked vs. unmarked categories. Fourth, I summarize some of the ways in which lesbians and gay men have been positioned differently with respect to cultural heterosexism.

Cultural Racism as a Template

Cultural heterosexist discourses are more sophisticated than earlier statements that configure homosexuality as a matter of innate inferiority. The literature on new forms of British racism offers a means of exploring the ways in which the equation of other = inferior has previously metamorphosed into a more subtle set of discourses that are not always immediately recognizable as discourses of domination. This literature emerged from the early 1980s and explored the ways in which immigration and antiracism were starting to be discussed by politicians and in the news media from the 1970s onwards. This is referred to as the *new racism* or *cultural racism*.[2] According to cultural racism, black immigrants were no longer considered to exemplify physical and mental inferiority, but instead they sought to patrol the thoughts of white Britons and thus bring about the downfall of the British nation in collusion with sympathetic white antiracists. White antiracists as well as immigrants are positioned in such discourse as "anti-British": the colonized were seen as colonizers. Antiracism was coded as racism; hence, those who subscribed to cultural racist discourse were able to position themselves as the true defenders against injustice.

It was supposed that this oppression of a white Britain and white Britons by the immigrants and their supporters occurred in several ways. First, immigrants were said to occupy areas of the inner cities, turning them (in the words of politician Enoch Powell) into "alien territories."[3] In a geographical sense, white Britons were said to be in danger of being displaced by the new arrivals. Second, it was alleged that the immigrants and their white colluders took hold of the apparatus of the local state by seizing control of the Labour Party, which held majorities on several urban local authorities and the Greater London Council. This control ostensibly led to the "banning" of black coffee, golliwogs, and the nursery rhyme "baa baa black sheep" by a "loony left," which was under the thrall of antiracist "agitators." In contrast, the "ordinary person" was "terrified" of the "Race Inquisition" that threatened to wreak terrible vengeance upon those who would not bow down to antiracist "fascism."

There was a clear discursive inversion or reversal in which "the people," who were to be understood as *white*, were said to be newly oppressed by the tyrannical immigrant/antiracist minority. This reversal served to reproduce racism, as the inferior/superior strand of traditional forms of racism continued in a modified form. Those who supposedly threatened to take over a vulnerable Britain remained an Other who should have "known their place." Accordingly, the ways in which immigrants were inferiorized in everyday life vanished from view, as they were constructed as powerful totalitarians. Such positioning as powerful legitimated their treatment as inferior.

Also crucial to the reproduction of racism were the accompanying significations of "Britain," "nation," and the "ordinary person." Insofar as they were to be defended from the incursion of the Other, these tropes were constructed as white. It was a white Britain who was allegedly at risk from the cultural influence and interference of the black immigrant, vulnerable in the face of antiracist tyranny. The "ordinary person" who was "afraid to speak" for fear of accusations of racism was the white Briton. Ironically, while being constructed as endangered by antiracist "fascism," white culture and nation remained normative within the social order.

The Bases of Cultural Heterosexist Discourse

These patterns and positions have been reproduced within heterosexist discourse. Racism and heterosexism are not identical in their means of operation, nor are they reducible to one another. However, cultural racism can be used as a starting point for the exploration of cultural forms of heterosexism because there are several thematic and discursive similarities. First, the shift from traditional forms of racism to cultural racism involves a change in understandings of ontology. The notion that black immigrants from the "colonies" are innately, biologically inferior gives way to the idea that those who previously "knew their place" now harbor a profound political threat. Cultural heterosexism mirrors this ontological shift. Second, there are similarities in discursive themes, patterns, and positions between these newer forms of heterosexism and cultural racist discourses. The tyrannical Other, tropes of fascism, Nazism and totalitarianism, "thought policing," fear of "speaking out," the "ordinary person," abuse of "taxpayers' money," and the image of the nation under siege are present in cultural racism and are reproduced in cultural heterosexist approaches.

Cultural racist discourses borrow from a range of (sometimes contradictory) ideological underpinnings, and cultural heterosexist approaches often utilize elements from these same positions. These are libertarianism, liberalism, authoritarian conservatism, and neoconservatism. In the discussion that follows, I will summarize the relationships between these and cultural heterosexist discourses, while elaborating upon the use of the specific discursive themes in cultural heterosexist texts.

Libertarianism

Libertarianism provides a notion of the individual who is detached from all social structure, self-directed, autonomous, and a possessor of a "negative" freedom—the freedom of action without restraint. The libertarian individual tends to be White, heterosexual, and male, as others (including gay men, lesbians, and/or women and/or "ethnic minorities") are regarded as members of "collectivities" who threaten "individual" sovereignty. Whereas for libertarianism the "individual" is upheld as the primary unit in both moral and ontological terms, the Others who occupy "collectivities" are constructed as inferior and dangerous. They are considered to be inferior because the "individual" is afforded moral superiority, and to be dangerous because they threaten the sanctity of that individual.

In libertarian writings, "individual" and "collective" are constructed as mutually exclusive and antagonistic terms. Within this logic, the collective seeks to impose on the male, heterosexual individual in a number of ways. Firstly, collective members appropriate the wealth held by the individual by means of taxes, and they use these taxes to fund social services and programs that further their collective interest, such as the Human Rights Commission or the Ministry of Women's Affairs. The collective is identified with the state, since both exist in opposition to the individual, and therefore the collective is said to have the coercive potential of the state at its disposal. Second, it is argued that collective members make false claims for resources upon the heterosexual male individual, and that these are based on assertions of systematic disadvantage that are fundamentally untrue. From a libertarian standpoint, such assertions are purely a means of receiving state largesse and thereby imposing upon the individual.

Third, members of collectivities threaten to police the actions of the individual, thereby infringing upon his (sic) liberty. Not only are the fruits of the individual's labor under threat from the collectivity's illegitimate demands, but the individual's very inner, possessive self and mind are under siege from policing by the state-supported Other. For example, human rights legislation is understood as prohibiting the freedom to discriminate and as censoring the freedom to speak. Feminists, lesbians, and "politicized" gay men are constructed as "Politically Correct gays and feminazis," tyrannical "fascists of the Left" who seek to coerce the libertarian individual.[4]

These aspects of libertarian logic rely to some extent on the idea of the "level playing field." Before the abstract male heterosexual individual is coerced by "politicization," the existing social order is considered to be "un-politicized": it is simply an expression of a desirable neutrality. It is not acknowledged that heterosexuality is itself always already a part of a political, "politicized" order. Instead, a libertarian argument suggests that "politicization" occurs only when members of a collectivity seek to directly limit the liberty and freedom of the heterosexual, male individual. Discourses of political correctness share this logic, with the implication that he/man language (for example) does not express relations of power, while attempts to "ban" it are expressions of a repressive power that infringes upon individual liberties.

Liberalism

Some aspects of liberal thought provide epistemological bases for cultural heterosexist discourse.[5] The concept of toleration has its roots in liberalism. It has as its basis a distinction between a powerful "we," who tolerate something with which "we" do not fully agree, and a tolerable, less than agreeable "they," who are on the receiving end of the tolerator's benevolence.[6] In heterosexist discourses, the tolerators are heterosexual and the tolerated are gay and/or lesbian.

As in the libertarian understanding, the liberal individual is regarded to be independent of any social structures that may define, constrain, or mold that individual. Accordingly, those who adopt liberal positions tend to avoid an analysis of the ways in which as subjects we are always embedded within particular relationships of power. In her writing about "race," Ruth Frankenberg[7] refers to a position that she terms "color blindness." According to color blindness, we are "all just people" for whom ethnicity is and should be irrelevant and insignificant. We are not "all just people." Instead, aspects of our selves are highly significant to life in a society where subjectivity is constituted through hierarchies of power that operate from above and below. As Henning Bech argues, "existing as a homosexual is synonymous with existing under certain *conditions...*which bear on that existence" (original emphasis).[8]

The insistence that "we are all just people" or that "everyone is the same" is an insistence upon ignoring the ways in which lesbian identities or gay identities exist within specific relations of domination. Such an insistence reinforces heterosexuality as normative by leaving intact its dominant, unmarked position and by rendering homosexuality less visible and viable.[9] The generic liberal subject remains, like the libertarian subject, male, White, and heterosexual.

Liberal assumptions and rhetoric are central to the position that I have referred to elsewhere as *excess equality*.[10] Excess equality posits that there is or was a time when lesbians and gay men had "equality" with heterosexuals, but that such a time has been "gone beyond" with the seeking of "special privileges." Excess equality relies upon an abstract notion of equality with no consideration of the ways in which some identity positions are systematically inferiorized within the society in which we live. The excess equality position erases the ways in which heterosexuality is privileged and obligatory. In other words, a society in which one's lesbianness or gayness is a criterion for subordination, and in which dominance is naturalized and regarded as apolitical, is taken to exemplify "equality." In turn, moves to overturn that subordination are considered to be moving "beyond" equality. Liberalism's individualism downplays structural inequalities thereby allowing appeals to equality to function conservatively. The "equality" promised can express and hide already existing relations of domination as it is constructed in the name of such domination.

Authoritarian Conservatism

Authoritarian conservatism is present in both ontological and cultural forms of heterosexism. This is not necessarily surprising, as these forms of heterosexism are not pure oppositions, and traces of the former reside in the latter. Authoritarian conservatism has as its basis an image of a fragile social order at risk from the failings of a hedonistic, fickle, and potentially amoral populace. Restraint is required, especially with respect to sexuality and the construction of "masculinity" and "femininity," in order that the collapse of a precariously balanced "civilization" be prevented. In authoritarian conservative positions, men and women are taken to have particular "natures" as active and desiring and passive and obedient, respectively, and these natures dictate particular positions and places within society, with women being subordinate to men (although women are often regarded as more morally pure—on this see Dworkin 1983).

Homosexuality is taken to exemplify sex out of control, and is coded as abnormal and in need of eradication. Individual lesbians and gay men are in need of conversion to heterosexuality if possible, or moral restraint if not. It is argued that the law should enforce conservative moral positions on abortion, sex education (again, promoting restraint), and punishment, and all legislation should send "messages" about the correct means of conduct.

Within cultural heterosexism, the discourses that utilize terms such as "special rights," "thought policing," "equality," "tolerance," and "political correctness" often function in the service of authoritarian conservatism. Anna Marie Smith suggests that conservative movements resignify terms such as "equality" and "tolerance" from their liberal meanings into a set of "reactionary" meanings, and that this is a part of the hegemonic project of such movements.[11] For example, in a letter to the editor, J. Hooker wonders whether he can "expect tolerance...when I rail against the revolting perversion of homosexuality."[12] Here, the liberal notion of tolerance is recuperated into authoritarian conservative discourse ("revolting perversion").

In contrast to Smith, however, I would argue that what is going on here is not solely a conservative *re*definition of these liberal or quasiliberal terms. Instead, the coming together of liberalism and authoritarianism results in part from shared precepts. While liberalism does not hold to ideas about homosexuality requiring restraint, both liberalism and authoritarianism refuse to acknowledge the materiality of the subordination central to the relationship between heterosexuality and homosexuality.

Neoconservatism

The term "neoconservatism" has perhaps had a wider currency in the United States of America than elsewhere. It can be used to refer to some of the crossovers between libertarianism and authoritarian conservatism. The main themes include opposition to affirmative action and to lesbian, gay, and feminist "politicization" of the nuclear family, as well as a concern with leftist "political correctness" coercively challenging the existing social order. Discourses of "political correctness" (PC) are a site of meeting for libertarian and authoritarian conservative positions because those movements and positions that are positioned as PC are understood to politicize the private realm, and to attempt "thought policing" of those who have been positioned as normative within traditional discourses and practices.

According to the logic of political correctness discourse as applied to sexuality, the heterosexual as a normative person is under threat from a resurgent homosexual Other who is expected to remain in the private sphere.[13] Those who use political correctness discourse in the service of libertarianism also tend to argue that "political correctness" mobilizes the resources and coercive powers of the state against libertarianism's heterosexual male individual. Political correctness discourse assists in the construction of this individual as heterosexual and male. It is white heterosexual men who are absent from the typifications in which the politically correct subject is constructed as a gay man or as a disabled lesbian of minority ethnic origin. Heterosexual men are left as the individuals who are "victimized" *by* "political correctness" when other identities are constructed *as* "political correctness."

Heterosexual women are positioned in somewhat more ambivalent ways than heterosexual men with respect to political correctness discourse. Women, per se, tend not to be characterized as politically correct. In order that the charge of "PC" be leveled, "woman" must be qualified by other aspects of identity such as feminist or lesbian.

Having summarized the linkages between these four ideological positions and discourses of cultural heterosexism, I will move on to review some of the specific discursive themes that characterize such forms of heterosexism. To this end, I make use of a paragraph from an opinion column written by Rosemary McLeod in the New Zealand magazine *North and South*. This magazine is written for a middle-class audience and is generally neoconservative in tone. McLeod's text encapsulates many of the discursive themes central to cultural heterosexism, and provides an example of the ways in which interlinkages occur. The themes are adopted, modified, and utilized within specific (con)texts, and they are able to be kept in circulation and hence reproduced because of their portability.

Themes in Cultural Heterosexist Discourses

> I have not heard about taxpayer-funded lunches for women at home with children at the Ministry of Women's Affairs. Still, they have a lot on their hands, what with organizing newsletters for disabled Maori lesbians…. Helen [Clark] will be happier when we pay higher taxes, too. The better to fund newsletters for disabled lesbians.[14]

In the above excerpt, McLeod refers to a catered meeting for lesbians in the public service hosted by the Ministry of Women's Affairs and that came to be known in the news media as "the lesbian lunch." Here, McLeod ties together several of the key themes within cultural heterosexist discourse. The first sentence contains the figure of the heterosexual who is "left out" of the new political landscape in which lesbians, gay men, and their "colluders" are in charge. In this case, the "left out" is the woman "at home with children." This image was widespread in coverage of the "lunch," sometimes with the implication that "deviant" women were being given privileges denied to "normal" women. The "left out" clearly resonates with the idea that lesbians (and gay men) are receivers of "special privileges" that are part of the move toward excess equality, and also with the argument that the homosexual subject has become an oppressor of the heterosexual populace.

The "taxpayers" who fund this "lunch" are understood as heterosexual, and the lunch represents taxpayers' money spent on Others. The libertarian formulation "tax-is-theft" echoes here, as the lesbian "collectivity" is seen to appropriate the wealth of the heterosexual "individual" taxpayer. The opposition between "taxpayers" and "Others" has been used in the context of British cultural racism, where taxpayers as white Britons were counterposed to immigrant and antiracist Others. Opinion columnist Karl du Fresne reconfigures "taxpayers' money" as "public money" in the context of a gay and lesbian pride parade: "the gay movement holds its hands out for public money to subsidise its self-indulgent, decadent frolicking."[15] In a letter to the editor, another writer also refers to "the homosexual exhibitionist minority demanding public money."[16]

The phrase "public money" not only reproduces the notion that tax-is-theft but it also serves to exclude lesbians and gay men from the construct of "the public." The phrase "the public" could be read as shorthand for "the public of New Zealand" and the construction of citizenship and nationhood as exclusively heterosexual. Members of the heterosexual taxpayer "public" are constructed as representatives of the New Zealand economy and by implication New Zealand society, while gay men and lesbians are the "nonpublic" and thereby noncitizens.

The third theme at work in McLeod's text is the equation "PC = disabled Maori lesbians."[17] While the PC element of this equation is not overt here, it is implicit, and it appears when this text is read intertextually with the others circulating in the news media at the same time.[18] The "disabled Maori lesbian" represents multiple marginality, unreality, and impossibility, and is therefore cited as the identity on which a Ministry of supposedly dubious value would be most likely to be wasting its time (and "taxpayers' money"). The last two sentences in the excerpt from McLeod's column also engage an equation in the form of a chain of equivalence. In 1993, the Labour Party, then in Opposition, underwent a leadership challenge in which Helen Clark replaced previous leader and former Prime Minister Mike Moore. Clark's challenge was characterized as a "pointy-headed lesbian plot," and a discursive chain of equivalence was constructed between the challengers in the Labour Party, homosexuality, feminism, socialism, intellectualism, and "political correctness." The chain reappears here, as links are remade between Labour, socialism ("higher taxes"), lesbians, and possibly even intellectualism ("newsletters"). The close association made between Helen Clark and lesbians during the 1993 challenge and debate is also reproduced clearly here.

Totalitarians and defenders

I have mentioned that the figure of the heterosexual "left out" resonates with the notion that the homosexual subject has become powerful and oppressive, having invaded the government sector and "public" space and proceeded to exclude and tyrannize heterosexuals. This idea is summarized in this excerpt from opinion columnist Karl du Fresne, writing in the capital city's evening newspaper:

> The scorn and ridicule the gay activists once bitterly complained of themselves they now deal out to others…. Of course all this is consistent with the tyranny of the minority, one of the great curses of the late 20th century, whereby small groups of people play on the conscience of much larger groups of people.[19]

Du Fresne's text epitomizes the inversion that lies at the heart of cultural heterosexist discourse: the marginal has become the tyrannical oppressor. As a sign, tyranny underlies cultural heterosexist discourse and it is often not visible, but in this excerpt it appears explicitly.[20] Having sought excess equality, "gay activists" now seek to tyrannize an innocent heterosexual populace. Such a position is logically dependent on the strand running through liberalism and libertarianism, which denies the specific ways in which lesbians and gay men remain marginalized. This form of discourse, then, can be seen as a strategy to reinforce dominance while subsequently denying it. Not only is the homosexual not marginalized, according to this narrative, but he or she has become powerful and dangerous. The idea of the homosexual as a dangerous invader is played out within cultural heterosexist discourse in three senses.

In the first sense, lesbians or gay men or both are seen to have invaded a series of state agencies, be they the Labour Party, the Family Planning Association, the Ministry of Women's Affairs, or various local authorities. One commentator argues that the first two of these organizations have been "hijacked by the homosexual propagation machine. We now have about 2 percent of the population, and their hangers on, pulling the strings to further their cause."[21] Again, the colluder figure appears in the form of the "hanger on."

Second, it has been argued that lesbians and gay men have become powerful through their occupation of "public" space. For example, gay and lesbian pride parades have been characterized as examples of the "promotion" of a homosexuality that should remain in "private" space. Central to this discourse is the rendering invisible of the ways in which performances of heterosexual identities are enacted in public spaces.[22] Heterosexuality is unmarked such that its visibility is invisible; expressions of heterosexuality are not regarded as heterosexual as such.

Third, it is argued that homosexuals have emerged from the private sphere of their closet and home to tyrannize the minds of heterosexuals. As "mind Nazis," lesbians and gay men come to "play on the consciences" of heterosexuals with the aim of policing their thoughts, speech, and actions.[23] Anna Marie Smith argues that this inversion in which the marginal becomes the invader has allowed those who oppose homosexuality to position themselves not as opponents, but as defenders. Opponents recast themselves as "defenders of the norm against the invaders".[24] As the concerns about "mindNazis" illustrate, not only are the spaces of government agencies or the city street considered to be in need of defence, but so too are the imagined, metaphorical spaces within the minds of conservative heterosexuals.

The language of totalitarianism implied in the term "mind Nazi" dovetails with this notion of defense: the norm and the minds of those upholding it are at risk from the totalitarian impulses of "politicized" lesbians and gay men. Such a norm needs reinforcement against the tyrannous invaders. Jean Bethke Elshtain[25] regards politicized "gay liberationists" as attempting "the remaking of human nature itself" and hence employing "a terrible engine of social control…absolute terror." A similar process is at work in cultural racist discourses, where immigrants and their supporters are seen to visit fascism upon an innocent white Britain.

The "Ordinary Person"

Images of totalitarianism and defense are dependent, too, on the image of the "ordinary person" who requires protection from the jackboots of the homosexual tyrant. The trope of the ordinary person has a tradition in conservative discourses. Within ontological heterosexism, the ordinary person is he or she who is not sick or sinful. In contrast, Ernesto Laclau and Chantal Mouffe[26] argue that in Reaganite and Thatcherite discourse, the category of "the people" as "those who defend the traditional values and freedom of enterprise" is counterposed to the subversives: "feminists, blacks, young people and 'permissives' of every type." It is this conception, in which the "ordinary person" and "the people" are those who oppose the politicized subversives, which appears in cultural heterosexist discourse, although there may at times be overlap with the older meanings. In both cases, the figure of the "ordinary person" serves to mark out boundaries of permissibility and impermissibility.

As controversy raged over a pride parade, two writers in *Metro* magazine constructed "the people" as heterosexual in their texts, suggesting that "people are sick to death of deviant homosexual behaviour being flaunted in public".[27] According to such a discourse, these "people" are putting lesbians and gay men on notice: "people" have had enough and the limit of tolerance has been breached. Another letter-writer[28] explicitly positions herself as the ordinary person, anticipating and disavowing a charge of homophobia in the process:

Not bigoted
Not homophobic
Just ordinary.

Inside/Outside; Unmarked/Marked

In that the "ordinary person" valiantly upholds a heterosexual norm against totalitarian assault, the invocation of such a trope relates to a set of interlinked dualisms: inside and outside, unmarked and marked. In discourses of invasion, heterosexuality is positioned as a primordial space "inside" of norms, which is able to be infiltrated by homosexuality as "outside." As I have suggested, this type of distinction is effected on at least three levels. The agencies and apparatus of the state are conceptualized as a threatened "inside," although one that has perhaps already been irreversibly infiltrated; "public" spaces in the landscape are at risk from entry from those who should remain "in private" and not "promote" their sexuality in public; and the conservative heterosexual mind is under threat from coercion and "thought policing."

Within the logic of such discourse, heterosexuality is under threat of dismemberment from an insurgent homosexual "outside." Once firmly established as a norm, heterosexuality is vulnerable to being overturned, with heterosexuals having their thoughts policed by "politically correct" lesbians and gay men. The figure of the heterosexual who is policed or "left out" is a particular point of concern for cultural heterosexism. Heterosexuality being positioned as *outside* is untenable to heterosexuality as an institution because it disrupts the social order and norms that heterosexuality should be *inside*.

According to cultural heterosexism, those upholding the norm are likely to be usurped by those who do not deserve power; if "we" open the gates to "them" then "they" will displace "us." This fear is epitomized by the comments of one city councillor who expressed concern that the homosexual subject has overstepped the boundary and is making inroads into heterosexuality. He argued that AIDS memorial pride parade floats were a cover for the "homosexual community" to "recruit": "there was a parade I think two years ago, when one of the placards read 'we recruit', now to me, that is deliberately provocative".[29] Having misunderstood the deliberate parody of conservative discourses represented by the sign "we recruit," the complainant understands the slogan as evidence of a concerted attempt to destabilize a heterosexuality that he seeks to defend.

The dualism of inside/outside is related to a distinction between the marked and the unmarked. As Monique Wittig has suggested, heterosexuality is constructed as a general, unmarked category. Those who identify and are identified as heterosexual are not positioned within discourses as heterosexuals so much as "people," and heterosexuality is merely "sexuality." The performances of heterosexual identity are not recognized as such, even if specific performances (such as sex in public) are regarded as problematic in themselves. In their discussion of conservative Christianity and "lust," Patricia Jung and Ralph Smith[30] argue that "whereas lust merely *disorders* heterosexual behaviour, lust *expresses...the disorder* of homosexual behaviour" (my emphasis).

The second aspect of this distinction between markedness and unmarkedness is the connection of markedness with politics and power, and unmarkedness with an apolitical stance. Wittig argues that those who employ dominant, unmarked positions "claim to say the truth in an apolitical field." Dominant positions, such as heterosexuality, come to be seen as zones free of power relations—hence Elshtain's position in which only challengers to dominance, and not that dominance itself, are regarded as being "politicized." This alignment of the "political" with the marked category is also visible in those discourses of political correctness into which lesbians and gay men are abjectly incorporated. As a linguistic term or signifier, "political correctness" was ripe for resignification in ways that marginalized subordinate groups. This is because the term itself implies that particular positions are "political" (and therefore "politically correct") and that others are apolitical and even commonsensical.

Gender Differences within "Tyranny"

In the discussion so far I have sketched out some of the themes that have been employed within texts to refer to both lesbians and gay men. While the dualism of heterosexual/homosexual has provided the framework for my investigation, gender and sexuality are never fully discrete or separable; instead, they are always mutually informing and intertwined. It should come as no surprise, therefore, that lesbians and gay men are sometimes represented differently in given moments. Anna Marie Smith suggests that when homosexuality is considered as an expression of same-sex sexual acts, the gay man has been seen as somewhat more of a threat than the lesbian. Smith argues that during British debate in the 1980s over Section 28 (a law prohibiting local authorities from "promoting homosexuality"), homosexuality was for the most part considered to be an expression of sexual acts. This was also true for the debate surrounding the decriminalizing of sex between gay men in New Zealand in 1985. In Britain and New Zealand, debate focused upon the sexuality of gay men, who were considered to be conduits for the spread of AIDS. British MP Lord Halsbury, for example, stated that lesbians are

> not a problem.... They do not molest little girls. They do not indulge in disgusting and unnatural acts like buggery. They are not wildly promiscuous and do not spread venereal disease.[31]

In such discourse, lesbian sexuality is rendered invisible, and to a degree impossible, precisely because it is not phallic.[32] Within this perception, however, lies the genesis of a construction of lesbian identity as threatening. The lesbian's repudiation of a male-centered sexuality has often been seen as threatening to men. While gay men's sexuality is regarded as a problem, it is "what lesbians *refuse* to do" (i.e., have sex with men) that attracts attention.[33]

Rosemary McLeod ties lesbians into the trope of fascism by positioning them as man-haters who have gained power through what she terms the "sex abuse industry." For another columnist the "Femi-Nazis" and "frustrated dykes" who would censor "sexy billboards" and "come after us [heterosexuals] in the privacy of our own thoughts" are embittered and vengeful because they go without men—precisely because they have "spent their lives trying to get a date with a real man" and failed.[34] In these examples, lesbians' alleged "political correctness" and fascistic tendencies are constructed as an expression of their repudiation of heterosexuality and supposed animosity toward men. One letter-to-the-editor writer refers to a gay and lesbian TV show segment titled "Lesbian Cooking with Libby" by invoking the image of a lesbian as a castrator:

> can someone in the know explain to me why lesbians should cook any differently than the rest of us? I can only surmise that "Libby" and her ilk are maybe working on a new cookbook–100 ways to prepare and serve a mountain oyster.[35]

Yet, in some texts, lesbian identity is not overtly constructed as powerful and highly visible. The archetypal "politically correct" identity is often constructed as lesbian and also in terms of disability and ethnic minority membership: the "Chinese-speaking Maori lesbian with a limp."[36] I have suggested that in this formulation, being lesbian becomes a marginal and somewhat incredible possibility, and lesbian identity is seen as somewhat ridiculous. Julia Penelope (1980) suggests that making the lesbian seem in some way unreal is a means of dissipating a sense of lesbian threat to patriarchy and heterosexuality. The lesbian-as-tyrant and the lesbian-as-impossibility can then be seen as two sides of the one patriarchal coin.

An examination of other examples of homosexual "tyranny" leaves the reader sometimes unclear about whether gay men, lesbians, or both are included in the textual formulation in question. Lesbians have been located quite explicitly as "politically correct" and/or "man-haters." Many of the media texts that include gay men, however, use the term "gay" or "gays." Both of these terms have an ambiguous markedness that can make it difficult to discern whether lesbians are supposed to be included. The term "gay" can be used to refer to men or to men and women. As an example of the former possibility, one writer refers to "gays" and to "lesbians."[37] In an example of ambiguity, Rosemary McLeod[38] refers to "gays such as Ms. Murrie-West," however, elsewhere she writes specifically of lesbians, and her comments on "gays" are accompanied by a cartoon image of a man.[39]

Sometimes, the term "gay" is clearly intended to include lesbians: one article that refers to "gay and lesbian marriages" has as its title "Push on to legalise gay marriage."[40] The term "homosexual" has a similar ambiguity to "gay." In one column in which he argued that "homosexual activists" were policing heterosexuals' speech, Karl du Fresne[41] started by using the term "homosexual" in a seemingly inclusive sense, but at the end of the column he referred to his association with "homosexuals and lesbians." MP John Banks differentiates between men and women in his argument that the Labour Party had been overrun with "homosexuals" and "lesbians."[42]

Such ambiguities make it difficult to separate the representations of gay men from those of lesbians for the purpose of analysis, unless the sexes of the homosexual subjects concerned are explicitly stated. That they are often not stated illustrates the ways in which lesbians have become partially incorporated under the term "gay."[43] There are clear similarities here between the use of the term "gay" and the ways in which "man" is often said to include women.[44] In the few cases where gay men are mentioned specifically rather than merely implied, another paradox is reproduced. The lesbian is on the one hand somehow unreal and on the other a tyrannical man-hater. The gay man, in contrast, is weak and yet powerful. Sarah Boyd[45] implies this weakness through her oxymoronic reference to the "PC softy" in her discussion of a gay male MP. In another example, a television presenter stated of a meteorologist's reluctance to disagree with a colleague: "It's just too PC for me: limp-wristed as my friend would say."[46] The paradox here is that while weak and "limp-wristed," the gay man who hijacks language and orders heterosexuals what to say and what to think is regarded as powerful.

In some ways, these paradoxes of weakness/tyranny for gay men and unreality/tyranny for lesbians reflect the distinction between older and newer, ontological and cultural forms of heterosexism. The weak gay man and the unreal or invisible lesbian are old figures: the former dates back to the medicalization of the late nineteenth century if not before, and the latter is reminiscent of comments made by law makers since the nineteenth century to the effect that it was better to pretend that lesbianism did not exist lest more women come to hear about it.[47] The image of the tyrannical gay man or lesbian, in contrast, is the central theme of more recent cultural heterosexist discourses.

Tyranny is attributable to either gay men or lesbians, or to both, depending on who is speaking or writing, and sometimes it is unclear whether the tyrants in question are "gay" or "lesbian." The libertarian magazine *Free Radical*,[48] for example, refers to "feminists and gays as 'fascists of the left,'" and elsewhere in that magazine lesbians are attacked vehemently.[49] While opposing pride parades as "exhibitionism" by "homosexualists," journalist Warwick Roger[50] appears to find gay men to be less of a problem generally than lesbians. He speaks highly of writers James Allan, Witi Ihimaera, and Peter Wells, while explicitly positioning them as gay. However, his references to lesbians are all negative, and often involve seeing lesbians as the harbingers of a threatening feminism. Rogers "hasten[s] to add that I published Carroll du Chateau's mid-80s From Feminism to

Fascism...and for my trouble was subject to a lesbian-led invasion of my office."[51] Elsewhere he refers to "lesbianese feminazis,"[52] and asks whether "there [have] been any outbreaks of mad cow disease at the Women's Studies department at Waikato University?"[53]

These connections between lesbian identity and feminism are frequent, and "lesbianism and feminism are often used to stand in for each other within popular culture."[54] When material about lesbians and feminists is read intertextually, the discourses surrounding them become indistinguishable at times. In one text, the term "feminazi" may be employed to refer to lesbians quite specifically, and thus other texts that use "feminazi" echo with the meaning "lesbian," although lesbians may not be specifically mentioned. In the coverage of the Labour Party leadership challenge, for example, all of the party's feminist woman MPs who supported Helen Clark were implicitly positioned as lesbian, whether or not this was in fact the case.

Conclusion: the Denial of Domination

Cultural heterosexism has as its basis two paradoxes. In the first, heterosexuality is positioned as normative while, at the same time, a social order typified by heterosexuality is said to be essentially neutral. The normativeness of heterosexuality is expressed through the tropes of the ordinary person, the public and the taxpayer, and through the double standard that marks homosexuality as an illegitimate occupier of a range of spaces while rendering heterosexuality invisible. The privilege of the right to visible invisibility that is accorded to heterosexuality in certain contexts is not regarded as a "special privilege," but as simply a reflection of the way things are. On the other hand, it is made out that the world as it is expresses an equality between subjects, and that this is a desirable equality. In the language of libertarianism, a level playing field exists on which all must compete and can take equal chances. An infringement of this level playing field, this essential equality, constitutes totalitarianism.

It is at this point that the second paradox comes into play. Those who are positioned outside the norm in the first paradox become the tyrants and totalitarians in the second. Here, an inversion takes place and marginal homosexual identities become the oppressors of a normative heterosexuality and of individual heterosexuals. Those who identify with cultural heterosexism regard themselves as newly oppressed by lesbians and gay men whom they regard as a "special interest group" that has won "special rights."

The trope of "special rights" signifies a move "beyond" the "equality" that is said to characterize the social order. Because it is asserted that this social order is equal, any recognition that homosexuality is inferiorized and that remedies may be needed can be constructed as an appeal for "special rights." According to this logic, if lesbians and gay men seek "special rights," then they can be viewed as illiberal. In addition to seeking such rights, the homosexual politicizes this supposedly equal social order, it is argued, introducing politics where previously there were none.

Perhaps a liberal notion of equality that masks the realities of domination on the basis of homosexuality has become the new ground on which the struggles of lesbians and gay men are judged from within conservatism. I am suggesting that less frequently are lesbians' and gay men's alleged medical or moral inferiorities the basis for heterosexist discourses. Instead, the central concern is the deviation from a particular definition of equality. This definition of equality is not what it seems, for it incorporates a dualism of norm and Other that is partially hidden from view. In this logic, to reject an implicit subordinate status is to reject equality and to express a desire to go beyond it. "Beyond equality" lies the search for special privilege and the oppression of conservative heterosexuals, the "ordinary people." This position goes hand in hand with a denial of the ways in which lesbian and gay identities do have a degree of specificity that exists, moreover, with respect to domination. To acknowledge this and to refuse to concede to the claim that we are all "just people" is to be seen to move away from "equality" and toward a form of tyranny. Yet, to concede to the "just people" claim can only serve to reinforce the privileged position of heterosexuality, because the ways in which this privilege is naturalized and rendered invisible remain unchallenged.

In the "excess equality" view, lesbians and gay men "have" equality, although we want more and are supposedly well on the way to achieving it. With "political correctness" on our side, gay men and lesbians are no longer *victims* of our own misfortune, but we have become *oppressors* of the heterosexual innocent who feels (according to one-letter-to-the editor writer) "obliged to bow, in the name of political correctness, to [the] strident minority trying to impose its will on society."[55] The circle is complete. According to cultural heterosexist discourses, the homosexual, previously confined to the private sphere, now invades the heterosexual imagination and the minds of individual heterosexuals.

Perhaps the greatest irony of this position for me was my experience of "living" the dissertation project out of which this chapter evolved. When others asked about the topic of my work, I often wondered what to say. The first half of the title reads "Deregulating the Heterosexual Imagination." I used the phrase "deregulation" as an ironic way of suggesting that while so many areas of New Zealand's economy and society have been "restructured" and "deregulated" under the neoliberal "reforms" of the last twenty years, the heterosexual imagination remains in need of deregulatory attention. Heterosexuality remains an "organizing institution," as Chrys Ingraham argues,[56] it still "circulates as taken for granted, naturally occurring and unquestioned."

My responses to questions about my dissertation topic were often limited by a strategic assessment of how the questioner would respond to being told that I was examining aspects of heterosexism and media representations. If I judged the questioner to be conservative, I talked in vague terms about media and ideology; if sympathetic, I mentioned sexuality and the media; and if the questioner appeared to be a kindred spirit, I launched into a tirade about various media texts. If I could not tell what the questioner's beliefs would be, I was cautious. There was an element of panoptical power at work: I was "watching myself" in case I gave information that would elicit negative responses. Rosemary Hennessy and Chrys Ingraham explain the precarious position that I felt at times was my own:

> Any lesbian or gay men anywhere in the culture poses the dangerous knowledge that the heterosexual norm is arbitrary. So long as heteronormativity remains unquestioned, it is sacred. And exposing the arbitrariness of the sacred…is always potentially fraught with risk.[57]

I felt that to mention homosexuality may incite hostility, but that to mention heterosexuality in other than naturalistic terms may well have been construed as a personal attack, as "going too far," given the assumption that a critique of heterosexuality is a charge against heterosexual individuals.[58] I was not, it seemed, doing much "deregulating" at the level of these interpersonal discussions. If a radical lesbian and/or gay male politics has indeed become a powerful, unquestionable orthodoxy as those who engage cultural heterosexist discourses allege, I am left wondering about my reticence.

References

Adams, Ian. 1998. *Ideology and politics in Britain today.* Manchester: Manchester University Press.

Altman, Dennis. 1993 [1971]. *Homosexual: Oppression and liberation.* New York: New York University Press.

Arblaster, Anthony. 1984. *The rise and decline of western liberalism.* Oxford: Blackwell.

Auger, P. 1994. The meaning of gay rights, letter to the editor, *Metro*, June 17.

Bech, Henning. 1997. *When men meet: Homosexuality and modernity*, Cambridge: Polity.

Bell, David and Gill Valentine. 1995. Introduction: orientations, in David Bell and Gill Valentine (eds.) *Mapping desire: Geographies of sexualities.* London: Routledge.

Boyd, Sarah. 1995. An MP making waves, *Evening post*, August 12, 12.

Brickell, Chris. 2000. Heroes and invaders: gay and lesbian pride parades and the public/private distinction in New Zealand media accounts, *Gender, place and culture*, 7(2): 163–178.

———.2001. Whose "special treatment?" Heterosexism and the problems with liberalism, *Sexualities* 4(2): 211–236.

Butler, Judith. 1991. Imitation and gender insubordination, in Diana Fuss (ed.) *Inside/out: Lesbian theories, gay theories.* London: Routledge.

Carter, R. 1995. 2% pulling the strings, letter to the editor, *Sunday star-times*, November 12, C4.

———.1998. Letter to the editor, *Metro*, January, 16.

Coote, Michael. 1997. None so queer, *Free radical*, August/September, 22–26.

Davey, Lois. 1996. Cooking a lesbian meal, letter to the editor, *Sunday star-times*, September 1, A10.

Due, Linnea. 1995. *Joining the tribe: Growing up gay and lesbian in the'90s.* New York: Doubleday.

Du Fresne, Karl. 1995. Here comes the annual look-at-me orgy, *Evening post*, 1 February, 6.
————.1997. Mr. Blumsky, tell the heroes to hike, *Evening post*, October 8, 10.
Dworkin, Andrea. 1983. *Right wing women*. New York: Perigree.
Elshtain, Jean Bethke. 1982/1983. Homosexual politics: the paradox of gay liberation, *Salmagundi*, 58–59, 252–280.
Express. 1998. Pearls: what did she say? March 19, 8.
Evening post. 1994. Political correctness, editorial, June 21, 6.
Frankenberg, Ruth. 1993. *White women, race matters: The social construction of Whiteness*. Minneapolis: University of Minnesota Press.
Free radical. 1995. The horror file, April, 24.
————.1998. He's still here!! Aaaaaaaaaaaaargh!!!!!!!!!!!!," advertisement, May–June, back cover.
Frye, Marilyn. 1983. *The politics of reality: Essays in feminist theory*. New York: The Crossing Press.
Gilroy, Paul. 1990. The end of antiracism, in Wendy Ball and John Solomos (eds.) *Race and local politics*. London: MacMillan.
Gordon, Paul and Francesca Klug. 1986. *New right, new racism*. Britain: Searchlight.
Hall, R. 1996. After the parade, letter to the editor, *Metro*, May, 16.
Hennessy, Rosemary and Chrys Ingraham. 1992. Putting the heterosexual order in crisis, *Mediations*, 16(2): 17–23.
Hooker, J. 1995. Tolerance for pragmatists, too? Letter to the editor *New Zealand Herald* 11 February: 1/8.
Ingraham, Chrys. 1994. The heterosexual imaginary: feminist sociology and theories of gender, *Sociological theory*, 2(12): 203–219.
Jackson, Stevi. 1997/1998. Whose sexual agendas? *Trouble and strife*, 36, 59–64.
Jung, Patricia and Ralph Smith. 1993. *Heterosexism: An ethical challenge*. New York: State University of New York Press.
Laclau, Ernesto and Chantal Mouffe. 1985. *Hegemony and socialist strategy*. London: Verso.
Laurie, Alison. 1987. Lesbian worlds, in Shelagh Cox (ed.) *Public and private worlds: Women in contemporary New Zealand*. Wellington: Allen and Unwin.
Leonard, Heather. 1998. Not bigoted, letter to the editor, *Metro*, January, 15.
Lesbian History Group. 1989. *Not a passing phase: Reclaiming lesbians in history 1840–1985*. London: The Women's Press.
McLennan, Catriona. 1996. Push on to legalise gay marriage, *Dominion*, January 18, 1.
McLeod, Rosemary. 1993. Old fashioned questions, *North and south*, April: 40.
————.1994. A jolly good wimmin, *North and south*, March: 34.
————.1995. Go tell your sexual abuse stories to a tetraplegic, *Dominion*, June1, 8.
————.1997. Putting all-girl sex in the pulpit, *Dominion*, April 10, 8.
McRae, Anne. 1993. The right to know? letter to the editor, *North and south*, November, 30.
Marshall, John. 1981. Pansies, perverts and macho men: changing conceptions of male homosexuality, in Kenneth Plummer (ed.) *The making of the modern homosexual*. London: Hutchinson.
Maw, Jackie. 1995. It's a wimmin's lot, *Free radical*, 16, 19.
Roger, Warwick. 1996a. Answers on a postage stamp please, *Evening post*, April 8, 4.
————.1996b. Why do we always ignore the obvious? *Evening post*, April 29, 4.
————.1997. Coverage of hero parade over the top, *Evening post*, March 10, 4.
Sandel, Michael (ed.) 1984. *Liberalism and its critics*, Oxford: Blackwell.
Scherer, Karyn. 1995. We must do better, says Labour Whip, *Evening post*, October 11, 1.
Seidel, Gill. 1988. The British new right's "Enemy Within": the antiracists, in Geneva Smitherman-Donaldson and Teun van Dijk (eds.) *Discourse and discrimination*. Detroit: Wayne State University Press.
Smith, Anna Marie. 1991. Which one's the pretender?: Section 28 and lesbian representation, in Tessa Boffin and Jean Fraser (eds.) *Stolen glances: Lesbians take photographs*. London: Pandora.
————.1994. *New right discourse on race and sexuality*. Cambridge: Cambridge University Press.
————.1997. The good homosexual and the dangerous queer: resisting the new homophobia, in Lynne Segal (ed.) *New sexual agendas*. London: MacMillan.
Turner, J. and K. Turner. 1998. Letter to the editor, *Metro*, January, 18.
TVNZ. 1997. *Holmes*, TV1, 25 September.
Weir, Lorna. 1995. PC then and now: resignifying political correctness, in Stephen Richer and Lorna Weir (eds.) *Beyond political correctness: Toward the inclusive university*. Toronto: University of Toronto Press.

Wittig, Monique. 1992. *The straight mind*. London: Harvester Wheatsheaf.
Zwicky, Arnold. 1997. Two lavendar issues for linguists, in Anna Livia and Kira Hall (eds.) *Queerly phrased: Language, gender and sexuality*. New York: Oxford University Press.

Notes

1. Butler, 1991: 23
2. Seidel, 1988; Gilroy, 1990
3. Gordon and Klug, 1986: 15
4. *Free radical*, 1998: back cover
5. I use "liberalism" in the sense of the liberal tradition in the broadest sense (Adams 1998: 35). While this tradition has several sometimes competing strands, fundamental to all are the concepts of "individualism," "equality," and "rights." For more detailed discussion of the antecedents of, and tensions between, different strands of liberal thought, see Adams (1998); Arblaster (1984); and Sandel (ed) (1984)
6. Altman, 1993: 59
7. Frankenberg, 1993
8. 1997: 102
9. See Due (1995: 256) for a slightly different formulation of this point
10. Brickell, 2001
11. Smith, 1997: 229
12. Hooker, 1995: 1/8
13. Brickell, 2000
14. McLeod, 1994: 34
15. Du Fresne, 1997: 10
16. Carter, 1998: 16
17. The Maori are New Zealand's indigenous and colonized people who now represent about 12 percent of the country's population
18. See Brickell, 2000; 2001
19. Du Fresne, 1997: 10
20. For an interesting analysis of the ways in which 'tyranny' constitutes the superordinate gloss of much discourse on 'political correctness,' see Weir (1995)
21. Carter, 1995: C4
22. Brickell, 2000
23. Hall, 1996: 16; du Fresne, 1997: 10
24. Smith, 1991: 131
25. Elshtain, 1982/1983: 253
26. Mouffe, 1985: 170
27. Turner and Turner, 1998: 18
28. Leonard, 1998: 15
29. TVNZ, 1997
30. Jung and Smith, 1993: 24
31. Smith, 1994: 208
32. Frye, 1983: 157
33. Jung and Smith, 1993: 129
34. Maw, 1995: 19
35. Davey, 1996: A10. A "rocky mountain oyster" is a bull's testicle — hence the connotation of castration
36. *Evening post*, 1994: 6
37. McRae, 1993: 30
38. 1997: 8
39. 1995: 8; 1993: 40
40. McLennan, 1996: 1
41. 1995: 6
42. Scherer, 1995: 1
43. Zwicky, 1997
44. Laurie, 1987: 147

45. 1995: 12
46. Wood, cited *Express* 1998: 8
47. Marshall, 1981; Lesbian History Group, 1989: 2
48. May–Jun 1998: back cover
49. Coote, 1997; *Free radical*, 1995; Maw, 1995
50. 1997: 4
51. 1997: 4
52. 1996b: 4
53. 1996a: 4
54. Bell and Valentine, 1995: 11
55. Auger, 1994: 17
56. 1994: 203
57. Hennessy and Ingraham, 1992: 18–19
58. Jackson, 1997/8: 62

2
The Paradox

Crossing the Borders of Gendered Sexuality: Queer Masculinities of Straight Men[1]

ROBERT HEASLEY

The personal ad began, "Must be gay? Guess again girlfriend!" Alan[2] is a 35-year-old male who ran this ad in search of a woman. He wants a woman who is attracted to a man who is open to expressing his feelings and listening to those of his partner. Alan is comfortable being in women's space and conversing on topics that are often more appealing to women than most men he encounters. Alan is heterosexual in his sexual experience and his erotic desires. At the same time, he is a member of a support group of men who identify as gay and bisexual, as well as having members, like Alan, who identify as straight. Alan publicly advocates an end to homophobia and heterosexism, and attends retreats and workshops with gay and bisexual men. Many of his physical mannerisms are "feminine"—he uses his hands when he talks, becomes excited and enthusiastic when he shares ideas, his soft voice rises to a higher pitch during these moments, and he cries more, and more openly, than the average guy. "Must be gay ... " has been a common refrain Alan has heard from women he has dated about why they did not initially pursue him, and one he has heard from males about their perception of Alan's sexual orientation. Alan is one example of a straight male who "crosses the border" of both masculinity and sexuality to become what I have come to think of as a "queer-straight" male.

Disrupting Traditional Ways of Being Masculine

Queer-straight males are those who disrupt hetero-normative constructions of masculinity, and in the process, disrupt what it means to be straight, as well as gay. Many straight men experience and demonstrate "queer masculinity," defined as ways of being masculine outside heteronormative constructions of masculinity that disrupt, or have the potential to disrupt, traditional images of the hegemonic heterosexual masculine (Heasley, Sage. Vol. 7.3 January 2005). Hegemonic masculinity is represented culturally in the icons of religion, sports, historical figures, economic and political leaders, and the entertainment industry.[3] In these arenas, males are presumed to be straight and hold stereotypically masculine beliefs, attitudes, and values unless and until they present themselves, or are presented, as other. Males who do not conform are problematized, often seen as odd, as struggling, humorous, or sad.

Consider the boy in middle school who enjoys playing the violin, is a veracious reader, prefers to talk with friends about ideas and intellectual challenges, and displays little if any overt sexual interest in girls. He may even openly admit that he prefers having female friends to male companionship, although he does not see girls as sexual objects or someone to win over for the purpose of having a girlfriend. I once overheard Sean, a seventh grade boy who was a childhood playmate of my daughter, say to her as they played a board game on a rainy day in the living room, "When I am hanging out with you and not the guys from school, I feel like I get to just be me." Although this particular boy was capable of doing hegemonic masculinity when he was with other boys (he primarily socialized with other boys when in public, and was readily accepted as "one of the guys") this was not a true representation of his masculinity. His relationship with my daughter allowed him to be "himself." If he had been this "self" in a more public arena, other boys would likely have questioned not only his masculinity, but by seventh grade, his sexuality as well. When in public, Sean hid this authentic masculinity in the shadows of the hegemonic.

I recently met with a group of college age males who had formed a student-led men's discussion group at a private liberal arts college. The name of the student group, The Multi-Orgasmic Men's Society (MOMS), made it clear that they were males who liked to talk about sex. The objective of the group's leadership, however, was that it would be a forum for males to discuss sexuality intelligently, and from a feminist, including a nonhomophobic, perspective. The group met weekly to raise questions about what it meant to be a male in the context of relationships, to break down stereotypes, to view sexual relationships as something more important than what *Maxim* or most other men's magazines encouraged. Discussions ranged from the use and meaning of pornography in their lives, to masturbation, anal stimulation, and for some of the males, how it felt to be perceived as gay.

During our meeting, I asked the students about why they considered themselves feminists and what value the group had to them personally. They said that feminism just made sense, that they wanted to date and have female friends who considered themselves equal to men and they wanted to be actively involved in ending sexism as well as homophobia, for both social justice reasons as well as personally as a way to have more meaningful relationships with other males regardless of sexual orientation. They expressed relief that through the group they were able to find other college men who were able to talk openly and honestly about sexuality, intimacy, and relationships, and to discuss such topics without ridicule or hype. Prior to this group's formation, most of the students had never experienced an environment where such discussions with male peers were possible. When they told other men (and women) about the group and what they talked about, they often faced questions about their gender attributes (were they all sissies?) and their sexual orientation (must be gay!). The two, gender and sexuality, are so closely linked as unmarked identities for straight males that to cross the border of either has implications in both arenas of identity.

Crossing the border into queer-straight maleness represents ways of being that extend the boundaries of the hetero-masculine and bring attention to, and in the process legitimize, the rich potential of masculinity and of heterosexuality. It is a process of queering that disrupts compulsory heterosexuality[4] and provides evidence of males "de-naturalizing" what is perceived as normative heterosexuality[5] and hegemonic masculinity.[6] The experience of queer-straight males also contributes to our ability to challenge institutionalized representations of hetero-masculinity, challenging what Ingraham (1999) refers to as the "meaning" given to heterosexuality itself, particularly as it is located in the context of masculinity. In much the same way that a feminist critique of the limits imposed on women has broadened ways of conceptualizing female-ness,[7] and female sexualities, acknowledging the ways hetero-masculinity is being queered by men in everyday life helps to expand the range of acceptable ways of being masculine, helping us realize that we can "turn up the volume"[8] on the multiple ways of being gendered and sexual for males.

Given the monolithic perception of heterosexualized masculinity, most men and women fail to conceptualize, let alone experience and value, other desirable ways of being straight and male than the typical "tough guy" that is so deeply rooted in the past 7,000 years of patriarchal social order.[9] It is a case of not being able to see the trees due to the assumptions made about the forest as one construction—that all straight males are the same, in terms of gender and their experience of sexuality. And, it is the power of the doubly uncontested identities of masculinity and heterosexuality that exist without conscious critique that contribute to the power resulting from those identities. At the same time, the very dominant positionality of hetero-males leads to a situation whereby those males who are not conforming can make change happen by troubling the hegemony. They can also be harshly sanctioned.

Sanctions on Queer-Straight Males

To act outside the idealized image of the hetero-masculine is to be suspect. And being suspect means being labeled, stigmatized, and ultimately punished. Psychologists have often labeled straight identified males who cross the border in their mannerisms, behaviors, and associations that did not fit the regimen of straightness, as "latent homosexuals." Such a term conjures up an image of "homo in waiting." This leap to label derives from both a rigid adherence to a reductionist approach to viewing all human sexualities as fitting into one of three categories, hetero–bi–homo-sexuality, or landing somewhere on the six-scaled continuum of sexual orientation proposed by Kinsey et al. (1948). It is also a result of the binary perception of gender,[10] with specific qualities associated with the two allowed options of male and female.

Gender-associated qualities are linked closely to perceptions of sexuality. Women are gendered as passive, vulnerable, and nurturing, while males are supposed to be aggressive, emotionally self-contained (meaning nonexpressive), and less nurturing. Gendered sexuality is reinforced by language. For instance, use of the word "luscious" by a male, or a male referring to another male as "pretty" (meaning it as a compliment), are virtually unheard of in the world of straight males; such terms are encoded not only as feminine but also as gay. Everyday sexual experiences of males draw on an inherited vocabulary that reflects the hegemonic masculine. Male discourse about such aspects of sexuality as masturbation reifies the violence inherent within hetero-masculinity, with use of terms such as jacking, choking, jerking, spanking, and beating. Such language, within the context of the interpersonal violence that is part of male culture, limits ways in which males perceive their male-ness, and their heterosexuality.

Males who do not fit comfortably into the hetero-masculinized discourse either by default (a heterosexual male who simply cannot "do" straight masculinity), or conscious effort (males who make a decision not to conform) are neither latent anything, nor are they homosexual. Their way of being is only problematic to those men who occupy the narrow space of hegemonic hetero-masculinity, and women who buy into that limited conceptualization of masculinity. Such problemization is reinforced by mental health professionals who fail to recognize the range of ways of being gendered and sexual.

Kevin, a 25-year-old heterosexual male talked with me about his intentional effort to move into queer identity through conscious nonconforming behaviors, attitudes, and beliefs that associate him with gayness and the feminine, saying,

> I think of myself as less masculine—no, that's not right, I think of myself as more masculine than traditional males. I mean, I can express my masculinity (and heterosexuality) in a wider range of ways than maybe most men can.... This sort-of leaves me feeling sorry for how narrowly many straight men experience their masculinity and their sexuality.

Kevin has participated in workshops where being naked with men and sharing massage and intimate touch has been part of the workshop experience, intended to break down the barriers and fears that males have about closeness with other males. This is not your typical 25-year-old hetero-male experience; however, it is one that, for Kevin, provided an opportunity to safely challenge fears and image a changing sense of self, of what it means to be heterosexual and masculine.

His conscious decision to be queer, to disrupt the meaning of heterosexuality and masculinity through embracing what is perceived as gay and feminine, has led him to be open to more sensual relationships with males in his life, as well as to feel closer in his identity with females. If Kevin's story was to appear in the media, or be examined by his parents (who do not understand his pursuit of queerness), his experience would likely be problemitized. Not only would Kevin be seen by the media as strange or different, but his actions may raise fears and anxieties for his family, who, after all, are put in a position of explaining Kevin's choices and behaviors to others. His queerness, although liberating for Kevin, becomes a stigma and a perceived burden to his parents.

At the same time, his pursuit of an intimate relationship with a woman may be second-guessed by the woman, as in the story of Alan at the beginning of this chapter, as though she cannot be certain she can trust him around his heterosexuality. And his male friends, who may not be prepared for relationships with other guys that are intimate and close—and who might be more comfortable with him if he just wanted to talk, but not touch, to do, but not feel—are confronted with whether they can be associated with a border-crossing queer-straight guy.

We conform to gender expectations because they are comfortable, familiar, and reinforced by others (we are rewarded for not breaking the norms), as well as unquestioned (we perceive there really are no desirable alternatives to the normative expectations). We do gender policing and ultimately become self-regulating. For males, such policing has been particularly restrictive.[11]

Boys suffer what can be profound consequences when departing from the norms and crossing the border into what is perceived as feminine as well as gay. The psychological diagnosis of gender dysphoria has been used to label boys who show signs of being "sissies," encouraging parents and teachers to see boys (or girls) acting outside of traditional gendered norms as needing intervention based on the child's presentation of self, not necessarily on any harm or threat the child poses to himself or anyone else. The hegemonic masculine is broadly supported by social institutions, as not only the ideal way to be a boy or man, but ultimately the only way. The typically hetero-masculine male, in contrast, faces no societally imposed intervention based purely on presentation of self.

The heterosexual male who has sex with another male is represented in film or novels as someone who is struggling with sexual identity, who must be at least bisexual (and in a religious context as someone who has sinned). The "sensitive" (translation: "sissy") young boy in films such as "Stand By Me" is portrayed as needing the protection and guidance of an older, heteronormative masculine boy. He needs the older male in the same way girls need a strong male. Likewise, in sociological and psychological literature, straight males-with-queerness may be identified as deviant, or pathologized for being gender inappropriate or sexually confused. On the street and in their schools, family, or workplace, openly queer-straight males may be stigmatized, seen as a curiosity, finding themselves positioned along with gay males in a world that is "other," and thus vulnerable to homophobic oppression.

Consider the male who identifies as a feminist and gay advocate. He is apt to be perceived as gay, and may not feel welcome in the company of stereotypically straight males. This is particularly the case if he also refuses to participate in traditional male culture, for example, if he does not attend sports games, or questions the value of competitive and contact sports, or prefers lesbian/feminist vocalists such as Indigo Girls, Melissa Etheridge, or another girl-band. Consider the fate of the straight male who is sexual or sensually close with another male, and openly acknowledges the relationship, even while defining as straight.

Recognizing Queer-Straight Ways of Being

These examples suggest a queering of hetero-masculinity in a variety of ways. However, we have no language or framework for considering the ways in which straight men can disrupt the dominant paradigm of the straight-masculine, a language that could provide legitimacy to the lived experience.

In an earlier article (Heasley, 2004), I proposed a typology of straight-queer males—males who disrupt both heterosexuality and hegemonic masculinity—as a contribution to the expansion of the conceptualization of straightness and of masculinity, in order to represent a truer picture than has been articulated of straight males' experiences and ways of being. Such a typology is needed for several reasons. It provides a way to expand upon the very notion of what is legitimized as being hetero-masculine and it allows us to "trouble" gender and sexuality as suggested by Judith Butler (1990), Michel Foucault (1978), and others. More specifically, it allows us to acknowledge a broader range of what exists, affirming elements of sexualized masculinity that have historically been treated as an exception and, in the kindest rendition, perceived as "nontraditional" male.

"Traditional males" are the ones society understands. Even if there are problems associated with the image, there is acceptance and legitimacy accorded to the typical-ness of his presentation. The "nontraditional" male, however, presents an unknown. Even though there are problems associated with the image of the traditional man, there is acceptance and legitimacy accorded to the typical-ness of his presentation. The "nontraditional" male, however, presents an unfamiliar package, even if the qualities he exhibits are seen as desirable, such as being an attentive, nurturing father. His difference demands justification, explanation. Being "non" means "not having." Applied to gender and sexuality, the implications are profound. The very labeling of a subject as the absence of something (such as labeling women as "non-men") reifies the dominant group while subjugating the subordinate. "Non" erases. And in the process, it problematizes other. For a straight-queer man, there is no place for awareness of self in relation to what is. He becomes the negative deviant, he is isolated, and in the process, is vulnerable to reactions in the form of stigma, labeling, and isolation by the dominant group. "Non" has no history, no literature, has no power, and no community. "Non" requires an invention of self.

By creating a typology of queer masculinities of straight males, we give space and language to lived experience, and set the stage upon which narratives of straight-queer men can find a home. My own experience of being a straight-queer man has contributed to my interest in creating a language through which I could come to know myself, and come to have agency in the knowing.

Recently, a new acquaintance, a straight male, told me that if he did not know I was married with three children, he would have assumed I was gay. Since hearing this is not an uncommon experience for me, I asked him the question I usually ask men (and women) who assume my sexual orientation to be gay—why? His response was typical—I talk with my hands, my voice is not deep, I care nothing about major sports, I am clearly a feminist and talk about gender, rape, violence as well as questioning male socialization (of course, I also teach and write in the areas of gender and sexuality!). He has also seen me greet close male friends by kissing them on the lips, hugging deeply, and at a social gathering, dancing together. "Must be gay… !"

It has always bothered me that I had come to define myself (and be defined by others) as "nontraditional." Yet, unless I were to give up what I feel to be my authentic self, I just could not "do" traditional (meaning, hegemonic-straight-masculinity) without changing: (a) what I find comfortable in terms of my body, (b) the intimacy I desire in my relationships with other men, (c) my sexual/sensual awareness, and (d) my politics that are informed by feminist and queer theory.

Writing in the mid-1970s, Bob Brannon introduced four themes that framed ways of being masculine: No Sissy Stuff, Sturdy Oak, Big Wheel, and Give 'Em Hell.[12] These themes continue to be in evidence today, as institutions from the military to the media emphasize these qualities for becoming "successful" males. Implicit in these categories is the assumption that all males are raised to be heterosexual. Brannon's four themes created a framework for breaking down types of masculine representation, all of which fit nicely into what Connell (1987) would later call hegemonic masculinity. The sexuality of males in Brannon's categories has only one dimension, hetero-masculinity. Given the extensive discourse about gender and sexuality that has taken place over the past thirty years we can now look at male's experience with an eye on straight-queerness and its disruption of the normatively gendered sexual.

Consider the following categories as an attempt to capture the ways this disruption takes place and an emerging legitimization of queerness within the hetero-masculine.

A Typology of Straight-Queer Masculinities

1. Straight sissy-boys
2. Social-justice straight-queers
3. Elective straight-queers (or the elective queer)
4. Committed straight-queers
5. Stylistic straight-queers
6. Males living in the shadow of masculinity (including Informed Inactive, Scared Stuck, and Uninformed Inactive)

These categories are nonlinear and nonhierarchical. They are clearly not exclusive; aspects of various males' lives are likely to fit with greater or lesser degree of comfort in one or in all categories depending on such factors as context and life stage. Each category, however, carries with it unique characteristics that queer the meaning of the heteromasculinity.

Straight Sissy-Boys
These are straight males who just cannot "do" straight masculinity. The sissy-boy appears to others as queer, although that is not his intention,

nor identity. He often experiences a response from the dominant culture, and perhaps from queers, as if he were queer. These males experience homophobic oppression for their apparent queer-ness, particularly as boys and young males when they are taunted and even attacked. They are likely to be isolated from straight male culture, and/or choose to separate themselves from the dominant male culture. Straight sissy-boy males may associate primarily with girls/women as opposed to actively engaging in gay male friendships and social networks, perhaps in part because of a desire to not be seen as being gay, beyond what is already perceived by others. Such males have varying degrees of homophobia or comfort/discomfort with homosexualities. Being perceived as gay by others is not necessarily a conscious choice and thus they may not have a conscious openness to the effect they have on queering their environment. Yet, just the existence of males who appear as "nonstraight" because they do not fit the image of the normative hetero-masculine serves to disrupt that masculinity and sexuality, simply by the sissy-boy showing up as straight.

Examples

Alan's story, introduced earlier, of running a personal ad with the headline, "Must be gay? Think again sister" suggests elements of the sissy-boy male. He has learned to value his presentation that leads others to perceive him as being gay. He uses it in his ad to find a partner.

My own experience as a young male helps me identify with this category as well, having been perceived as a sissy as a child, within my family and school. My inability to perform masculinity to meet my father's expectations gave impetus to his referring to me as a sissy and discounting my positive attributes, as well as contributing to his verbal threats and physical attacks. In elementary school, I did not participate in competitive sports, although the few times I attempted to do so, I was inevitably a "last pick" by whomever was captain of the recess baseball game. In high school, I avoided the hallways where the guys who harassed the sissy-boys and sexualized the girls hung out (that they were the same hallways is in itself a statement about the status of the sissy male, used by hegemonic males as part of their performance to affirm their heterosexuality).

I found safety in my role as a student volunteer in the library, on the forensics team and debate club, and in taking private acting classes after school (all experiences that have served me well as an adult, but experiences I took on, in part, as a means of avoiding the land mines of straight masculinity). I was also vulnerable to adult males who pursued young boys for sex. As a sissy male walking the streets of my town or hitchhiking (the normal way boys in my family got from town to home in a rural area), older men made sexual advances, at least in part, I suspect, due to my apparent vulnerability. I did not look like the type of young man who would beat them up!

The irony of having to struggle with attacks by straight peers for being a sissy, dismissal by a hegemonically masculine father for not being male enough, and being vulnerable to sexual molestation by adult males because of a sissy presentation, suggests that males in this category can, and do, experience challenges from nearly every angle.

It was easy, however, to find girls to date. Like Alan, I was attractive as a friend to girls due to the very qualities that made me vulnerable to male dismissal and abuse; although it was necessary to establish my heterosexual interest in "making out" (which I enjoyed!), I was not likely to pursue sexual interaction beyond what a particular girlfriend initiated.

Social Justice Straight-Queer

Males in this category take action publicly in support of those who identify as gay, lesbian, bisexual, or transgender and at the risk of being marginalized by straight males and/or being responded to as if they were gay. Thus, their actions represent risk-taking, placing themselves in a position of possibly being threatened, stigmatized, or violated as a result of association with gayness. A key element in this category is the deliberate public expression by straight males, verbally or through action, in ways that disrupt both heterosexuality and masculinity.

Examples

Eric is a middle-school age boy who consciously acts as a public advocate when as a new kid on a soccer team, he chooses to be friendly with Thomas, a classmate whose sissy-boy characteristics have left him shunned by the other boys. When I talk with Eric, he is aware that he is challenging homophobia by acting as an ally for Thomas, and taking risks as a new kid at this school. At the same time, Thomas pursues such behaviors as listening to girl bands on his walkman (does not attempt to adapt to normative hetero-masculinity), even though he is threatened. Simply by refusing to adapt, both boys contribute to queering hetero-masculinity because they are a threat to the status quo.

In another example, Jake is a straight male in his mid-twenties, and is very close with his brother who is gay. He attends social events and retreats with primarily gay and bisexual males, and actively participates in public demonstrations in support of gay rights.

Both Eric and Jake disrupt the meaning of masculinity and straightness; they show up in masculine space (competitive sports, for instance) and pursue heterosexual dating relationships, and yet are not comfortable with the often homophobic behaviors associated with the hegemonic straight masculine. Social justice queers can be trusted to not "go along" with male norms in order to gain approval of other straight males. Rather, they use the privilege they have as straight males to interrupt the hegemony of the hetero-masculine at the interpersonal or social system level, and join the queers as an ally.

Elective Straight–Queer

Elective straight–queer identity can be seen as straight men performing queer masculinity. Males in this category elect to move into queer masculinity as a means of liberating themselves from the constrictions of heteronormative masculinity. Such males can move with varying levels of comfort back into "straight masculinity" without necessarily losing power within the dominant culture. They "flirt" with queerness, taking on queer characteristics, kissing, dancing, dressing, and moving the body queer-ly, but within the context (setting) of the queer world where it is safe, for instance, the gay bar. Men in this category move into queer space and may take on queer ways of interacting, not based primarily on a social justice principle, but just for the purpose of personal enjoyment, comfort, and desire. Moving into queer space may permit them to be more fully themselves, providing the opportunity to discover the breadth of their masculinity and their sexuality, exploring ways of being associated with what had previously only been presented as "other."

Example

Andy is a straight 30-year-old male and identifies as somewhat of a gay spirit. He has never found himself sexually aroused by males. In high school and most of college, he was what he called a "typical" straight guy, participating in homophobic put-downs, and hanging out with other guys while sexualizing relationships with women. After becoming friends with and starting to hang out with a gay male co-worker during college, he began to see the fun of being in gay space. For the past five years, Andy's social life has primarily focused on going clubbing (dancing at nightclubs) and partying with gay males. His former workmate became his roommate, and now most of his best male friends are gay. He has attended gay strip shows that included performances of sexual acts and says the experience has allowed him to let go of his own inhibitions when it comes to his body and dancing, and to find comfort in an environment of men. One benefit of having a gay social life, he says, has been accumulating "a great wardrobe" that contributes to the flamboyance he brings with him to his position as a popular art teacher in a progressive high school. Andy was recently married, with his gay friends among others in attendance, to a woman who initially did not pursue dating him because she assumed he was gay.

Committed Straight-Queer

Committed straight-queers practice at being queer with the intention of personally benefiting from moving toward queerness as an integral aspect of their sexuality and their masculinity. While the elective straight-queer may or may not be interested in learning about queer-ness to expand his own sexual and gender boundaries, this is clearly the intent for committed straight-queers who see queerness as a desirable way of being, see benefits for their own life and potentially (at least for some) for society in terms of moving toward changes in institutions such as the family, religion, and the law. Committed straight-queers like queer space and ways of being. They distance themselves from what they see as the constrictions of the hegemonic straight masculine. If they move into the straight-masculine at all, it is more likely to visit, to participate in, for whatever reason, but not to identify with straight-masculinity.

There has been a similar movement by males who "get it" about feminism and have a determination to change the way they experience masculinity to incorporate identity with women, accessing women's culture and integrating ways of being that might be perceived by the larger culture as "feminine." Committed straight-queers look to queers for direction and ways of being.

Examples

Kevin, the young man quoted earlier as describing himself as "more masculine than traditional males" exemplifies this category. Over the last eight years, he has made a conscious decision to not present himself as a "straight-masculine" male. Kevin pursues intimate physical and emotional relationships with other males (straight and gay). He is open to being sexual with another male, although at 28, has not experienced an orgasmically sexual same-sex relationship. When he was 17, he entered a recovery program for recovering addicts where he developed a consciousness about his use of (heterosexual) pornography and his pattern of manipulating females in order to have sex, a pattern encouraged by his male peers. In the program, he heard the stories of women his age who had been sexually abused or raped, and began to understand the violence associated with much of male sexuality. He decided to become celibate, for an extended period of time, which included breaking his addiction to pornography. During this period, he also heard the stories of males in his therapy group who identified as gay. He began attending gay narcotics anonymous meetings, developing close friendships with gay men, both older men who mentored him, and younger males he came to mentor.

His recovery story is powerful in that he came to appreciate the role both hegemonic masculinity and heterosexuality played in his own life through knowing the experiences of others who lived on the margins. While Kevin does not desire that part of gay male culture that sexualizes relationships, he does desire that which he perceives as queer masculinity, the masculinity that is not dominated by or dictated to by men's control of women and other men, where sexuality becomes in both cases the tool of control—the threat of sexual and physical violence toward women who do not respond to male desires, and the threat of physical, and at times sexual, violence toward males who do not conform to heterosexualized masculinity. Kevin admits that he finds strength in stepping outside the cultural image of heterosexual masculinity.

In a second example, Tim and Jon, who met as Freshman year roommates, are college seniors who define as straight. They desire sex with women, talking specifically about their love of cunnilingus, vaginal intercourse, and the feel of women's bodies. They both have girlfriends with whom they are sexually active. Tim and Jon are best friends, and describe themselves publicly as being "nonorgasmic boyfriends." They say they like to queer straight space as a political act, but they also simply love being intimate and exploring the ways to be in relationship with each other. When alone, they have engaged in kissing and sexual play with each other. Jon states that this has allowed him to more fully practice his sexuality. Tim, a former high school football player, says that at some point he would like to have oral sex (both active and passive) with another male, and to experience anal penetration. Tim, a sexuality educator and advocate on his campus, introduced Jon to wearing skirts. Initially, they did this when they were at home and with their girlfriends, or at parties with gay and lesbian friends and other queer-straight males. More recently, they have occasionally worn skirts on campus, and at times, held hands when walking together.

Neither Tim nor Jon see themselves as bi-sexual or gay and they generally are not erotically attracted to other males. They do, however, question whether those categories make any sense for them or anyone. Tim and Jon are intentional in both their public and private exploration of queerness. They disrupt the hetero-normative masculine when alone in order to experience their private sexuality. When in public, their behaviors are political, but also a means to express gendered sexuality in a way that is increasingly comfortable and familiar to them.

Stylistic Straight-Queers

There are a growing number of straight males—film and recording artists, athletes, fashion models, and "metrosexual"[13] males—who intentionally take on a presentation of self that is traditionally associated with gay male culture. These "stylistic straight-queers" allow themselves to develop and display an aesthetic, such as stylish hair cuts and clothes, having facials and pedicures. In so doing, they are attracting the attention of gay men, as well as those straight males who can identify with the border crossing identities. They also get the attention of straight women who find themselves attracted to what is perceived as a "gay" aesthetic or a "gay" sensitivity.

Straight males in this category are taking risks of being rejected by hegemonic hetero-masculine males while at the same time they can gain commercial and sexual capital from the appeal to both straight women and a segment of the queer male population who themselves have been socialized to pursue straightness as the ideal (for themselves and for their sexual partner) in the way African Americans have had "blondness" romanticized and sexualized as the ideal.

While stylistic straight-queers have the benefit of using their straight-male privilege for commercial and relational gain, by moving into gay space in a public way they are also, even if unconsciously, participating in border crossing behaviors (or at least the appearance of such) and thus queering the hegemonic hetero-masculine. They are disrupting the meaning of straight and of masculinity, making it harder for the general public to infer sexual orientation from stylistic cues.

Examples

British soccer player and media celebrity David Beckham identifies as straight while assuming queer-identified characteristics. Known for his polished nails, going to gay bars, and publicly proclaiming his acceptance of gay male culture (as well as declaring his heterosexuality), Beckham currently has perhaps the highest profile in this category. Earlier examples included such performers as Mick Jagger (when he was still androgynous) and basketball player Dennis Rodman (when he was wearing wedding dresses). Straight male actors who play gay characters and perform sex scenes on the cable television series "Queer As Folk" and the actor who plays Will on the television show, "Will and Grace" are among the many males queering up masculine sexuality by their active participation in queer roles.

A recent issue of *OUT* magazine (April, 2003), marketed primarily to gay males with an emphasis on fashion, featured a photo section entitled "The Carlson twins take it off." Kyle and Lane Carlson started their modeling career with Abercrombie and Fitch, a mainstream clothing company that uses homoerotic imagery to sell their products. In dozens of interviews in a variety of media outlets, the Carlson twins make it clear that they are straight. At the same time, they appear in sexualized poses (without women) in magazines that appeal to gay men. In the issue of *OUT*, they are not only featured in sexually suggestive poses, as an exclusive for the magazine, but their family—including father, mother, siblings, and in-laws—is featured as well. The appearance of the Carlson family, from rural Minnesota, serves to queer not only masculinity but also straight families, at least stylistically.

Males Living in the Shadow of Masculinity

Straight males living in the shadow of the hegemonic hetero-masculine are men who avoid displaying difference, but are not completely comfortable with, and somehow do not "fit in" with the heterosexualized masculinity that is all around them. They may (or may not) "get it" in terms of disagreement with the traditional male role, at the intellectual, emotional, or physical level, but are unlikely to do anything to either change or challenge the status quo, or change themselves around how they do heterosexuality and/or masculinity. Often, these males are seen as "quiet."

I see them sitting in my classroom, often in the back, with baseball caps on backward, seldom speaking up, yet obviously engaged in listening. In their class essays on gender and sexuality, they often share personal reflections that are insightful, expressing a desire to see changes in how society constricts both masculine and heterosexual expression. But if there were no written assignments on the topic, I (like others in the class) would never know these males were able and willing to challenge hegemonic heteromasculinity. We can assume that their voices are not raised publicly due to fear of being labeled gay, not masculine, and because they lack role models for and personal experience with such public "outing."

Males living in the shadow of masculinity are unlikely to take risks in interrupting gender and sexual expectations, although they are also less likely to participate in the oppressive aspects of masculinized heterosexuality. In some ways, they may be seen as the "sweet guys" who do not engage at least in the more oppressive aspects of straight masculinity.

Although they do not display any "queer" public behaviors or express attitudes that put them at risk in confronting the dominant system, they still contribute to the queering of masculinity by not actively participating in the dominant system. Since we know that systems of oppression require agreement of members who have qualities identified with the oppressor group to participate in supporting the system, males in this category subvert the dominator group simply through their inaction, while at the same time avoiding any overt appearance of challenging the system.

Often, it seems, it is the women in their lives—their female friends, girlfriends, wives, or mothers—who see the tears, fear, or anger these males feel in response to the constrictive nature of the hetero-masculine. They are also more likely to see the playful male, the spontaneous and emotional male, the excited, gleeful male, who hides from public view for fear of punishment and rejection by those who dominate the system.

There is a wide continuum in terms of the knowledge and awareness about gender, or alternatives to heteronormativity among the men who might fit in this "shadow" category. One way of thinking about the variation among men in the shadows is by looking at the following three subcategories. Like the overall typology presented in this chapter, these subcategories are not exclusive, but rather represent an attempt to organize patterns that appear to have some commonalities among members of this large group. The categories are: Informed Inactive, Scared Stuck, and Unaware Inactive.

Informed Inactive Some men who hide in the shadow of masculinity are "informed inactives." They are informed about sexuality, gender, and masculinity and are likely to understand and support feminism as well as gay rights. They are straight, but not "narrow" in terms of knowledge and even attitudes on the subject of gender and sexuality. Yet they do not act overtly on what they know or how they feel. Males in this category may find ways to display behind-the-scenes support for queer gay men, but are not comfortable being queer-straight men, or putting themselves in positions publicly where they might be perceived as gay.

Thus, they are unlikely to display nonconforming behaviors, or appear in queer space unless accompanied by a girlfriend or female friend. They are also unlikely to take any personal risks, emotionally or sensually, with close male friends, or present themselves through body posture, language, or physical appearance as queer, particularly not while they are with straight male friends in public.

In private space, with close friends or with women, such males may take on a nonhegemonic male appearance or behavior such as talking seriously and respectfully about homosexuality, or they may cross-dress in front of a girlfriend, or talk cute/sweet using nonmasculinized language when in bed with their female partner, or even lying in their female partner's arms, being held and cuddled. Generally, this category represents men who are informed and knowledgeable, but who remain behind the scenes when it comes to changes in their presentation and experience of heterosexual masculinity, or public advocacy and support for changes in the system.

Scared Stuck Some straight men can talk the language of queerness, can quietly have gay friends but cannot "do gay"—cannot transcend into being physically close (not necessarily sexual) with another male. They would not feel comfortable if others perceived them to be gay, although they are comfortable with quietly being an ally to gays. Like the Informed Inactive men, they "get it," but are able to go a little further in terms of their interpersonal relationships. Yet, unlike males who are social justice queers, they are less likely to be public advocates, and unlike committed queer-straights, they are reticent to adopt personal qualities of being queer. Men in this category can accept queer-ness, and even intellectually embrace it, but hold back for whatever reason from doing the personal work that would be needed to allow themselves to become queer-straight identified. They lack the confidence or perception that they can go beyond the intellectual "acceptance" of queer masculinity for "gay men" but not for themselves. They may cheer others on, even have friends who are queer-straights, but do not move into the experiential sphere of queer masculinity. They appear to be stuck in the forms of traditional masculinity, to overtly know better, yet at the personal level, the default for such males is "normal" even if in intellectual and emotional respects, they realize "normal" is not what it is cracked up to be.

Unaware Inactive Another place on the spectrum of "shadow males" are those who are also inactive in any intentional queering. Such males may realize that they do not "fit" within traditional straight masculinity, and are not necessarily comfortable with the status quo, but they do not perceive that change is possible, individually or culturally. These males do not appear gay or connect to a queer world in any way, but they also do not do straight hegemonic masculinity. Having no awareness of what queer masculinity is, their life in the "shadow of masculinity" leads them to do enough straight masculinity to get by, which means wearing appropriate male clothing so that they do not stand out, knowing enough about normative hetero-masculine expectations to "pass." If they are on a construction crew or in a board room of men who act out hetero-masculinity in their language and behavior, they might choose to eat alone at lunchtime. If they are sitting with other straight men who are talking in hyper-masculine, sexist or homophobic terms, they will not attempt to change the topic, but neither will they participate. Rather, they fade into the background.

In college, they are the men who stay in their rooms, away from the noise of masculinity that ripples through the hallways (the "hey, look at me!" noise of the masculinized corridor). They do not do hyper-straight male language-do not use "cunt" or "let's go have a few brews" or know the names of NFL players. They avoid the hyper-male scene whenever possible.

Males living in the shadow of masculinity may be what Crane and Crane-Seeber (2003) refer to as sweet guys, but they also can be pretty shut down emotionally. Expressing straight male emotions such as anger does not fit for them, nor do they allow themselves "female emotions" such as crying when they are sad or expressing fear. It is safer to not say anything, not show anything, and attempt to get by. The body of these men is not represented in the image of straight or gay masculinities—there is no appearance or an image of "self," no public voice, only quiet knowing of being "different"—a self-identity of being "non." They may live inside the space of computers, musical instruments, books, or other such places that provide safety from the storm of heteronormative masculinity. Almost by the nature of living in the shadow, they seek each other out and "play" most of their lives with other men who quietly "go along" with the mainstream, but are never fully engaged in the dominant hetero-masculine world.

Jim, a graduate student, noted that this category reminds him of many of the boys he knew in high school, who,

> ...were not queer-acting at all but were simply not good at masculine privileged activities such as sports, hitting on girls, being the class clown, or knowing about cars. These were guys who were "straight" in appearance (and no doubt took time when dressing each morning that they appear straight) but were good at math or playing the trombone, things that were not going to get you a date with the homecoming queen. Some may refer to these boys as "dorks" or "nerds." These men are not forced to hide because of what they do (as young overtly queer acting boys must do). Rather, they are outside of normative masculinity because of what they are unable to do, the privileged activities and interests of boy culture. These boys know they are pretty low in the social hierarchy but would probably just understand themselves as unpopular as opposed to unpopular because they are not good at "boy stuff" (J. Fulton, personal communication, June 27, 2003).

These boys, as Jim suggests, would not be likely to do the analysis to understand their experience; they would not add a "gender component" to thinking about their relatively low status, and the particular form of isolation they experienced from those with the highest status. And they certainly are unlikely to add a sexual component to any thinking about their status, seeing that their position is not only a result of failure to perform hegemonic masculinity but also hegemonic heterosexuality. This is similar to how, given the general absence of consciousness about social class in the United States, those at the bottom socioeconomically are very aware of their relative status, but unlikely to pursue analysis at a level of acting out against the oppressive nature of the system and its institutions. The oppression is instead internalized to the point of hopelessness and lowered expectations.

Giving Legitimacy to Queer Masculinity

Border crossing can be dangerous, and in the midst of oppressive systems that threaten those who take the risk to cross it seems ominous and even undesirable. The queer-straight male holds a position that, regardless of where one falls in the typology presented here, is not institutionally supported. It is a status that may find support from other marginalized groups including women and gay queers, although even that may be a mixed bag, given that some forms of queer-straight masculinity, such as the elective or stylistic straight-queer, may result in men in these categories gaining social capital beyond what is possible for women or gay queers (who do not have the same options).

At the same time, there is little institutional support for straight-queer males, when compared to the privileges extended to hegemonic hetero-masculine males. At least not yet. And there is no clearly defined social movement for males that attempts to raise consciousness and invite the level of change that will queer straight masculinity. Not yet.

The benefit of building a typology of queer masculinities is to extend voice and legitimacy to the queer-ness that already exists within the straight male world. It is an attempt to contribute to the discourse initiated by the first wave of the feminist movement, and the actions of the earlier gay movement dating back to Germany in the nineteenth century that found currency in the United States in the mid-twentieth century. What has been consistent in both the feminist and GLBT movements throughout the past century is that the discourse on sexuality and gender in these communities has provided an appreciation for the diverse ways in which gender and sexuality take form. Naming the diversity within the construct of masculinity–and its relationship with queerness, gives voice and legitimacy to the queer-ness that exists within the straight male world. It will ideally provoke greater discourse on the topic and extend awareness of the influence of the hegemonically straight masculine not only over gay men, but straight males as well.

There are many questions to explore, such as what is the attraction of moving outside the hetero-masculine norm? What is gained? Is this "using" queerness as a cover—to avoid dealing with straight masculine environments where threats are great? Do elective queer-straight males in queer space privilege straightness at the expense of queers? Is this an honoring of queerness or a use? Is there a difference between queer experiences by straight males that takes place in private space vs. public space?

Queer forms of straight masculinity represent something much more than just men who are "nontraditional." Rather, they suggest a masculinity and male heterosexuality that extends the reach of societal perceptions of both, and one that for males in any of these categories, allows potential for evolving a broadened definition, resulting in expanded norms and expectations, for who straight men are and who they can be.

Why are the types of males discussed in this chapter disrupting hetero-masculinity? It is because they queer the environment of the hetero-masculine by, for whatever reason, not fully participating in the normative system. And they provide a hiding place for males who are queer and do not feel safe or competent in passing in heterosexualized masculine environments. Queer-straight males' respective refusal to actively participate in the dominant system serves to stall the system itself. Their absence, and, at the very least, their lack of full participation in hetero-masculine culture weakens the system of oppression that is an essential part of normative hetero-masculinity. At the same time, many of the queer-straight males identified with these categories actively challenge the assumptions of the hetero-masculine, the dichotomous thinking that has been a cultural stronghold and the core legitimizing force of gender and sexual oppression.

Creating a language for queer-straight males is in itself a queering of hegemonic hetero-masculinity. It is an attempt to change social attitudes around both male sexuality and masculinity and provide support for both those in the trenches of queerness and those males who are in the shadows. It turns the volume up, giving legitimacy and voice to a way of being for queer-straight males.

By looking closely to see, and validate, the queering that goes on by straight males, it is possible to recognize a range of ways in which males problematize hegemonic masculinity and heterosexuality, and by doing so, disrupt one of the most privileged identities in Western society.

References

Bem, S. 1995. Dismantling gender polarization and compulsory heterosexuality: should we turn the volume down or up? *Journal of sex research*, 32(4): 329–334.

Brannon, R. 1976. The male sex role: our culture's blueprint of manhood, and what it's done for us lately, in D. David and R. Brannon (eds.) *The 49th percent majority*, pp. 1–45 Reading, MA: Addison & Wesley.

Butler, J. 1990. *Gender trouble*. New York: Routledge.

Connell, R. 1987. *Gender and power*. Cambridge, MA: Polity.

Crane, B. and J. Crane-Seeber, 2003. The four boxes of gendered sexuality: good girl/bad girl and tough guy/sweet guy, in R. Heasley and B. Crane (eds.) *Sexual lives: A reader on the theoriesand realities of human sexualities*, pp. 196–217 New York: McGraw-Hill.

Foucault, M. 1978. *The history of sexuality*, Vol. 1. New York: Pantheon Books.

Heasley, R. Queer masculinities of straight men: creating a typology. *Men and masculinities*. Sage. Vol. 7. 3 January 2005.

Ingraham, C. 1999. *White weddings: Romancing heterosexuality in popular culture*. New York: Routledge.

Kinsey, A. C., W. B. Pomeroy and C. E. Martin. 1948. *Sexual behavior in the human male*. Philadelphia: W. B. Saunders.

Kindlon, D. and M. Thompson. 1999. *Raising Cain: Protecting the emotional life of boys*. New York: Ballantine Books.

Pollack, W. 1999. *Real boys: Rescuing our sons from the myths of boyhood*. New York: Random House.

Rich, A. 1980. Compulsory heterosexuality and lesbian existence. *Signs*. 5: 631–660.

Seidman, S. 1992. *Embattled eros*. New York: Routledge

Spring fashion: the Carlson twins take it off, *Out*, April 2003, 72–85.

St. John, W. 2003. Metrosexuals come out, *The New York Times*, June 22, 9–1, 9–5.

Notes

1. Portions of this chapter originally appeared in "Queer Masculinities of Straight Men: Creating a Typology" (Sage Vol. 7. 3, Jan. 2005). *Men and masculinities.* Sage.
2. Pseudonyms have been used throughout the chapter to create a coherent story, and are based on stories shared by men in interviews.
3. Connell, 1987
4. Rich, 1980
5. Seidman, 1992
6. Connell, 1987
7. Imagining a shifting reality around male heterosexuality expands the social construct of masculinity. Masculinity itself, like heterosexuality, represents a privileged identity. Ironically, feminist theorists have not attempted to expand the construct of "femininity," but rather, the boundaries around ways that girls or women can be. This may relate to the way femininity" is not a desirable category to expand while masculinity is, due to its privileged status.
8. Bem, 1995
9. Crane B and Crane-Seeber, J. 2003
10. Bem 1995
11. Connell, 1987; Kindlon and Thompson, 1999; Pollack, 1999
12. Brannon, 1976
13. As identified by an article in the *New York Times Style Section* (St. John 2003).

CHAPTER **6**

White Heterosexuality: A Romance of the Straight Man's Burden

MASON STOKES

© *Reprinted by permission of Duke University Press*

There is an unfortunate irony embedded in the recent spate of critical attention to heterosexuality, particularly if we see this attention as part of a larger academic interest in "unmarked" and "naturalized" categories. Scholars across disciplines and fields are busy interrogating those hegemonic structures whose power is derived from their uncanny ability to avoid the glare of the spotlight. The recent growth industry in "whiteness studies" provides the most obvious example of this trend, and the new critical heterosexuality studies seems to be following not too far behind. Both of these subfields of academic inquiry are long overdue and hold the potential to be enormously useful.

But here is the irony. While whiteness studies seeks to deny whiteness the uninterrogated racial default position, much of the new scholarly attention to heterosexuality exists in a racial vacuum where whiteness is once again allowed free and invisible reign as the always-assumed norm. In other words, the new heterosexuality studies has been slow to learn the lessons of the new whiteness studies. Scholars are demonstrating that heterosexuality does indeed have a history, but we seem less aware that this history might in fact be imbricated with various *racial* histories.

If, as Richard Dyer (1997) has suggested, "all concepts of race are always concepts of the body and also of heterosexuality" (20), then it is worth asking if the reverse is also true: are all concepts of heterosexuality always concepts of race? I want to attempt an answer to this question by linking an analysis of heterosexuality with an analysis of whiteness, working through their apparent commonalities in order to see each more clearly. These commonalities are rather obvious upon reflection. In a white-supremacist culture, whiteness—with its hysterical concern over racial purity—bears a necessarily anxious relation to reproduction, a relation mediated through the structure of heterosexuality. Whiteness needs heterosexuality in order to reproduce itself, in order to guarantee the pristine white future it depends upon; heterosexuality, on the other hand, needs whiteness—with its claim to an unblemished morality—as a safeguard against the moral taint of the *sex* in hetero*sex*uality, the taint that accompanies the messier aspects of bodies that go bump in the night. There is a way, then, in which whiteness and heterosexuality can be usefully seen as normative copartners, mutually invested in the power that percolates at the center of things. The Women's Christian Temperance Union (WCTU) understood as much when, in 1885, its Social Purity Division adopted the slogan "The White Life for Two," a phrase that economically figures this mutually beneficial relation between whiteness and heterosexuality.[1] Through its use of this slogan, the WCTU signaled the centrality of heterosexuality to the maintenance of both the white race and a "white" morality.

This story of heterosexuality and whiteness as partners in crime makes a great deal of sense; however, there is another, stranger dynamic worth exploring. For if heterosexuality is essential to the reproduction of whiteness, it is also the means through which whiteness can lose itself. In other words, there is a way in which heterosexuality actually poses a threat to whiteness. Although it is difficult for us to imagine this sense of heterosexuality as dangerous, given its almost completely naturalized status at the turn of the twenty-first century, a brief glance at the history of heterosexuality's "invention" over a hundred years ago serves as a useful reminder of its potential for mayhem. Jonathan Ned Katz (1995) traces the process of heterosexuality's birth in medical literature of the late nineteenth century, charting the ways in which heterosexuality made its gradual and deeply ironic journey from perversion—its first incarnation—to its modern status as an immensely powerful normalizing force.

According to Katz, "heterosexuality" first appeared in the American medical lexicon in 1892 in an article by Dr. James G. Kiernan (19). For Kiernan, "heterosexuality" signified the perverse, since it referred, in part, to male/female sexual behavior divorced from reproductive imperatives. Since reproduction normalized different-sex eroticism, sexual pleasure occurring outside of a reproductive context was seen by Kiernan and others as unhealthy, as pathological. At the time of Kiernan's article, Richard Von Krafft-Ebing was also using the word "heterosexual" in his landmark study,

Psychopathia Sexualis. Krafft-Ebing shares Kiernan's sense that "heterosexual" signifies a nonreproductive, pleasure-centered pathology, but, contrary to Kiernan, Krafft-Ebing begins to position heterosexuality as a normalized, healthy, different-sex erotic standard. Because Krafft-Ebing discusses heterosexuality alongside case studies of men troubled by homosexual desire, heterosexuality begins to assume its shape as a cure for deviance, as a thing to strive for. This process of normalizing heterosexuality was continued by Freud in his "Three Essays on the Theory of Sexuality," where "heterosexuality" comes to mean the healthy, natural endpoint of one's sexual maturation. As Katz writes, Freud "helped to constitute our belief in the existence of a unitary, monolithic thing with a life and determining power of its own: 'heterosexuality'" (66). Katz continues, "Freud's explicit uses of the word *heterosexual* helped to constitute a different-sex eroticism as modern society's influential, dominant norm" (66).

This unleashing of heterosexuality had jarring consequences for those invested in notions of racial purity. The move from a reproduction-based sexuality to a pleasure-driven heterosexuality brought with it the possibility of contamination, of racial corruption. If, in its early days, heterosexuality signified a newly defined, normalized eroticism—one liberated from procreative imperatives—it held the potential to break the allegedly closed circuit of white reproduction. It located desire outside family, race, and nation. This newly disattached desire brought with it problems of its own, given the inherently unstable quality of desire—part longing, part repulsion, part fascination, part horror. The result was that heterosexuality—imagined as the great white hope of racial reproduction and fueled by the contradictory logics of racial desire—found itself not quite up to the job. So often seen and experienced as a hugely powerful normative force, in its infancy heterosexuality was actually the weak link in this hegemonic chain.

A more detailed understanding of this weakness can be useful to those of us seeking an insight into the shape and texture of heterosexuality. In the pages that follow, I want to re-place heterosexuality in what I consider to be its essential American context: the shadowy landscape of American racism. More specifically, I want to borrow a particularly popular turn-of-the-century literary staging of these issues for the insight it might offer as to the true structure of heterosexuality. Thomas Dixon Jr.'s infamously racist novel *The Leopard's Spots: A Romance of the White Man's Burden* (1902) is a perverse text that captures a surprising truth about heterosexuality in its early days. Dixon's single-minded devotion to white-supremacist ideologies exposes things about sexuality—specifically heterosexuality as simultaneously a normative standard and a deeply ambivalent structure of desire—that might be left unseen in another work lacking Dixon's polemical drive.

Through a reading of Dixon's novel, I hope to support my answer to the question with which I began: yes, all concepts of heterosexuality *are* also concepts of race, whether we admit it or not. In the pages that follow, I want to see what happens when we admit it, when we recognize that heterosexuality can be best understood when we view it in its natural habitat, which, at least in the American context, is a habitat shaped by a torturous racial past.

The Leopard's Spots turns out to be an ideal window through which to glimpse the racialized emergence of heterosexuality, its gawky adolescence in the early days of the twentieth century. Published on March 22, 1902, *The Leopard's Spots* immediately leapt up the sales charts, selling over 100,000 copies within a few months.[2] It appeared at number five on *Bookman*'s list of best-selling novels for the month of June, and the sectional breakdown of the *Bookman* data reveals a strong southern response to the book. It was the number one best seller for that month in Atlanta, Dallas, and New Orleans, and number two in Norfolk. According to Raymond Cook's account of the novel's spectacular sales, it eventually sold over one million copies and was translated into several foreign language editions. Its success was largely responsible for establishing Doubleday, Page & Co. as a major publishing house and netted its author several hundred thousand dollars in royalties (Cook 112). A special holiday edition was published on December 19, 1903. Dixon's next novel in his proposed racial trilogy, *The Clansman* (1905), surpassed the sales of *The Leopard's Spots*. This, coupled with both novels' eventual adaptation into the film *The Birth of a Nation*, made Dixon a household name in America, if his first novel had not already succeeded in doing so. Dixon's brand of particularly virulent racial hatred had found a comfortable home in the American imaginary.

The Leopard's Spots actually tells two stories: the story of young Charlie Gaston, a handsome white southerner whose father was killed in the Civil War and who is just embarking on a career in politics, and the story of the white South's attempt to consolidate its white-supremacist ideology into a workable post-Reconstruction white-supremacist government. Charlie is the fulcrum on which these stories turn, since, in Dixon's hands, Charlie's love for white supremacy is simultaneously the story of his love for the beautiful Sallie Worth, daughter of an old-school Democratic kingmaker. In other words, Dixon has joined politics with romance. This fusion of genre turns out to be less than tidy, opening up all kinds of fissures in what is, to put it simply, a deeply odd book. *The Leopard's Spots* is fairly bursting at the seams with every anxiety known to the turn-of-the-century white South. These anxieties are, not surprisingly, both racial and sexual, as Charlie spends most of his time demonstrating.

For example, during his courtship of Sallie, Charlie is deeply troubled by her love of dancing, a love Charlie most certainly does not share. Charlie's refusal to attend a dance that Sallie has organized causes an early crisis in their relationship. On the surface, his refusal results from pride and is connected to issues of race and class. Admitting to his lack of a proper suit for the ball, Charlie tells Sallie that he "'can't afford to buy one for this occasion. I couldn't be nigger enough to hire one, so that's the end of it'" (251). Charlie may be poor, but he's still "White" as long as he refuses to play the role of someone able to afford finer clothes. Connected to the issue of attire, however, is a more fundamental reason for Charlie's refusal to enter the ballroom: his two left feet. As he tells Sallie, "'If I could only dance, I assure you I'd try to fill every number of your card. Not being able to do so, I simply decline to make a fool of myself'" (252). Tortured by the vision of Sallie dancing with other men, Dixon shows Charlie to be fully aware of what he is missing:

> He knew the dance was a social convention, of course. But its deep Nature significance he knew also. ...that it was the actual touch of the human body, with rhythmic movement, set to the passionate music of love. This he knew was the deep secret of the fascination of the dance for the boy and the girl, and the man and the woman. (341)

Thinking of Sallie in the arms of another man, Charlie "never knew how deeply he hated dancing before" (252). And while jealousy supplies one reason for his feeling, his admitted inability to dance suggests a more complicated picture.

Charlie is, to put it bluntly, the archetypal early-twentieth-century heterosexual man. Katz describes a basic conflict at the heart of the newly emerged heterosexuality, one in which the flesh and the spirit wage an unresolvable battle. As Katz puts it, "the heterosexual ideal displays, from its inception, a fundamental tension. Heterosexual affirmation encounters a basic conflict between the pleasures of the flesh and the yearning for a pure, fleshless spirit. The sexual in the hetero ideal was a troublemaker from the start" (30). Dixon portrays Charlie as the poster-boy for this tension:

> His whole life had been dominated by this dream of an ideal love. For it he had denied himself the indulgences that his college mates and young associates had taken as a matter of course .... He had kept away from women. He had given his body and soul to the service of his Ideal, and bent every energy to the development of his mind that he might grasp with more power its sweetness and beauty when realised. Did it pay? The Flesh was shrieking this question now into the face of the Spirit. (343)

Charlie is paralyzed by the heterosexual ideal, by its irreconcilable longings toward pleasure and purity.

Given Charlie's tortured inner debate over the relative merits of "ideal love" and sexual "indulgences," it is worth asking where sexuality appears in this novel, and what kind of sex it seems to be (or more accurately, what kind of sex it *does not* appear to be). Charlie cannot participate in "the rhythmic touch of the human body" (252) when it is shrouded in the "social convention" of dancing. He can, however, call up and respond to sexual energy in his political oratory, as his speeches become the repository for the desire thwarted by Charlie's inability to dance.

The novel, in effect, demands this transfer of (hetero) sexual energy into the realm of politics, where it can fuel a different kind of fire. And with this move, the shift from specifically heterosexual energy to something more like Eve Sedgwick's (1985) notion of homosocial desire is fully enacted. This shift is enabled by Allan McLeod, who is to become Charlie's chief political adversary, as well as a romantic threat to Charlie's aspirations in the direction of Sallie Worth. A protégé of Sallie's father, McLeod has long been an intimate of Sallie and works throughout the novel to secure her hand in marriage. Despite Sallie's indifference to McLeod, Charlie is clearly worried over this possible rival.

In one of his frequent periods of despondency over his hopes with Sallie, Charlie visits his friend Reverend Durham for advice. The lines between romantic and political rivalry blur considerably when Durham counsels Charlie on the proper course to be taken. Durham tells him that it is fine for women to despair over thwarted love, since for a woman such as Sallie "love is the center of gravity of all life" (308). With "normal men," however, things are different. As Durham puts it, "The center of gravity of a strong man's life as a whole is not in love and the emotions, but in justice and intellect and their expression in the wider social relations" (308). One almost feels in Durham's words a deliberate pull away from heterosexuality—away from those sexual energies that deplete one's masculinity. Charlie immediately seizes upon this advice, vowing to "fight this coalition of McLeod and the farmers every inch" (308). His romantic rivalry with McLeod seamlessly becomes a political rivalry. Charlie must quit thinking about Sallie and think instead about politics. Given the mechanics of this transfer, it makes sense that the political arena becomes the site of the novel's sexual confrontations and relations. As we shall see, this linkage of sexuality to Charlie's white-supremacist political future will become a staging ground for the making and unmaking of Dixon's white heterosexuality.

Before looking at the novel's romantic resolution, though, I want to focus briefly on Dixon's treatment of white women as threatened commodities—as needing white male (and consequently phallic) protection against black sexual terror—since it is in this atmosphere of threat that we begin to witness the tenuous structure of white heterosexuality in its early days. We can see this most clearly in the case of Tom Camp, a poor white man whose daughter Annie is engaged to marry a man by the name of Hose Norman. Within minutes of the couple being pronounced "man and wife" (125), the wedding party is interrupted by a gang of "Negro troopers" who carry Annie away as "Hose's mountain boys" come to the rescue waving pistols (126). Although Tom succeeds in knocking down one of the black terrorists (he takes off the wooden leg he acquired during the war and uses it as a club), the rest of the gang carries Annie into the woods.[3] An urgent colloquy between Hose's boys and Tom Camp leaves no doubt as to the price affixed to the woman in this system of exchange between men: "'What shall we do, Tom? If we shoot we may kill Annie.' 'Shoot, men! My God, shoot! There are things worse than death!'" (125). The boys shoot, and a bullet hits Annie in her temple, leaving "a round hole from which a scarlet stream was running down her white throat" (126). The men carry Annie back to the cabin and lay her "across the bed in the room that had been made sweet and tidy for the bride and groom" (127). Dixon's eroticization of Annie's wound—it suggests the imminent loss of her virginity that the black troop both interrupted and allegedly intended—makes it fitting that her bleeding body is carried to the bridal bed. And the troopers' entrance only minutes after the solemnization of the wedding vows creates the perfect juxtaposition through which to examine the heterosexual politics of this abduction scene. While Dixon asks the reader to imagine the black men as potential rapists, it is actually the white men who shoot Annie through the skull. It is the collective discharge of *their* guns that creates Annie's wound, a wound obviously suggesting her loss of virginity. Tom's order to shoot and the wound that results suggest not black sexual assault but incest, the inverse of—and defense against—miscegenation.

Yet, the timing of the scene points out a black usurpation of white male privilege, as Hose, whose name is significantly phallic, is denied his legitimate role as deflowerer. The entrance of the black troops simultaneously disrupts the narrative of white heterosexual union and produces the rape narrative, which seems to require that union as a necessary first step in the attempted sexual assault that follows. According to the narrative logic, the attempted rape can only occur once Hose and Annie are wed, suggesting that the victimization of Annie is not truly significant until it is simultaneously a crime against Hose, whose woman has been taken from him. For Dixon, Annie signifies only in relation to her conflicted status as a dead bride—both to Hose and, more generally, the white male South. And while I do not mean to conflate rape with sex, in Dixon's portrayal the scene is not sexualized until the entrance of the black troopers. Despite Hose's name, Annie's wound does not occur until blackness comes knocking.

As Annie's father attempts to comfort the boys who fired the bullets, however, he paints a picture not of death but of salvation:

> "It's all right, boys. You've been my friends to-night. You've saved my little gal. I want to shake hands with you and thank you. If you hadn't been here—My God, I can't think of what would 'a happened! Now it's all right. She's safe in God's hands!" (126).

Annie's martyrdom, which precipitates a rebirth of the Ku Klux Klan, becomes the excuse for a new wave of white terrorism of blacks, while the clear signal to white women is that they must fear not only the potential black rapist but also the avenging white mob that may find it necessary to sacrifice them in the name of racial purity.

Dixon's focus on death as an honorable alternative to rape by a black man dramatically underscores the extent to which women in this novel function solely as signifiers in exchanges between men. These exchanges are both ideological and erotic, as the ideological becomes a site of a differently directed erotic energy. Annie Camp is not a woman; rather, she stands in for such abstract notions as "the South" or the quintessence of "Southern womanhood." In either case, her character exists as an idea, not a person. Lying at the root of his portrayal is a displaced erotics, a transference of heterosexual desire in which racial domination becomes the narrative eros, as white women are denied bodies, while the bodies of black men are forced to work overtime.

Not content with one scene of supposed black sexual villainy, later in the novel Dixon again offers Tom Camp's family as the site of racial assault. Flora Camp, the daughter Mrs. Camp gave her husband to take the place of Annie, is allegedly raped by a childhood friend of Charlie Gaston, a black man named Dick (described in the novel's "List of Characters" as "an unsolved riddle"). Although we do not witness the rape itself, Dixon shows the reader the battered body of Flora, her skull crushed in with a rock. As with Annie, the rape is signified indirectly through a trickle of blood: "Down her little white bare leg was still running fresh and warm the tiniest scarlet thread of blood. It was too plain, the terrible crime that had been committed" (371).

It is interesting that Dixon stages both of these assaults at the site of the Camp family, primarily because the Camps occupy a clearly visible class position within the novel's array of white characters. Distinguished from the formerly aristocratic Gastons, but friendly to them, the Camps represent that degree of whiteness existing in closest proximity to blackness. Dixon seems to suggest that the black assault on whiteness will happen first at this border territory, this liminal state between border-transgressing blacks and the "best" that whiteness has to offer. The Camps, then, occupy the front line in the war to preserve the unsullied future of whiteness. It is therefore less than a coincidence that Tom Camp is the most virulent racist in the novel.

Within this context, Dixon's restaging of sexual assault—a repetition almost exact in its details—recalls Freud's notion of repetition either as the return of something that has been repressed or a mechanism through which one achieves mastery over a painful circumstance.[4] It is useful to see Dixon's narrative technique as an instance of the second possibility. Dixon as author seeks control over the trauma of his characters, a trauma not limited to this specific instance, but part of a larger anxiety over whiteness as a stable property, an anxiety that Dixon certainly shares.

This anxiety over whiteness takes its more specific shape in Dixon's concern over black male genitalia. That Dixon offers Dick as the "rapist" in the assault on Flora shows a revealing conflation of black men with actual genitalia. ("Dick" as slang for "penis" had currency in American usage as early as 1888).[5] As Frantz Fanon (1967) has written in an oft-quoted passage, this conflation reveals a white psychopathology in which "one is no longer aware of the Negro but only of a penis; the Negro is eclipsed. He is turned into a penis. He *is* a penis" (170). Given his name and the crime of which he is accused, Dixon's description of Dick as "an unsolved riddle" highlights, to an almost ludicrous extent, white male anxiety over black male sexuality. That Dixon goes to the trouble of naming his black male rapist "Dick" reveals the extent to which black men were felt as sexual threats not only by white women but by white men, who, as we shall see, felt it necessary to respond in kind.

In the wake of Annie's death, for example, Reverend Durham seeks to comfort Tom Camp over his loss by telling him that "your child has not died in vain," since "a few things like this will be the trumpet of the God of our fathers that will call the sleeping manhood of the Anglo-Saxon race to life again" (128). This "sleeping manhood," yet another phrase carrying phallic connotations (or in this case antiphallic connotations, given its slumber) does not remain asleep for long. Only twenty pages pass before the South's "sleeping manhood" takes the form of white-sheeted and hooded vigilantes organized under the banner of the KKK (an image of white racial erection if ever there was one). Anglo-Saxons respond to "Dick" with one of their own—an erection for an erection. Worried over myths of black sexual prowess, white men respond to black sexual threat with arousal. To protect their women from black "Dick," that "unsolved riddle," they must themselves be hard.[6]

And if we think back to the first sexual assault of the novel, where Hose Norman and his mountain boys fight off the black troopers, Dixon's hand shows more clearly still. Annie's new husband is interestingly named.

"Hose" carries a phallic association that, when coupled with "Norman"—suggesting as it does the hyper-whiteness of Scandinavia—combines to create an apt composite for Dixon's purposes.[7] These two assaults, taken together, reveal the story Dixon is primarily concerned with, as he pits Norman Hose against black Dick. Keeping in mind Gayle Rubin's (1975) description of the phallus as "a set of meanings conferred upon the penis" (190), "a symbolic object which is exchanged within and between families" (191), we can see this clash of male genitalia as an ideological struggle, one in which Dixon's concern over the protection of white female virginity leads to his imagining of male/male arousal.

This imagined male sexual contest over the bodies of white women exposes the intimate connection between male domination and racial power. In Dixon's view, the ultimate issue is one of "racial absolutism" (336), a state only achievable through male control over female sexuality. In a conversation late in the novel between Reverend Durham and a preacher from Boston, Dixon establishes the stakes being played for. In response to Durham's statement that his only goal is to establish and maintain absolute segregation in the South, the preacher suggests that the battle is already lost, since "'evidences of a mixture of blood'" (336) already abound. Interestingly, Durham dismisses this evidence as the lingering effects of "'the surviving polygamous and lawless instincts of the white male'" (336). Since these instincts are on the wane, he argues, the only threat to "racial absolutism" comes from the black man, who, through an accumulation of wealth and culture, may someday "'be allowed freely to choose a white woman for his wife'" (336). He continues,

> "The right to choose one's mate is the foundation of racial life and of civilization. The South must guard with flaming sword every avenue of approach to this holy of holies. And there are many subtle forces at work to obscure these possible approaches". (336)

This "flaming sword," wielded in defense of the "holy of holies," a phrase occupying a rather vague syntactic position within Durham's sentence, deserves attention. On one level, it simply refers back to "the right to choose one's mate." At the same time, however, given the syntactic proximity of the "flaming sword" and the "avenue of approach," the "holy of holies" becomes the very "thing" being fought over: female genitalia. In defense of this genitalia—for Dixon the key to racial integrity—stands, of course, the white phallus, trying hard to fight off the "many subtle forces" working to admit greater access to white female sexuality. And what might these "subtle forces" be? Female autonomy, for one. As Michael Rogin (1985) puts it, "The sword guards the female genitalia not only to protect the white woman from the black phallus but also to keep her from acquiring a phallus of her own" (176). While the "right to choose one's mate" is the key issue, it is not a right that extends to women. For if it did, the possibility would be raised that it is not simply "the lawless instincts of the white male" that threaten racial integrity, but the possibility of white female desire for black men, a desire that would render the "flaming sword" of the white South no longer so necessary.

Absent this white female desire, however, and given the increasingly better behavior of white men, the only avenue available for the contamination of whiteness is the black rape of white women, which explains its centrality both to Dixon's narrative and to more general cultural imaginings and deployments. In "'The Mind That Burns in Each Body': Women, Rape, and Racial Violence," Jacquelyn Dowd Hall (1983) argues that during the latter half of the nineteenth century, rape became a more overtly political weapon than it had been during the days of institutionalized slavery. While the white plantation owner's unrestricted sexual access to his black slaves was a cornerstone of the patriarchal plantation system, in the years following the war the idea of rape was to become a central image in a political discourse devoted to reinforcing a white male power that had to some degree been subverted by the South's defeat. The freedmen's newfound right to a position of power within their own families threatened that power formerly exercised exclusively by white men.

Hall sees lynching as a story men told themselves about the social and psychological ordering of their lives. This story casts them in the role of avenging hero, restoring to them a power that was rapidly slipping away. With this power comes an erotic twist, as lynching worked to call forth the apotheosis of frail, victimized Womanhood, forced into the public eye as a symbol both of sexual contamination and the need to protect. The so-called threat of black men renders white female sexuality hypervisualized. As Hall writes, "rape and rumors of rape became the folk pornography of the Bible Belt" (335).

To take Hall's formulation one step further, it is important to realize that "victimized Womanhood" was not the only erotic component in this folk pornography. While lynching worked in part to reinforce the political and social subjugation of women, it was a crime directed specifically at black male bodies. These bodies, I would argue, became a central part of the folk pornography that Hall describes. More specifically, the focus on castration as a part of lynching rituals brought the black penis to the forefront of the cultural imaginary. As Kobena Mercer (1993) has written, in an essay on Robert Mapplethorpe's photographs of black male nudes,

> In the fantasmatic space of the supremacist imaginary, the big black phallus is perceived as a threat not only to the white master ... but to civilization itself, since the 'bad object' represents a danger to white womanhood and therefore the threat of miscegenation, eugenic pollution, and racial degeneration. (353)

Scientific discourse on racial difference in the nineteenth century is filled with speculation concerning black male genitalia, with a particular focus on its alleged superiority in size to that of white males. This widespread speculation bespeaks a fascination (Mercer calls it a "primal fantasy") that, if not itself erotic, is certainly based in erotic energies.

The act of castration itself, for all its obvious horror, does give us one of the few opportunities to witness culturally sanctioned physical interaction between white men and black male genitalia. This interaction is, of course, highly conflicted, and, to borrow a phrase from Eric Lott (1993), can be described as an act of "love and theft," in which the castrated penis is both revered and reviled. In her reading of lynching narratives, Trudier Harris (1984) reminds us that even as white men "castrated the black men, there was a suggestion of fondling, of envious caress" (22). Or as Robyn Wiegman (1995) writes, "the white male desires the image he must create in order to castrate" (98). In an epigraph to her essay, Hall quotes a member of a lynch mob in 1934: "After taking the nigger to the woods ... they cut off his penis. He was made to eat it. Then they cut off his testicles and made him eat them and say he liked it" (329). This brutal moment tells the story all too well. The object of white male fascination is severed, only to be forcibly consumed by the black man himself, its threat and lure forever absorbed. The "Other's strange fruit" (to borrow Mercer's phrase) becomes less strange through the white men's control of it.[8]

Dixon accomplishes a similar negation by having Dick burned at the stake by a raging mob of white men, who finally succeed in diminishing his mythic power to "ashes and charred bones" (384). While being burned at the stake is a different type of violence than castration, it is not without its own phallic overtones. Dick, whose name already casts him as the black penis itself, is forced to become the visual manifestation of black erection— tied to a stake, forced to stand up to endure the fire that consumes him. As in the ritual of castration, this perceived struggle between white men and black men over the bodies of white women culminates in white male fascination with and terror of the black penis.

The larger result of this fascination is, as Wiegman points out in her work on lynching, the simultaneous blurring and reification of those lines demarcating the difference between heterosexual and homosexual desire. In Wiegman's words,

> we might understand the lynching scenario and its obsession with the sexual dismemberment of black men to mark the limit of the homosexual/heterosexual binary—that point at which the oppositional relation reveals its inherent and mutual dependence— and the heterosexuality of the black male 'rapist' is transformed into a violently homoerotic exchange. (99)

This slippage between hetero and homo desire, as well as its role in the maintenance of white supremacy as a political and social structure, takes on additional importance in the novel's conclusion.

Having examined the homosocial underpinnings behind Dixon's rape narratives, I want to discuss the homosociality that enables not rape, but marriage. Doing so will give us our clearest sense yet of the ways in which heterosexuality is functioning in this turn-of-the-century racial landscape. The novel's climax comes in a speech Charlie delivers to the Democratic Convention of North Carolina on the subject of how best to rule the Negro in the South. The speech is extremely important, since it decides an internecine struggle for control of the Democratic party. Charlie is the leader of a faction of young men ready to wrest control of the party away from its more traditional, and elderly, base. They hope to do so by foregrounding the "Negro question" and taking a hard line on the absolute necessity for Negro disfranchisement and white supremacy. The contest takes on personal significance for Charlie since Sallie's father, General Worth, is the de facto leader of the Democratic establishment, its current king-maker. The General has refused Charlie's request for his daughter's hand, standing in the way of the "Ideal love" that so consumes him.

Charlie's speech is clearly a narrative device for Dixon himself, as it brings together into one document the racial ideology upon which this novel is based. It begins,

> Whereas, it is impossible to build a state inside a state of two antagonistic races, And whereas, the future North Carolinian must therefore be an Anglo-Saxon or a Mulatto, Resolved, that the hour has now come in our history to eliminate the Negro from our life and establish for all time the government of our fathers. (433–434)

The speech continues in predictable fashion, touching upon Anglo-Saxon "conquest of the globe" (435) and the "filth and degradation of a Negroid corruption" (436). Reiterating that this is a "white man's government," Charlie concludes with a call to Aryan manhood: "'Citizen kings, I call you to the consciousness of your kingship!'" (442).

Dixon eroticizes Charlie's oratorical powers, as his resolutions bring the crowd "to the highest pitch of excitement, and his words, clear, penetrating, and deliberate thrilled his hearers with electrical power" (434). Charlie

> played with the heart-strings of his hearers ... as a great master touches the strings of a harp. His voice was now low and quivering with the music of passion, and then soft and caressing. (439)

In the midst of it all, of course, sits Sallie Worth, "her face ... aflame with emotion, her eyes flashing with love and pride" (434).

Charlie's oratorical prowess finally overcomes the General's political opposition to his views on the race question as well as his opposition to
Charlie as Sallie's suitor. As he tells Charlie after the speech, "My boy, I give
it up. You have beaten me! I'm proud of you. I forgive everything for that
speech. *You can have my girl*" (443, emphasis added). Charlie's emotional
appeal for a new South built upon the truths of white supremacy and Aryan
domination secures him Sallie as a gift from her father. This exchange creates a kinship system that effectively unites the Old Democrats with the
New, establishing a revitalized and expanded power base for a white-supremacist overthrow of republican/fusionist rule. Before the novel's last
page, Charlie is elected Governor, and he and Sallie are married on the
morning of his inauguration.

What is intriguing about the marriage ceremony, however, is its redun-
dancy; Charlie and Sallie had actually been secretly married some thirty
pages earlier. And it is this move from a secret heterosexuality to a public heterosexuality that exposes the impossibility of Dixon's white nation. Dixon's
implied but repressed logic goes something like this: as long as a black threat
to the state exists, Charlie and Sallie's marriage must remain a secret. Only
with the victory of white supremacy—and the implied expulsion of the black
threat—can that marriage become public, can the name of heterosexuality
be spoken. Why is this the case? In Dixon's novel it is not whiteness that
stands in for heterosexuality but blackness, which becomes, through the
black troopers and black Dick, the transcendent sign of men who desire
women. Blackness, as heterosexuality writ large, disrupts the homosocial
kinship economy among white men. It stands as a too visible reminder of the
reproductive possibilities that so threaten Dixon's white state. And so, the secret marriage between Charlie and Sallie cannot withstand the public gaze
until it is removed from the haunting presence of blackness, which is to say,
from the haunting presence of heterosexual desire. With the expulsion of
blackness and its attendants (reproduction, miscegenation, the body), whiteness can reign supreme as a homosocial economy of racial power.

That whiteness exists only in the realm of the homosocial is made clear
by Sallie's role in the marriage that ends the novel. As she tells her husband
in the novel's final pages, "I do not desire any part in public life except
through you. You are my world.... I desire no career save that of a wife"
(468–469). In other words, while Sallie is absolutely necessary to this con-
solidation of white-supremacist power, she must quickly disappear from it.
Like Annie, Flora, and Dick, she is merely a transitional phrase within a heterosexual and white-supremacist grammar. Her vow of public silence at her
most public moment speaks both to her necessity and her ultimate irrelevance. Yet, given that irrelevance, where is there for white male sexual desire
to circulate at novel's end? With the creation of the white-supremacist state

that Dixon and his white characters long for, desire between white men is really the only option left. The heterosexual union that reigns on the novel's final page is a dodge, its narrative insistence speaking to its fragility, as well as Dixon's anxiety. If the creation of the white-supremacist state depends upon the forcible exclusion of black men, and the death or silence of white women—both exclusions signaling the desperate expulsion from the novel of heterosexual desire—then the inaugural ball must find a way to celebrate a new homosociality, one no longer dependent upon mediating figures. But, of course, a homosociality absent mediating figures is nothing of the sort. Deprived of black Dick, and deprived of Sallie, General Worth and Charlie are left in a place of barren whiteness neither wanted to imagine, dancing with themselves.

Although I suggested in my introduction that whiteness and heterosexuality can be usefully imagined as normative copartners, Dixon's surreal novel tells a different story. In Dixon's anxious hands, heterosexuality actually threatens whiteness because it breaks the closed circuit of white reproduction. This twist most often takes the shape of overt homoeroticism, a homoeroticism that appears to be the necessary byproduct of a gradually solidifying heterosexual imperative. As heterosexuality emerges as both a biological and a political requirement, it becomes, in many ways, more visible. And this visibility causes a certain anxiety, as it simultaneously produces the specter of heterosexuality's necessary corollary, homosexuality. Charlie becomes the perfect emblem of this anxiety, as he doubts his ability to live up to the requirements of heterosexuality, yet recognizes the relation between those requirements and the political future of whiteness. Judith Butler (1993) gets to the heart of this in an oft-quoted and still resonant passage about drag, performance, and heterosexual anxiety:

> To claim that all gender is like drag, or is drag, is to suggest that 'imitation' is at the heart of the *heterosexual* project and its gender binarisms, that drag is not a secondary imitation that presupposes a prior and original gender, but that hegemonic heterosexuality is itself a constant and repeated effort to imitate its own idealizations. That it must repeat this imitation, that it sets up pathologizing practices and normalizing sciences in order to produce and consecrate its own claim on originality and propriety, suggests that heterosexual performativity is beset by an anxiety that it can never fully overcome, that its effort to become its own idealizations can never be finally or fully achieved, and that it is consistently haunted by that domain of sexual possibility that must be excluded for heterosexualized gender to produce itself. (125)

This "domain of sexual possibility that must be excluded" is seemingly omnipresent in Dixon's novel—the clash of Dick and Hose that then leads, of necessity, to the burning of Dick at the stake. And this excluded sexual domain is also, as Judith Roof (1996) argues, a constitutive part of narrative itself. Positing Freud's "Three Essays on the Theory of Sexuality" as something of a first text of modern heterosexuality, Roof writes:

> The reproductive imperatives of the story produce heterosexuality as the magical, motiveless mechanism that turns everything right, while homosexuality and other perversions—also necessary elements—make all fail to cohere, exposing the story's parts in a meaningless, short-circuited, truncated, narrative gratification that heterosexuality seals up again. (xxii)

Roof's gloss on Freud resonates with my own reading of Dixon, particularly the extent to which, in Dixon's story, that magical heterosexuality actually does a pretty miserable job of making everything okay at story's end, of making all cohere.

As it turns out, this is entirely appropriate. The heterosexual whiteness that reigns in the final pages of Dixon's novel must necessarily be homoerotic at its core, a byproduct of Dixon's antiamalgamationist fervor. As Robert J. C. Young (1995) writes,

> same-sex sex, though clearly locked into an identical same-but-different dialectic of racialized sexuality, posed no threat because it produced no children; its advantage was that it remained silent, covert and unmarked…. In fact, in historical terms, concern about racial amalgamation tended if anything to encourage same-sex play (playing the imperial game was, after all, already an implicitly homo-erotic practice). (25–26)

In other words, the white nation is a homosocial nation. As long as it is really Charlie and General Worth who are married at novel's end—not Charlie and Sallie—then whiteness can remain pure, since only male–male relations can avoid racial contamination. Here, then, heterosexuality threatens the very whiteness that it pretends to protect. Through its new pleasure-centered dispersal of sexual energy, heterosexual desire threatens the fall of the white state.

A question remains, however. Can Dixon's story be taken as a representative fable about the political structures of racial and sexual desire, or is it finally only an idiosyncratic example of one man's rather hysterical response to perceived racial threats? In other words, what does the novel tell us beyond itself? Can its bizarre lessons fuel a more general speculation about the cultural construction and propagation of whiteness and heterosexuality at the turn of the century? One way of answering these questions, if only briefly, is to think about Dixon's use of the elements of conventional hetero-romance as a framework for his less than conventional "romance of the white man's burden"—in other words, to trace the plight of convention when coupled with racial extremism. Dixon's conflation, for example, of a wedding scene with an attempted rape suggests that the one is necessary for the maintenance of the other, a relationship that Dixon would certainly contest. The troopers threaten white marriage at the same time that they bolster its reason for being—as an institution whose function was, at least partly, to preserve and claim white female chastity as well as to insure the unsullied future of whiteness. The troopers' transgression against the newly constituted Norman heterosexual couple is the ultimate transgression, precisely because, in Dixon's hands, it reveals the homosocial underpinnings behind both white supremacy and heterosexual marriage.

Likewise, Dixon's suture of the Charlie/Sallie romance plot onto the "political plot" clearly indicates the politics of romance within a white-supremacist worldview. This narrative move suggests that hetero-marriage is necessary for the creation of a white-supremacist state. That this marriage is more accurately a marriage between men than between a man and a woman dramatizes, as clearly as I think possible, the interdependence of white supremacy and masculinist control, and it does so in a way that queries the heterosexual constitution of that whiteness that it seeks to enthrone.

In short, Dixon's novel makes it difficult to think about white supremacy without simultaneously thinking about white male heterosexual desire. This overdetermined conflation of politico-social hatred with conventional hetero-love produces the novel's narrative desire, that "affective or social force" (2), to borrow a phrase from Eve Sedgwick, that tries so desperately to hold both the novel and its motivation together. But given the complexity of that desire, we are not surprised to discover that the new world Dixon creates already shows signs of wear and weakness. To construct that world through the slippery field of plot and language is to risk a contamination from within, as the heterosexual whiteness that reigns in the novel's final pages is revealed to depend upon other—less hetero, less white—properties. Although Annie and Flora Camp are nowhere to be seen at Charlie's inauguration, or his wedding to Sallie, their presence is most acutely felt. Annie and Flora, martyred by Dixon for his cause; Dick, burned at the stake—these are the constitutive elements of heterosexual whiteness, dead ravaged white women and burnt black flesh. Dixon, I think, would be the first to acknowledge the role of Dick's lynching in his grand scheme. The trail of dead and brutalized women, however, is another matter, and one he would most likely refuse to admit. Whether sacrificed to the pressures of narrative, or the dictates of heterosexual whiteness, or more probably both, these white women cannot attend the novel's closing ceremony, a ceremony that Dixon could not imagine without them.

In his desperate attempt to plot the marriage of whiteness and heterosexuality, Dixon offers us, a hundred years later, an angle of vision on heterosexuality that we have had difficulty finding. One of the problems with the study of heterosexuality—as with whiteness—is that, in our effort to decenter these hegemonic categories through critical attention to them, we too often end up *re*-centering them as critical fetish. Having mastered the tricks necessary to insure their largely invisible reign, heterosexuality and whiteness betray a protean ability to find a way back *in* through the *out* door. The gravity at the center of things is strong indeed. Thinking about heterosexuality through the lens of whiteness, however, throws heterosexuality off its game; it exposes the kinks that make up the allegedly straight, the weirdness that defines the normal. This decidedly queer and off-center heterosexuality offers itself up to the critical gaze with less resistance than heterosexuality in its normative mode. It strikes me as a good place to continue thinking about the ways in which heterosexuality—inextricably entangled in the web of American racism—is as much a burden as a boon.

References

Baldwin, James. 1965. *Going to meet the man.* New York: The Dial Press.

Butler, Judith. 1993. *Bodies that matter: On the discursive limits of "sex."* New York: Routledge.

Cook, Raymond Allen. 1968. *Fire from the flint: The amazing careers of Thomas Dixon.* Winston-Salem: John F. Blair.

D'Emilio, John and Estelle B. Freedman. 1997. *Intimate matters: A history of sexuality in America,* 2nd edition. Chicago: University of Chicago Press.

Dixon, Thomas Jr. 1967 [1902]. *The leopard's spots: A romance of the white man's burden—1865–1900.* Ridgewood: The Gregg Press.

Dyer, Richard. 1997. *White.* New York: Routledge.

Fanon, Frantz. 1967 [1952]. *Black skin, white masks.* Trans. Charles Lam Markmann. New York: Grove Press, Inc.

Freud, Sigmund. 1957 [1920]. Beyond the pleasure-principle, In John Rickman (ed.) *A general selection from the works of Freud,* (Trans. C. J. M. Hubback), pp. 141–168. New York: Liveright Publishing Corporation.

Gunning, Sandra. 1996. *Race, rape, and lynching: The red record of American literature, 1890–1912.* New York: Oxford University Press.

Hall, Jacquelyn Dowd. 1983. "The mind that burns in each body:" Women, rape, and racial violence, in Ann Snitow, Christine Stanswell and Sharon Thompson (eds.) *Powers of desire: The politics of sexuality,* pp. 328–49. New York: Monthly Review Press.

Harris, Trudier. 1984. *Exorcising blackness: Historical and literary lynching and burning rituals.* Bloomington: Indiana University Press.

Katz, Jonathan Ned. 1995. *The invention of heterosexuality.* New York: Penguin.

Lighter, Jonathan E., ed. 1994. *Randon House Dictionary of American Slang.* New York: Randon House.

Lott, Eric. 1993. *Love & theft: Blackface minstrelsy and the American working class.* New York: Oxford University Press.

Mercer, Kobena. 1993. Looking for trouble, in Henry Abelove, Michele Aina Barale and David M. Halperin (eds.) *The lesbian and gay studies Reader,* pp. 350–59. New York: Routledge.

Rogin, Michael Paul. 1985. "The sword became a flashing vision:" D.W. Griffith's *The birth of a nation, Representations* 9: 150–195.

Roof, Judith. 1996. *Come as you are: Sexuality and narrative*. New York: Columbia University Press.

Rubin, Gayle. 1975. The traffic in women: notes on the "political economy" of sex, in R. Reiter (ed.) *Toward an anthropology of women*, pp. 157–210. New York: Monthly Review Press.

Sedgwick, Eve Kosofsky. 1985. *Between men: English literature and male homosocial desire*. New York: Columbia University Press.

Stokes, Mason. 2001. *The color of sex: Whiteness, heterosexuality, and the fictions of white supremacy*. Durham: Duke University Press.

Wiegman, Robyn. 1995. *American anatomies: Theorizing race and gender*. Durham: Duke University Press.

Young, Robert J. C. 1995. *Colonial desire: Hybridity in theory, culture and race*. London: Routledge.

Notes

1. D'Emilio and Freedman, 1997: p. 153
2. Cook, 1968: p. 112
3. This business with the wooden leg is almost too rich. As Sandra Gunning notes, Tom's status as an amputee signals an obvious "dephallicization of the white male" (39). Yet, his use of his prosthesis as a club can be read as an attempt to reclaim a phallic power taken from him by war. Significantly, it is only in the presence of the black troopers that he can in fact accomplish such a reclamation.
4. See Freud (1957), "Beyond the pleasure principle," 147–150.
5. The *Random House Dictionary of American Slang* cites the following passage from a work called *Stag Party* as the first use of "dick" in the manner I am tracing here: "Student (turning her fairly around and putting his dick where his finger was)—Nice, isn't it, ducky?" (Lighter 583).
6. A minor moment late in the novel shows this to be not solely a racial drama. When Reverend Durham learns that Allan McCleod has been spreading scandal about his wife, his automatic impulse is to respond with violence. Again, however, Dixon renders this move in terms of male sexual arousal. Taking a sword down from the wall, Durham notices "how snugly its rough hilt fitted his nervous hand-grip! He felt a curious throbbing in this hilt like a pulse. It was alive, and its spirit stirred deep waters in his soul that had never been ruffled before" (453). Although Durham is about to defend his wife's honor, his throbbing hilt and deeply stirred soul-waters are caused by Allan, not by his wife.
7. Although "Norman" actually references Normandy in Northern France, the settlers of Normandy were Vikings from Denmark, Norway, and Iceland.
8. James Baldwin (1965) brilliantly dramatizes this dynamic in his short story "Going to Meet the Man," where he describes a lynching in brutal detail:
   The man with the knife took the nigger's privates in his hand, one hand, still smiling, as though he were weighing them. In the cradle of the one white hand, the nigger's privates seemed as remote as meat being weighted in the scales; but seemed heavier too, much heavier, and Jesse felt his scrotum tighten; and huge, huge, much bigger than his father's, flaccid, hairless, the largest thing he had ever seen till then, and the blackest. The white hand stretched them, cradled them, caressed them. (247–248)

CHAPTER 7

The Mermaid and the Heterosexual Imagination

LAURIE ESSIG

For hundreds of years, mermaids were a Christian riddle, overburdened with the social significance of any riddle. The question was not whether mermaids were real. Everyone agreed that they were. What was at issue was her soul. Since the mermaid was not fully human and only humans had souls, many concluded that she did not. On the other hand, there were plenty of eyewitness accounts of mermaids converting to Christianity, usually just before torturous deaths at the hands of their fully human captors. Thus, the wild and inhuman mermaid always also held out the tantalizing possibility of union with humanity.[1]

Nowadays, the mermaid presents us with a different kind of riddle.[2] It is a riddle that I encountered again and again while researching an event called "The Mermaid Parade."[3] During nearly every interview, whether with the mermaid or mermaid watcher, the question was posed: "Does the mermaid have a vagina?" At first the question puzzled me. It seemed rather obvious that even if the mermaid did have a vagina, it would be the vagina of a fish, or, at best, a dolphin, thereby rendering it off limits to human desire. But the persistence of the question forced me to rethink what was really being asked. The absence or presence of a vagina, like the absence or presence of a soul, is a riddle not about mermaids, but about us, about our culture and our beliefs and, ultimately, what it means to be human. In our post-Christian era, the limits of humanity are centered not around the soul, but on the vagina. The mermaid's vagina stands in for our larger cultural obsession with women's bodies and their accessibility to men.

In other words, the mermaid is both a cultural fantasy and a cultural nightmare. She swims at the edge of the heterosexual imagination as a potential lover and a potential monster. In her potential lover incarnation, the mermaid is innocent and nearly childlike in her devotion to her man and her heterosexual desires.[4] As a potential monster, the mermaid is not only without a vagina, but she is a seductress bent on using men's desire for her to drown them. In this way, the mermaid is conflated with the Sirens, who lured human males to their watery deaths without ever offering them true pleasure in the form of insertive heterosexual intercourse.[5]

So it is that any mermaid today must learn to negotiate her position as half monster/half seductress through her sexuality, her heterosexuality to be exact. In order to be fully human, she must be heterosexually embodied and available. In order to be a monster, she must be heterosexually embodied and unavailable. Because she is potentially both, because her vagina is both present and absent, the mermaid is a powerful figure in heterosexual fantasy and desire. In this chapter, I want to sketch the shape of the mermaid in the heterosexual imagination by considering how she pops up in American culture in general[6] and the Coney Island Mermaid Parade in particular.

Mermaid Movies

In the 1930s, Hans Christian Andersen's century old tale of "The Little Mermaid" was making its way through the Disney studios along with "Peter Pan" and "Alice in Wonderland." Andersen's 1837 tale is an attempt to answer the Christian riddle of whether or not the mermaid has a soul. In this version, it is the promise of a human soul and eternal life after death that lures Ariel to the surface. The Prince's love is merely the means to salvation. When Ariel learns from her grandmother that humans

> "…have a soul that lives eternally—yes, even after the body has been committed to the earth—and that rises up through the clear, pure air to the bright stars above!" she immediately claims that she "…would willingly give all the hundreds of years I may have to live, to be a human being for but one day, and to have the hope of sharing in the joys of the heavenly world."

Again, Ariel wants an immortal soul, not a white wedding. And Andersen gives it to her, at least the possibility that she shall gain one by performing "good deeds" in a purgatory in the air, a liminal space between earth and heaven, animal and immortal.[7]

Disney put the tale aside for another fifty years. In the rational and scientific 1930s, the question was not whether the mermaid had a soul, but why anyone would have ever been "primitive" enough to believe in her existence. By the 1980s, Americans were far less enamoured with science. Angels and manifestations of the Virgin Mary were at a fever pitch. At the same time, sex was everywhere and the real issue at hand, that is, the question of the mermaid's genitalia, could be asked, even in a children's movie.[8] So it was that in 1989 Disney reworked Andersen's Christian tale of sacrifice and souls into a heterosexual romance. The company's sense of timing and narrative structure could not have been more perfect. The animated feature was a blockbuster, bringing in $84 million dollars in North America alone.[9]

The vagina is in fact the heart of "The Little Mermaid." The story centers on Ariel, the daughter of the Sea King, Triton. Ariel wants legs, but the legs are in fact a euphemism for a human vagina.[10] This fact becomes obvious when Ariel's desire for "legs" is intensified by her desire for a human male in the form of Prince Eric. At this point in the plot, the notion of mermaid as a monster/seductress gets divided into two separate characters: the monstrously feminine Ursula and the now voiceless but fully human Ariel.

Ariel is offered access to humanity/a vagina by the sea witch, Ursula, who is also an octopus. Ursula's femininity is signified by large breasts, full red lips, and a throaty cabaret voice full of sexy innuendo. These stigmata of femininity are in direct contrast to the virginal Ariel, who has agreed to give Ursula her voice in exchange for a chance to be kissed and potentially penetrated by Prince Eric. Without a voice, Ariel's childlike features (oversized eyes, extremely thin body) are dramatized and she appears in the human world helpless and dependent.

When the Prince's kiss is misdirected to Ursula, in human form, Ariel loses her legs/vagina/humanity and is forced back into the impenetrable sea. Her father comes to her rescue by surrendering his rule, in the form of a highly phallic trident, to Ursula. Now the nightmare of the Phallic female is played out, with Ursula immediately losing all emotional control and destroying her own smaller floating phalluses, two electric eels named Flotsam and Jetsam. At this point, Ursula's grotesquely feminine form enlarges itself, thereby taking up too much space. Prince Eric deals with the engorged Ursula by ramming a ship's prow through her middle. After deflating and defeating the monstrous feminine, Eric restores the trident/Phallus to its rightful owner in the form of the father/Triton. Triton, grateful for the return of his trident/Phallus, rewards Eric by giving Ariel legs/a vagina and the heterosexual romance comes to a happy ending with a white wedding and its imagined consequence, legitimate sexual intercourse.[11]

Five years before Ariel came out, an adult movie about a mermaid helped propel Daryl Hannah and Tom Hanks into stardom. The movie, "Splash,"[12] resolves the issue of the mermaid's vagina in a novel way. On land, the mermaid has legs/a vagina. In water, she has a tail. But if the issue of the vagina is resolved in "Splash," the issue of the mermaid's monstrosity drives the narrative. The movie's dramatic tension turns on the possibility that the sexually desirable female will be revealed as a monster.

Hannah's character, Madison, first appears as a mer-girl who nearly drowns Hank's character, Allen, because of her desire to be with him. Seeing her swimming off of Cape Cod, young Allen jumps off a ferry to be with her and she pulls him farther and farther into the sea. The adult humans save the boy from drowning, while the little mermaid watches in sorrow. But Allen is not actually saved from the mermaid's spell. Instead, he grows into a man who is incapable of living a "normal" life. His character complains at a friend's wedding of his own inability to be like everyone else, to fall in love with a woman and get married. Allen's desire for the mermaid, now unspoken, has turned him into a freak.

The mermaid as freak is a large part of this movie. Madison cannot reveal her "secret" to Allen for fear of losing him. In fact, Madison cannot even say her true name to Allen because it is too painful for normal humans to hear. Renamed Madison, after the avenue, she passes as normal, but her true name and true self are always visible as "The Big Secret." There are other forms of freakishness in the film. Allen's brother, Freddy, is played by John Candy. Needless to say, Candy's large size marks him as a bodily freak. Yet, Freddy is also a sexual freak. He drops coins on the ground to look up women's skirts, worships pornography, and refuses to "work hard" or "settle down." Freddy's sexual freakishness elicits another form of sexual freakery, lesbianism. His story, "A Lesbian No More," is published in *Penthouse*. The lesbianism in the story serves as a marker of female sexual freakishness, as shocking as a mermaid's tail since it implies a vagina that is not accessible to men. It is a theme that surfaces again when Madison goes out dressed in Allen's clothes. In a suit and tie, wingtips and oxfords, even Daryl Hannah looks butch.[13]

When Madison's freakishness as a mermaid is revealed, however, the response is not desire, but revulsion.[14] Imprisoned in New York's Museum of Natural History,[15] Madison as mermaid is made the object of scientific inquiry. She represents the heterosexual nightmare, the perfect woman who is, in fact, a monster. Madison's perfection as a woman is not only in her long, blonde hair and thin body, but also in her childishness coupled with aggressive sexual desire. Madison is childish because she is completely igno-rant of human customs, including human language. This childlike state is coupled with her seemingly insatiable desire for her man.

In the end, Allen's revulsion is once again turned into desire as he dives after her into the water and gives up the human world. Madison has, of course, reverted to her mermaid state, while Allen remains human, but aquatic. Thus, the story ends with the revulsion at a tale retranslated into desire and devotion, but the vagina question is now unresolved. The viewer is forced to satisfy herself with romance and love since the question of insertive intercourse remains unclear. Will he, with his human genitalia, have sex with her fish vagina? If not, Allen's taking the plunge and renouncing the world of humans/humanity/life seems to have been a mistake, the age-old mistake of sailors who drown in pursuit of women who are, after all, monstrosities.

Mermaids Marching

The Mermaid Parade, like the mermaid movies, is about heterosexuality, but not heterosexuality's center. Instead, the Mermaid Parade is about the limits of heterosexuality, how far heterosexuality can go before it becomes as freakish as homosexuality or a fish's vagina. The Mermaid Parade, then, is a manifestation of the heterosexual imagination at its very limits.

The Parade sprang forth from Coney Island USA, a group of artists who got together in 1980 to preserve the culture of Coney Island. The driving force behind the organization was Dick Zigun, a young man who had recently completed his MFA at Yale and came to Coney Island because he was interested in American popular culture and making art that had a "social political purpose." Zigun and the others wanted to create some kind of event that could both raise the profile of their organization and make a difference in the spirit of the neighborhood. Someone suggested a mermaid parade. The impossibility of mermaids marching appealed to the ironic sense of humor of the group as well as their commitment to "doing something for the neighborhood."

Since its debut in 1983, the Mermaid Parade has grown into one of the city's largest and most televised events. The reasons for the parade's popularity are complex. Many years the head mermaids are stars, like David Byrne and Queen Latifah, but even when there are no stars, the crowds show up. The parade has a certain appeal for the city's pagans because of it ritualistic offerings to the sea, but few people seem to be there for religious reasons. In fact, nearly all the participants and observers mentioned two things: bared breasts and the age-old question of whether or not the mermaid has a vagina. These two locations, the visible female breast and the fishily unclear genitalia, are the real source of the Mermaid Parade's popularity. The parade, like the mermaid in general, is about heterosexual desire. The heterosexual desire is part of an imaginative landscape where desire is always for a female whose humanity is never fully established. It is here, at the limits of humanity and heterosexuality, that the Coney Island mermaids gather.[16]

My first clue that the Mermaid Parade was about the limits of heterosexuality came when I learned that the parade organizers wanted Monica Lewinsky to be the head mermaid for the year 2000 parade.[17] The choice seemed absurdly overdetermined. After all, who better to represent the mermaid than the young seductress whose ability to be sexually desirable without using her vagina nearly brought down the President of the United States? Although Lewinsky never did come to the parade in person, the spirit of her scandalous image did. Lewinsky represents the edge of heterosexual desire, the absolute limit of legitimate sex, the line between titillating and nauseating. It is this line between desire and revulsion that drives many of the Parade's participants.

Consider Bambi,[18] who describes herself as a "professional mermaid." Even as a child, Bambi fantasized about being a mermaid and would tie her feet together in the swimming pool to simulate a tail. Bambi has participated in the Mermaid Parade for the past eight years. Like many of the parade's participants, Bambi is an artist, both performance and visual. She is also a sex worker and sees the mermaid as part of that. "I consider it (being a dominatrix) a very loving and therapeutic and nurturing act and the mermaid is a big loving creature." Bambi thinks of her life and her work as about "birth, disappointment, and then rebirth" and considers herself a role model and inspiration for young girls everywhere.

> I feel like my whole life story could be an inspiration for any girl anywhere. I mean there I was born in the Midwest and everything is so normal and I would just dream about joining the circus and becoming a whore because it just seemed so glamorous, you know, all the costumes and perfume and stuff. And now I'm doing it...

The specific message that Bambi, who is tall and thin, with bleached blonde hair wants to spread is to get girls to be both beautiful and free of insecurities about their beauty.

> Too many women are crippled by self-loathing. They look into the mirror and are crippled by it. It's all about invention and re-invention. I'm into using my own flaws to make myself more powerful.... Once I just stared into the mirror for twelve hours, you know, really looking. After that.... I wasn't afraid of my flaws anymore.... But I don't think the answer is to give up on beauty. I mean, women love all this stuff: costumes, make-up. We just need to give up our neurosis.... Women lose more men by being neurotic. Men want women to feel secure.

Bambi's girl-centered message is partly about embracing that which is female in our society. In other words, Bambi wants girls to feel empowered by girly things, by stiletto heels and pasties and the male gaze. Bambi's message is also, of course, a heterogendered and heterosexist one. Women are to embrace beauty, but in order to be more attractive to men. Men must renounce beauty. Bambi does not like the idea of men dressing up. Men need "to stay virile." Bambi worries that if she ever had a son that she would have to be very careful about playing dress-up with him. "I would have to try really hard to not make a little boy into a freak, to say, you're Neptune, not a mermaid…" At the same time Bambi is fearful of making her son into a freak/cross-dresser, she embraces the category of freak as long as heterosexuality is firmly established. Bambi calls herself a freak and even laments her lowly status as a self-made freak versus a born one.

Kate Fallon[19] is also a regular participant in the Mermaid Parade. Like Bambi, Fallon fantasized about being a mermaid from a very young age. Also like Bambi, Kate has worked off and on in the sex industry. For her, becoming an adult mermaid was about embracing the "freak within."

> You go through your whole life knowing you're different form other people. And it's really hard for younger women…. And then you just reach a point, like around thirty, right? Where it's just like: "Fuck you. I'm different." You give up on trying to be normal. So at the parade I'm just like here I am, look at me, I'm a freak…. The pleasure of the mermaid is that she's not quite human, she's a monster. Think of the sirens, who are so closely related to the mermaid. They're beasts, they're a destructive force, they're alluring yes, but they'll destroy you…. It's about idolizing this weirdo you keep under wraps all the time. You have to keep under wraps because of your office job and your in-laws. It's about saying fuck my employer, fuck my in-laws. It's about encouraging people to be a gorgeous freak.

The embrace of freakishness for Kate, as for Bambi, is about figuring out the limits of heterosexuality as well as the limits of women's humanity. For both of them, there is an understanding that the desirable female is also always potentially an inhuman monster. And both women see a certain power in the female as a monster. Bambi has created a photographic exhibit called "Geek Pin-ups." In the photographs, Bambi poses herself (usually at Coney Island) as a pin-up from the neck down and a geek from the neck up. For instance, several photographs feature Bambi completely nude and bereft of body hair, but with the head of a chicken or a space alien or a bearded lady. The point of the photographs is to pair the desirable with the repulsive.[20]

Another mermaid who is pushing the limits of the heterosexual imagination by embracing both the seductress and monstrous aspects of the mermaid is Lin Gathright.[21] Gathright has explored heterosexual desire as a sex worker and a filmmaker. Her short film, "Hello Kitty," has won her prestigious awards and the wrath of many women for treating a "date gone wrong" in a comic fashion. Gathright sees her film and her performance as a mermaid as exploring the boundaries of heterosexual desire.

> I first started to be a mermaid as a child in New Orleans. As a child (of ten) for Mardi Gras I begged and begged my mother to go as a mermaid and she refused…. She was really against my being a mermaid. My mother is sort of hung up about sexuality especially from me…. And it was just too sexy for her…. So I went as my own particular invention…. Of course the costume was sexy. I wore this bikini top and a towel around my hips and beads and a wig and a crown.

As a young adult, Gathright played a mermaid again for the opening of an arts center. She sat in a baby pool in a big plastic clamshell with a green sequined tail, a blond wig, and pasties. Gathright used her position at the entrance to tease the well-heeled guests by flirting with the men and teasing the women with plastic crabs and accusations of having the other sort of crabs. For Gathright, it was

> so much fun. They were so uptight…. The pleasure was in getting a rise out of people…. When I was ten the fantasy was to swim and have all these magical powers and be free. I'm less conscious of that stuff now—the swimming a thousand miles away whenever you want to. But it's still about freedom. There's a lot of freedom in being naked, in being sexual.

Gathright's willingness to be at the edge of heterosexual desire, to be both sexy and horrible, is also played out in a geek act she does with Bambi. Gathright plays the "Wild Ocelot" to Bambi's mermaid/geek. In a leopard skin dress ala Fred Flintstone, Gathright serves Bambi live goldfish, squirming bugs, and a freshly opened can of cat food, all of which Bambi eats with relish.[22] Both women talk about the "fun" of being beautiful and disgusting at the same time. Indeed, Gathrights's role as the "wild ocelot" comes from a comment made by her mother when Gathright was receiving considerable male attention walking down the street in a sundress. Her mother reportedly uttered in disgust, "I don't think we could be getting more attention if I was walking down the street with a wild ocelot." The fact that this comment, infused with pride and disgust in a heterosexually attractive daughter, was turned into a bug-eating geek act is a good indicator of how many of the Coney Island mermaids embody the heterosexual imagination.

The shifting line between desire and repulsion is also what draws many of the event's spectators. Consider how a middle-aged, white, married couple, one a newspaper editor, the other a stockbroker, described their reasons for coming to the Parade for the last five years.[23] The man discussed his love of the topless women and how it is a little exhibitionism that is not hurting anyone. The woman talked about living and growing up in respectable neighborhoods, but being attracted to the "honky tonk," "sleezy," and even "criminal" side of Coney Island. Another observer, a young, black high school guidance counselor, said he loved the parade because "there are tons of freaks." When asked to define "freaks," the man said the freaks are "people who are different, interesting, eye candy. It can be a performative thing. I'm a freak... "

According to another observer, a white law student, it is the freakish atmosphere of Coney Island that makes the mermaids attractive.

> Before I saw a parade, I thought of mermaids as more pristine. And didn't really like them. Like Daryl Hannah who was so beautiful and naïve and stupid (in "Splash")…. In a Coney Island sense, the mermaids are these dirty, but beautiful, beings. They're saucy and sexy and messy and slutty and really beautiful creatures …. Here they're like the rest of us in this dirty, sexual way. It's like the ocean and it's all warm and alive and you don't know what's going on down there and the mermaids are the queens of this unknown realm. And the mermaids are exclusively female. I don't believe in mermen.

This embrace of the mermaid as freak was voiced again and again. A middle-aged white lawyer gushed that "the Mermaid Parade is a great big statement that being abnormal is an okay thing. It's even a good thing." A young white man who describes his job as "pushing paper for the man" claimed that if he ever participates in the Mermaid Parade, he will "drink a lot of beer and get even fatter, you know? Because the idea of the parade is that everyone can show their body no matter what their body looks like."

But if the Mermaid Parade is about the celebration of freakishness, it is a freakishness firmly rooted in the normalcy of heterosexuality. Besides a smattering of cross-dressing mermaids and one lesbian couple in a mermaid contingent, the mermaids were heterosexually embodied.[24] Of the twenty parade participants I interviewed that day, all identified themselves as heterosexual. Nearly half of them also worked in the heterosexual sex industry (e.g., erotic dancer, dominatrix, and pornographic film actress). When asked to describe how the mermaid embodies their desires, many female participants described their love of being attractive to men. For instance, three white mermaids in their early twenties were being surrounded by a crowd of ten or so men who wanted to stare at and take pictures of their bared breasts. When asked whether they liked all the attention, they all three said they loved it. One of them said that the men's attention would give them their "narcissistic kicks for at least a month." She also described that the reason she loved being a mermaid was because they are so "beautiful and feminine. There's nothing androgynous about them."

The men were attracted to the mermaids for a different reason. For them, the mermaid is desirable precisely because she is unattainable. As one participant, a young white woman, explained it, "the mermaid is really the ultimate sex symbol because you can never obtain her. You can only chase after her tail and men love that. They're hunters. They love to pursue what they can't have." Another participant, a middle-aged white college professor, described his attraction as about fear, not of drowning, but of not obtaining union with the mermaid.

> I suppose there's a little fear, because of the water.... I'm fearful of drowning, sharks, sea creatures and mermaids, but.... I don't think of mermaids as scary but as a life force, seductive, but not deadly, but also about how love can hurt and how they can't actually be together.... It's really scary putting yourself out there. Unrequited love. And that's the tragedy. That it's your own doing, you know? That you would fall for someone you can't have. It's heart wrenching.

So it is that the Coney Island mermaids transform their freakishness into (hetero)sexual attractiveness. Their difference, that is, their tails/inaccessible vaginas, are the attraction. By having a tail, the mermaid, like the lesbian, becomes that which cannot be obtained and is therefore all the more desirable.

But the Coney Island mermaids, like the fantasy of lesbians in "Splash," are in fact, humans and, as such, have human vaginas that can, potentially, be penetrated. Thus, the Parade resolves the issue of the mermaid's vagina and thus her humanity by making its lack a prop in heterosexual desire. Because she might not have one, or to be more precise, because she might not give it to the male spectator, the mermaid is all the sexier. Perhaps no Coney Island mermaid represents this fact better than Patrick Bucklew.[25]

Bucklew is a middle-aged, heterosexual white man who is known as Mangina because of his invention of a prosthetic vagina of the same name. Bucklew came up with the "mangina" two years ago both as a piece of art and a way of dealing with a painful break-up. The mangina utilizes the scrotum to create a labia (Bucklew calls this the "lotum"). Bucklew wears the device on stage and invites people to insert their fingers into him/it. Bucklew says that he is "... trying to figure out what it feels like to be a woman, because I was so hurt after the break up with my girlfriend. I'm trying to feel what it's like to be that open and vulnerable." Wearing the mangina, then, is about trying to figure out heterosexuality. As Bucklew puts it, "I'm not a hermaphrodite, not a transsexual, not a homosexual. I'm just a man with a vagina."[26]

When Bucklew went to the Mermaid Parade (in 1998), he went as Fish Mangina. He built himself a large fish hat and wore a suit that allowed him to expose his "mangina" to those who wanted to see it. Even wearing his prosthetic vagina, Bucklew desired the mermaids as potential objects of penetration. "I think the mermaid is very sexy. Water is sexy…there's the whole mystery of it…. The genitalia aspect and what's going on downstairs and is there some sort of access?" Like many of the other men, Bucklew's desire was coupled with fear.

> Water really scares me. I have a fear of the depth of the ocean. I won't go swimming too far, but I don't think I'm afraid of mermaids. I can't be afraid of a woman of any form. Even if she drowned me, it would be worth it to be with a woman. I'll go there.

Mermaid Marriage

Although Coney Island mermaids like Bucklew and Bambi push the limits of the heterosexual imagination, they also remain firmly within it. These mermaids on the edge of respectable heterosexuality are able to explore a suspect topic like sex with a different species precisely because they are so clearly heterosexual. Their desires are firmly located within the only truly legitimate sexual practices in our culture, the desire for heterosexual intercourse, for the insertion of a penis into a vagina, even if that vagina belongs to a fish.[27] Indeed, the freakishness of Coney Island mermaids, who are not only predominantly heterosexual but also White and middle class,[28] is rooted in a deep and abiding belief in the normalcy and legitimacy of their true selves, regardless of their performances as and even embrace as freaks. In this way, the freakish Coney Island mermaids can marry their images to the wholesome fun of Disney's Ariel and Daryl Hannah's Madison. They can get caught in the act of being naughty, but it is a naughtiness that is rooted in their "normalcy" and "legitimacy" as middle-class, White, and most importantly, heterosexual members of American culture. Perhaps no event symbolizes this marriage of freak and pin-up, monster and girl-next-door than an actual mermaid wedding that took place at the Coney Island USA SideShow.

The wedding was that of Bambi the mermaid to a biker by the name of Indian Larry.[29] Despite the wedding's status as a "freak show" at a literal freak show in Coney Island, Bambi described the event as a "fairytale come true." According to Bambi, Larry looks like a "psychotic murderer" because of his heavily tattooed body and biker leathers, but he is, in fact, a "prince," her soul mate and true love. The way Bambi describes love and her mermaid marriage is very like the far more legitimate Disney narratives.

> In the original *Little Mermaid*, the Hans Christian Andersen one, it's about giving up her soul, her very soul, but it's worth it because it's for love. And love is the nearest we get to heaven on earth…. It's about the real life ending to my fairy tale life.

Bambi's love, then, is predicated on the highly recognizable and legitimate trop of heterosexual romance. Despite that which marks her as a freak, that is, her tail, her sex work, and her performance art, she is also simultaneously the heroine of a true-life love story. She is, deep down, the sweet, beautiful, and even innocent girl we all want her to be, and the fact that she is also a bug-eating, sex worker with a mermaid's tail, is just a disguise, a costume that we must see through in order to see how fully normal and heterosexually embodied and human she really is.

And so this fish tale, like all good heterosexual romance, ends with a white wedding. The wedding brings women fully into humanity by attaching them to men and sanctioning their bodies, yes, even their fishy vaginas. In its current cultural form, the wedding is white, that is pure, from racial taint and the taint of any sexual practices other than insertive heterosexual ones.[30] That is why on a warm, June day in a place on the edge of New York, in a space on the edge of the heterosexual imagination, a group of people gathered together to see a man and a woman married. The crowd, exclusively white, was made up primarily of the tattooed, the pierced, and of blue and pink and green and platinum hair. Many in the crowd were dressed as mermaids. Many wore the leather chaps and bodices and boots of s/m practitioners and/or bikers. Nearly all of them were armed with cameras and a certain ironic grin, a grin rooted in their faith that they were overturning the normalcy of weddings and embracing the freak within.

When the bride arrived, in a beautiful white tail with appliqued pearls, a large pearl in her belly button, and clam shell pasties, the crowd, myself included, gasped at her beauty. She was the embodiment of all our cultural desires and none of our fears. She was simultaneously sexy and sincere, a bad girl in a naughty, playful sense, but in no way a monster who might lead men to their doom. More importantly, the back of her tail revealed two human legs and the promise of a human vagina. We all watched, with tears in our eyes, as the bride mounted the stage at the center of the room with her bridal party, four mermaids and one merman by the name of G-spot. As the ceremony proceeded and Bambi and Larry vowed their eternal love, the room grew quiet and solemn. After all, we were witnessing the transformation of a mermaid into a human, a humbling moment of heterosexuality's ability to make even the only half-human mermaid fully human. That the transformation took place at the edges of the heterosexual imagination, at the edges of legitimacy, only increased its poignancy and potency. This act of union with the mermaid fulfills the promise of Christianity and more modern notions of self by endowing the female body with both a soul and humanity. More importantly, this act of union with the mermaid fills in the edges of the heterosexual imagination, an imagination predicated on union with the Other. That the Other might just remain Other, that she might not transform her tail into a vagina, only makes the union that much more sacred and sexy.

Notes

1. Theodore Gachot. 1996. *Mermaids: Nymphs of the sea,* p. 16. San Francisco: Harper Collins. The mermaid was catalogued in the bestiaries of the Middle Ages, and there are several instances of mermaids being converted to Christianity or at least being taught to kneel before a cross. See "Folklores and Legends" at rubens.anu.edu.

2. That the mermaid is still a powerful symbol of our culture is evident in the fact that a web search for mermaids will reveal over 35,000 sites. The mermaid is also the national symbol of Denmark and the symbol for countless commercial enterprises, from erotic escort services to water filtering systems. For a website dedicated to the inaccessibility of the mermaid's vagina for human men, see www.machaon.ru/st.valentine/mermaids

3. The "Mermaid Parade" is an event that occurs at Coney Island every June on the first Saturday after the Summer Solstice. Each year over half a million people gather to celebrate mermaids, sea creatures and folk, and the official beginning of summer. The research was conducted for my forthcoming book *Coney Island and the edge of pleasure.*

4. Of course, even in her guise as potential lover, the monstrous is always lurking not too far beneath the surface. For example, in "Splash" the mermaid as a child tries to drown the boy child who grows up to be her lover.

5. Gachot.

6. Popular images of mermaids are examined through two movies, "Splash" and "The Little Mermaid," which were mentioned by nearly everyone I interviewed when I asked whether there were any books or movies about mermaids that were important to them. One young woman spoke about being so moved by Hannah's performance in "Splash" that as a young girl of eight or nine, she imitated Hannah's character and poured a box of salt into her tub. To her disappointment, the result was not a mermaid's tail but itchy skin and a scolding from her mother. The people I interviewed were all either participants in or observers of the annual Coney Island Mermaid Parade.

7. Hans Christian Andersen. 1993. *The little mermaid.* New York: Jelly Bean Press.

8. Like any cultural cipher, the mermaid has multiple meanings. Margaret Starbird argues that Disney's Ariel is a composite of Mary Magdalene, Aphrodite, Athene, Demeter, and the Holy Sophia. The sacred aspect of Ariel is evident in her red hair (like Mary Magdalene's), a painting in her collection of human artifacts of Georges de la Tour called "Magdalen with the Smoking Flame," and the fact that the heresy of the Holy Grail is that Mary is descended from mermaids. See www.members.tripod.com/RamonKJusino/littlemermaid. In deconstructing Disney, the authors read "The Little Mermaid" as a tale about capitalism's superiority over socialist economies and a piece of corporate propaganda aimed at the soon to be Disnified Western Europe and the soon to be capitalist Eastern Europe. According to this analysis, the film centers not on a vagina, but on debt. On this view, Ariel, who is a child of the East, longs for the goods of the West, but can only gain those goods by going into debt to the Sea Witch. The Sea Witch represents the specter of dictatorship that might descend over the East if the debts are left unpaid, while Eric represents the benevolent West that can destroy the Sea Witch/dictatorship, thereby putting Triton/reasonable leaders of the East, in his/the West's debt. Byrne, Eleanor and Martin McQuillan. 1999. *Deconstructing Disney,* pp. 22–36. London: Pluto Press.

9. Aol.eonline.com.

10. At the beginning of the film, before she has a human focus for her desire, Ariel sings of wanting a vagina/human form in the song "Part of Your World." The lyrics show her lack of satisfaction with the material possessions of the human world, how she's got "gadgets and gizmos aplenty," but she wants legs since "flippin' your fins don't get too far, Legs are required for jumpin', dancin'" and one can assume "fuckin.'" "The Little Mermaid," Disney Studios, 1989.

11. It is interesting to note that Ariel's wedding presents a problem for Disney's claim to wholesome entertainment because she is, in fact, a child of fifteen. After "The Mermaid's" appearance in 1989, Disney made sure that its "teen romance" movies did not end in a wedding/clearly sexual coupling. Consider "Beauty and the Beast," "Aladdin," and "Mulan." *Deconstructing Disney,* p. 68.

12. "Splash," Touchstone Films, 1984.

13. It is interesting to note that in Andersen's version, *The Little Mermaid,* there is also a scene of cross-dressing. The prince "had her dressed in male attire, that she might accompany him on horseback …". Of course, Ariel is actually a freak because she is mute. It is her inability to

speak, like Madison's unspeakable name, that removes her from normalcy/humanity. Andersen, pages not numbered.

14. Obviously, lesbianism in the film is attractive as a prop for heterosexual intercourse. The point of Freddy's story is making the lesbian accessible to heterosexual desire, just as Madison's cross dressing is presented between scenes of heterosexual lovemaking. Like the Mermaid, the lesbian is only desirable to the extent that she has a vagina that is accessible to men. Otherwise, she figures as a monster.

15. The Museum of Natural History as the place for the mermaid's imprisonment is extremely appropriate given its history as a place for the erotic display of difference. Indeed, the Museum and others like it were founded on the scientific impulse to display the racial Other as more animal, more feminized, and more sexualized than the Museum's white and middle-class audience. See, for example, Haraway Donna, 1989. *Primate visions*, New York: Routledge.

16. My research of the Mermaid Parade included nine in-depth interviews of participants. The interviews lasted an average of two hours and were open-ended, but always included questions about the mermaid's sexuality as well as her race. In addition to these interviews, I conducted 33 interviews at the 2000 Mermaid Parade with participants and spectators alike. I was also an official judge at the Mermaid Parade, which provided me with an extremely good view.

17. Interview with Dick Zigun, March 18, 2000.

18. Interview with Bambi, May 30, 2000.

19. Interview with Kate Fallon, June 6, 2000.

20. I saw the photographs in Bambi's home, but they were recently in a public exhibit.

21. Interview with Lin Gathright, June 7, 2000.

22. I saw this act performed on July 28, 2000, at Tirza's Winebath, a weekly burlesque show run by Coney Island USA.

23. All interviews with spectators were conducted on June 24, 2000, the day of the Parade.

24. Again, as a judge I was able to see all the participants from the vantage point of a reviewing stand. Not surprisingly, the judges were encouraged to ignore conventional rules of fairness and impartiality. In fact, we were encouraged to take bribes (usually in the form of cold beer) and vote for friends.

25. Interview, July 25, 2000.

26. Obviously, Bucklew's statement "just a man" to signify heterosexual is a way of denying manhood to those who are not.

27. The Monica Lewinsky as mermaid image comes into sharper focus when we consider how the President did not consider any other sort of sexual interaction as "sexual intercourse."

28. Coney Island is not a primarily white space. In fact, on any given day in the summer, whites are clearly in the minority. In terms of neighborhood population, according to the 1990 U.S. Census, the neighborhood was about 47.9 percent white (not including "white Hispanic"). But on the day of the Mermaid Parade, nearly everyone is white. All of the entries in the Parade were white except for one headed by two women whom I had interviewed earlier as acquaintances who participate in the Parade, Laurie Ourlicht (Interview May 24, 2000) and Carola Burroughs (June 23, 2000). Both women grew up mixed race in the 1950s and discussed the role of the mermaid, as half human and half inhuman, in representing that experience for them. I discuss the role of race in deciding the mermaid's qualifications as fully human more thoroughly in my forthcoming book, *Coney Island and the edge of pleasure*. The Parade participants and observers were also nearly all college educated and lived in either middle class and/or culturally prestigious neighborhoods. The neighborhoods mentioned most often were the East Village, Williamsburg, and Park Slope.

29. Bambi was kind enough to allow me to attend her wedding, which took place on Saturday, June 3, 2000. The wedding did not consist of legal registration, in part because of some lingering problems with the IRS for Indian Larry. Bambi said that the civil ceremony did not matter to her because state recognition is "not what makes it sacred." On the other hand, she also said they will make it legal sometime in the near future, perhaps in Las Vegas. Interview, May 30, 2000.

30. See Ingraham Chrys. 1999. *White weddings*. New York: Routledge.

3
The Promise

CHAPTER **8**

"Someday My Prince Will Come": Disney, the Heterosexual Imaginary and Animated Film

CARRIE L. COKELY

Disney is a $6.8 billion corporation.[1] This worth is not only the revenues generated from theme parks, film, videos, and merchandise but also represents the revenues generated from Disney's holdings in major television networks, magazines, radio stations, newspapers, and major film production companies. As it has grown into a multinational corporation, Disney has increasingly come to signify so much to so many, and stands as a pillar of U.S. popular culture.

While cultural critics have begun to critique the many faces of Disney,[2] these faces remain largely unexamined by the general public as sites of cultural production and reproduction. Since American consumers typically equate Disney with the magical, the wholesome, the imaginary, they overlook the ideological messages that are embedded within the films, the parks, and the products. Instead, consumers dismiss these messages as mere fantasy. Consequently, Disney remains an underexamined educational site, educating both the children who consume the culture through films, cartoons, and books, as well as the mass population of adults who have invested in Disney as a means of recapturing their youth.

While the most obvious way to experience the "magic" of Disney is to visit the ultimate theme park, Walt Disney World, only a small number of middle and upper class families may have the resources to actually travel to Disneyland and experience the "happiest place on earth."

However, many more families can access the "magic" of Disney through films in movie theaters as well as in their own homes. In the United States today, between 85 and 90% of families own a VCR making the viewing of home movies popular, especially among children.[3] Among the 34 G-rated, full-length, animated films that Disney has released, seventeen have been released on video as well, for a "limited time." These seventeen videos alone account for over 220 million video unit sales since their release. Clearly, the Disney videos, and with them the popular Disney ideologies, have been well received by the general public.

Much of the magic that is produced by Disney is entangled with notions of romance, true love, and the white wedding. While promoted as stories of adventure, of youthful rebellion, and of coming of age, the majority of Disney animated films center on the theme of the marriage plot: finding true love and, inevitably, marriage. By examining these films, we are able to uncover not only the ways in which heterosexuality operates within this site of U.S. children's culture but also the ways in which heterosexuality is institutionalized in the United States.

Critiquing the institution of heterosexuality is not new. Second-wave feminists argued that heterosexuality is an organizing institution containing multiple forms of oppression, rather than a naturally occurring phenomenon.[4] Adrienne Rich, in her groundbreaking essay on compulsory heterosexuality, argues against heterosexuality as naturally occurring, asserting that heterosexuality is, instead, compulsory, constructed, and taken for granted. For Rich, the institution of heterosexuality serves the interests of patriarchy and male dominance.[5] Monique Wittig, in her essay "The Category of Sex" argues that heterosexuality is a political regime, again serving the interests of male dominance through the marriage contract.[6] More recently, Chrys Ingraham, in her essay "The Heterosexual Imaginary: Feminist Sociology and Theories of Gender," puts forth the notion of the heterosexual imaginary as "that way of thinking that conceals the operation of heterosexuality in structuring gender (across race, class, and sexuality) and closes off any critical analysis of heterosexuality as an organizing institution."[7] All three of these authors recognize the ways in which heterosexuality is learned and organized, as well as the interests that are served by keeping heterosexuality in place and unexamined as "natural." Using these frameworks to examine heterosexuality as an institution that structures race, class, and sexuality allows for the exploration of the "simultaneity of oppression and struggle."[8]

The Research Project

This project is an attempt to apply these ways of thinking to Disney's animated films. In completing this project, my objectives are threefold: (1) to explore the ways in which the heterosexual imaginary is at work in Disney's animated films; (2) to expose the ways in which heterosexuality, as an institution, not only serves to organize gender but also keeps in place hierarchies surrounding race, class, and sexuality; and (3) to examine the ways in which Disney's animated films "work as a form of ideological control to signal membership in relations of ruling."[9] This project utilizes content analysis to examine the films *Snow White* (1937), *Cinderella* (1950), and *Sleeping Beauty* (1959), from the old generation of animated films, as well as *The Little Mermaid* (1989), *Aladdin* (1992), and *Pocahontas* (1996), from the new generation of animated film, in order to grasp the ways in which the heterosexual imaginary operates across time.[10]

Once Upon a Time …

It is with these words that Disney begins to cast its spell. For the masses, Disney is the producer of the stories, the films, the magic, and innocence of childhood. Yet, as Jack Zipes tells us, Disney merely adapts many of its more prominent stories from preexisting European tales. He states,

> It was not once upon a time, but at a certain time in history, before anyone knew what was happening, that Walt Disney cast a spell on the fairy tale, and he has held it captive ever since. He did not use a magic wand or demonic powers. On the contrary, Disney employed the most up-to-date technological means and used his own "American" grit and ingenuity to appropriate European fairy tales. His technological skills and ideological proclivities were so consummate that his signature has obfuscated the names of Charles Perrault, the Brothers Grimm, Hans Christian Andersen, and Carlo Collodi. If children or adults think of the great classical fairy tales today, be it *Snow White*, *Sleeping Beauty*, or *Cinderella*, they will think Walt Disney.[11]

In these adaptations, Disney, even today, sticks to the formula that has proven successful time and again for the studio's animated films. The central component to this formula, the magic one may say, is embodied in romance, finding true love, and marriage. In short, the magic is very much entangled with the naturalization of heterosexuality. This is evidenced over and over in the six films that I examined. *Snow White*, *Cinderella*, and *Sleeping Beauty* all sing about the dreams they have of their one true love.

Snow White (1937)	*Cinderella* (1950)	*Sleeping Beauty* (1959)
Some day my prince will come Some day we'll meet again And away to his castle we'll go To be happy forever I know Some day when spring is here We'll find our love anew And the birds will sing And wedding bells will ring Some day when my dreams come true.	A dream is a wish your heart makes when you're fast asleep In dreams you lose your heartaches, whatever you wish for you keep Have faith in your dreams and some day your rainbow will come smiling through No matter how our heart is grieving, If you keep on believing, the dream that you wish will come true.	I know you, I walked with you once upon a dream. I know you, The gleam in your eyes is so familiar a gleam. Yes, I know it's true that visions are seldom all they seem. But if I know you, I know what you'll do. You'll love me at once the way you did once upon a dream.

In all three of these examples, it is the females who are hoping and dreaming of their one true love, who they have not yet met. The belief is that if you just wait long enough, wish hard enough, and keep on dreaming eventually he will come for you. This puts forth the notion that it is so "natural" for women to want to be married that it consumes not only their dreams, but that it also spills over into their waking thoughts as well.

While they do not dream of it per se, the theme of finding a true love, that worked so well in the films of the 1930s and 1950s, remains in the newer Disney films. Ariel, the main character in *The Little Mermaid*, dreams of being human and a part of that (his) world. For her true love and happiness is bound up in a world of which she can only dream, the human world. In her song to her Prince she exclaims,

> I don't know when
> I don't know how
> But I know something's starting right now
> Watch and you'll see
> Someday I'll be
> Part of your World.

The Little Mermaid (1989)

Aladdin's Princess Jasmine, while more rebellious than the others we have seen, still when forced to think about whom to marry exclaims, "Father, I hate being forced into this. If I do marry I want it to be for love." Again, we see the notion of finding true love and settling for nothing less than this dream. Finally, Pocahontas consults Grandmother Willow concerning matters of the heart. In doing so, Pocahontas relates a dream that she had,

> Pocahontas: My father thinks it's the right path for me, but lately, I've been having this dream, and I think it is…
> Grandmother Willow: Oh, a dream! Let's hear all about it.
> Pocahontas: Well, I'm running through the woods, and then, right there in front of me, is an arrow. As I look at it, it starts to spin …
> Grandmother Willow: A spinning arrow, how unusual.
> Pocahontas: Yes, it spins faster and faster and faster until suddenly it stops.
> Grandmother Willow: Hmmm, well it seems to me that this spinning arrow is pointing you down your path.
> Pocahontas: But what is my path? How am I ever going to find it?
>
> *Pocahontas* (1996)

In and of itself, this dream does not seem like the dreams we have seen in the other films. However, later in the film Pocahontas realizes that the arrow, and her path, is pointing to John Smith. Long before she consciously knew, she was apparently destined to fall in love with John Smith. This again solidifies the females as concerned with matters of the heart and relationships, which are exclusively heterosexual.

Messages like this mask the ways in which heterosexuality is institutionalized. Also masked is the possibility that females may have aspirations separate from marriage. This is demonstrative of Jo VanEvery's claim that "the hegemonic form of heterosexuality is marriage."[12] In a society organized by heterosexuality, there are few acceptable options for women outside of marriage. As Stevi Jackson asserts, "the ideology of heterosexual romance tells us that falling in love is the prelude to a lasting, secure, and stable conjugal union."[13] Despite escalating rates of divorce and single motherhood as well as declining marriage rates, individuals, especially women, still hold up marriage as a goal and dream of the romantic fairy tale wedding.

And They Fell Madly in Love …

While dreaming of love is nice, it is nothing without the romantic meeting between the Princess and her Prince Charming where it is love at first sight. This meeting without exception is present in all the films. What constitutes this romantic meeting? The Duke in *Cinderella* sums it up best when, in talking to the King, he says,

No doubt you saw the whole pretty picture in detail.
The Young Prince, bowing to his sampling.
Suddenly he stops, he looks up.
Behold! There she stands, the girl of his dreams.
Who she is or where she came from he knows not, nor does he care.
But his heart tells him that here is the maid destined to be his bride.
Oh, a pretty plot for fairy tales, but in real life no.

Cinderella (1950)

Despite the Duke's disclaimer that this does not happen in "real life" as he speaks, we see the Prince spot Cinderella and they play out the scene exactly as the Duke describes, thereby contradicting the Duke's belief that it could never happen in "real life." Also of interest is the fact that in all of the films, it is the "Prince" figure who initiates the meeting between himself and the Princess. While it may be the Princess who dreams of finding her true love, it is the Prince who is responsible for the union. *Sleeping Beauty's* Prince Phillip seeks her out in the forest, following her beautiful singing. Upon seeing her, he knew she was the one he was going to marry. Aladdin sees Princess Jasmine from afar in the marketplace and proceeds to meet her and win her heart. This pattern continues in the other three films as well.

Throughout each of these scenes what becomes important is the idea that true love can conquer all. As the Duke tells us, "Who she is or where she came from he knows not, nor does he care." Regardless of status, background, class, or race, the two must and will be together. This is especially clear in *Sleeping Beauty*, *The Little Mermaid*, and *Pocahontas*. *Sleeping Beauty's* Prince Phillip informs his father that he has fallen in love with a peasant girl and is going to marry her. For Phillip, it does not matter that she is not a princess and has no money. What is important is that they will be together. In *The Little Mermaid*, Prince Eric and Ariel are not even the same species: he a human, she a mermaid. However, he is determined to be with her and she with him despite the wishes of everyone else. Finally, in *Pocahontas*, she and John Smith meet and fall in love in spite of the wishes of Pocahontas's father and the orders of the Virginia Company. Although the two groups of people, the Native Americans and the English, were at war, John Smith and Pocahontas could put aside their differences in the name of romantic love.

Masked in this discourse of true love and romance is the underlying message that it is indeed the male who is the "aggressor" in a heterosexual relationship. The rules for heterosexuality are put in place. In each and every case, it is the male character who finds and seeks out the female character for marriage. Many times this happens without her consent. The male character announces to the audience that he is going to marry that particular girl, the one of his dreams. The females, on the other hand, are forced then to wait for the man of their dreams to come take them away from their unbearable situation. Held up as true love, however, this model is rarely viewed as anything less than perfect.

And they were Married the Very Next Day...

In addition to the masking of heterosexuality as an organized rule-based system, these films naturalize the patriarchal system inherent in the institution of marriage and give clear messages as to who is "fit" for marriage. All three of the older films, *Snow White*, *Cinderella*, and *Sleeping Beauty*, consist of the marriage of a prince to a princess. While the females are often working as servants or taking on the role of a peasant for one reason or another, we must not forget that they are indeed royalty. It is through marriage that the princess is returned to her status as royalty. While the marriage brings the female out of servitude/peasant conditions, the male has really nothing to lose in the marriage contract. In fact, he is legally gaining a female to care for him. While it may appear that the female is benefiting the most from marriage—after all, she is given royal status and wealth—this advantage comes at a cost. It is these patriarchal relations that are masked in the magic of these films.

In *The Little Mermaid*, Ariel is already a princess, but through her marriage to Prince Eric she is able to become part of the human (read civilized) world of which she has always dreamt. It is the female who gives up her father, her sisters, and her identity, in the name of true love. Prince Eric, on the other hand, gives up nothing and has everything to gain.

Aladdin is a twist on the Disney classics for Aladdin is the peasant and Jasmine is the Princess. For Aladdin, marriage to Jasmine brings wealth, status as royalty, and power as Sultan. Jasmine gains nothing from the deal, and, in fact, needs her father to change the law in order for the marriage to even occur. While Pocahontas does not marry John Smith, during their relationship she is in a position to lose her family and tribe as she allies with and cares for John Smith. Even in the cases where the women are supposed to be rebellious and strong, the same patriarchal relations are secured in these films.

Also contained in these tales of love and marriage are messages surrounding guidelines as to who is really "allowed" to be together in marriage. In all the films in which a marriage occurs, the couples have similar socioeconomic backgrounds—they are in the ruling class. With only one exception, *Aladdin*, we see a Prince marrying a Princess. As described above Aladdin is not royalty, but he is still allowed to marry the Princess. This is most likely the result of the fact that through most of the film Aladdin masquerades as Prince Ali in order to win the Princess's heart. At the end of the film the genie tells Aladdin, "No matter what, you'll always be a prince to me." Upon hearing this, the Sultan agrees that Aladdin has indeed "proven his worth" and can therefore marry Princess Jasmine. In this case, although Aladdin is not royalty, he has proven that he is worthy to be royalty and can be elevated to that status through marriage.

Marriages also occur in the cases where the couples share the same racial background. With only one exception the ethnic and racial background of the main characters in these films is white European. While Aladdin and Princess Jasmine are of Arab descent, they physically resemble their white European counterparts in previous films enough that they are rewarded with marriage. The one film in which marriage does not occur, *Pocahontas*, is the first time that we see an interracial couple depicted in an animated Disney film. It is no accident that the two were not wed in the end. The United States has a long history of discouraging interracial relationships and has even had miscegenation laws prohibiting these marriages in some states. To produce the "magical" romance of the Disney film, the filmmakers need to rely on notions of innocence and purity. The interracial marriage between Pocahontas and John Smith does not count as innocent or pure and contradicts this necessity. As Ingraham points out, "weddings are code for whiteness."[14] Those that occur outside the realm of acceptable whiteness, as interracial couples often are, are prohibited from participating in the traditional "white" wedding and marriage.

Third, marriage occurs for the "beautiful people." This becomes increasingly evident in these films when we examine those individuals the beautiful people are placed in relation to, namely the villains that work to keep the couple apart, as well as the parental figures. The older films, *Snow White, Cinderella,* and *Sleeping Beauty,* as well as *The Little Mermaid* from the new generation, construct opposition between female characters, usually the young heroine, an evil queen, and some kind of fairy. The ways in which each of these women are constructed reveal cultural codes that align the audience with the young and old females and set the viewer up to see those females in the middle as dangerous. The young heroine represents beauty and youth. They are the embodiment of the traditional woman. Even those heroines who are rebellious—Ariel, Jasmine, and Pocahontas—ascribe to hegemonic notions of femininity in order to get their man. A prime example of this is present in *The Little Mermaid.* In order to become human Ariel makes a pact with Ursula the sea witch. In exchange for legs, Ariel must give Ursula her voice. When Ariel expresses concern as to how she will get Prince Eric to notice her and fall in love without her voice, Ursula explains the following:

> You'll have your looks, your pretty face,
> And don't underestimate the importance of body language!
> The men up there don't like a lot of blabber

They think the girl that gossips is a bore
Up on land it's much preferred for ladies not to say a word
And after all dear what is idle prattle for?
Come on they're not all that impressed with conversation
True gentlemen avoid it when they can
But they dote and swoon and fawn
On a lady that's withdrawn
It's she who holds her tongue who gets her man!

The Little Mermaid (1989)

Through this monologue, Ursula not only emphasizes the importance of adherence to "proper" expressions of gender but also the reward that this adherence will bring—a man. It becomes evident that Ariel and the others are deemed worthy of marriage and will "win" the man of their dreams by adhering to traditional gender behaviors and patriarchal norms pertaining to femininity.

The middle-aged villain, on the other hand, is depicted as a strong and dangerous woman, in direct opposition to the young heroine. The villain is self-assured and confident in expressing her beauty, her sexuality, and her power. She often outwits and overpowers the young heroine as well as some of the men in the story. Consequently, these women are depicted as threats to the established heterosexual, patriarchal order and as a result are deemed unworthy of marriage.[15] It then becomes necessary for these women to be defeated by the male hero of the story in order for the traditional order to remain intact. This is the part of the film where the audience cheers as the villain is massacred in return for evil deeds that interfere with true love.

Finally, the grandmother figure is usually depicted as a godmother, a fairy, or a servant. These women are in contrast to the middle-aged villain in the story. They are nurturing, cooperative, generous, and kind. They are willing to make sacrifices for the greater good and appear harmless and nonthreatening.[16] Yet despite this, they pale in comparison to the young heroine and therefore are not worthy of marriage either. They live vicariously through the young heroine and are therefore gratified by helping her achieve her quest for marriage.

In the final two films from the new generation, *Aladdin* and *Pocahontas*, while the young heroines remain in traditional roles deeming them worthy for marriage, the villains and parental figures are male. This then sets up the conflict and struggle between the young male heroes, the parental figures, and the villains. Like the female heroines, the male heroes also exemplify hegemonic discourses of gender. These men are sensitive and caring while at the same time able to protect their love and are smart enough to outwit those trying to stand in their way. While the female villains are dangerous due to the fact that they flaunt their sexuality, the male villains are dangerous due to their greed and lust for power. Heterosexuality and patriarchy operate in a way that masks the power and benefits males derive from these systems. In their blatant quest for power the male villain threatens the established order. The male figure in these stories is actually the parent, rather than a fairy. While not in conflict with the male hero, this parental figure is more of a representation of what the young hero can become. In each of these stories, the father figure is married, although we never see the mother figure, and expresses desire for his daughter to be married because she will need someone to protect her. This is exemplified through the comments of both Princess Jasmine's father and Pocahontas's father.

> I'm not going to be around forever. I just want to make sure that you are taken care of, provided for.
>
> Sultan to Jasmine, *Aladdin* (1992)

> My daughter, Kocoum will make a fine husband. He is loyal and strong and will build you a good house with sturdy walls. With him you will be safe from harm.
>
> Chief Powhatan to Pocahontas, *Pocahontas* (1996)

In other words, once the daughter marries the control exercised by the father will be passed along to the new husband, thereby perpetuating the patriarchal order. Just as the female is rewarded by marriage, the male hero is also rewarded. He is "given" the woman of his dreams to care for in marriage. However, this unequal relationship remains hidden in the films, masking again the inherent inequalities in the institutions of heterosexuality and patriarchy. Film theorist Mas'ud Zavarzadeh (1991) argues that the masking or naturalizing of these processes is necessary in order to maintain the interests of the ruling classes. He writes,

> Capitalist patriarchy...requires an idea of femininity that reproduces its relations of production and thus perpetuates itself without any serious challenge to its fundamental social norms .... None of these [feminine] traits are in themselves and "by nature" definitive of femininity and are all in fact political attributes required for maintaining asymmetrical power relations and thus the exploitative gender relations between men and women .... These traits, however, are not produced in a material vacuum: a society "desires" that which is historically necessary for its reproduction and can be made intelligible to its members.[17]

Consistent with this argument, these Disney animated features are constructed in ways that keep in place the dominant ideologies surrounding heterosexuality, gender, and patriarchy. These messages are then consumed by the general population and are necessary for the reproduction of the hegemonic order.

And They Lived Happily Ever After ...

The love of the young hero and heroine is sealed and the film ends with the romantic fairy tale kiss. In those films where the couple is married this takes place in the context of the wedding, in the case of Pocahontas and John Smith, their symbolic kiss occurs before John Smith leaves for England. While the two are not legally bound together in marriage, Pocahontas tells John Smith that they will always be in each other's hearts, again exemplifying the romantic notion of true love.

In the other films, the endings consist of the couple "riding off into the sunset together." In the three older films, the Prince and Princess are either riding on (*Snow White* and *Sleeping Beauty*) or have a carriage pulled by (*Cinderella*) white horses as the sun sets in front of them. Ariel and Prince Eric in *The Little Mermaid* ride into the sunset on their wedding ship while Aladdin and Princess Jasmine are on the balcony of their palace, again as the sun sets. The setting sun symbolizes the end of the single life and the beginning of their life as a couple. Once again the filmmakers invoke the notion that romance and, in the end, marriage is "the prelude to a lasting, secure, and stable conjugal union."[18] We are left with the line, spoken or unspoken, "and they lived happily ever after" by virtue of the fact that true love won out and a marriage took place. But only for those individuals "allowed" to marry according to the dominant ideology of heterosexuality expressed in these films.

Beyond Happily Ever After ...

There is no question that Disney brings a great amount of pleasure to adults and children through these films and others like them. To derive this pleasure from these films, one must be firmly situated within the dominant ideologies of heterosexuality and patriarchy that are reinforced through these films. Those of us who are located within these structures not only establish our identities through cultural productions, such as films, but are also able to reaffirm those identities.[19]

Cultural theorists Adorno and Horkheimer assert, "the claim of art is always ideology too."[20] Therefore, representations of sexuality or romance seen in these Disney productions are often dismissed as entertainment (a form of art) and fantasy but do indeed reinforce the dominant beliefs surrounding race, class, gender, and heterosexuality. Disney then, through these films, as well as through other forms of "magic," is merely filtering the world through the culture industry. As a result of this, individuals willingly choose to participate in the hegemonic order and in doing so reinforce the dominant relations of ruling that are tied to heterosexuality, patriarchy, and capitalism.

But what about those who choose not to participate in the hegemonic order? Or those who are unable to identify with the characters on the screen, who do not see the "realities" that are produced as their own. In thinking about the heterosexual imaginary in animated films, those who may not be witnessing these representations as their own are gays and lesbians. While invested in the notions of true love, romance, and partnerships, many gays and lesbians do not experience these ideologies in the same way as the heterosexual viewing audience. Even though they have been socialized to participate in patriarchal and heterosexual social arrangements, there are differences in how gender is practiced in same-sex partnerships. Since the partners are the same sex there is not always the same gendered inequality that exists in a heterosexual partnership rooted in relations of patriarchy.

Secondly, in viewing the films, the gay, lesbian, or transgendered viewer may have a hard time finding a character that is similar to him/herself. In the older films, there are no portrayals of or even allusions to gay/lesbian characters. Even in *Snow White,* a story that revolves around seven male dwarfs who live together in the woods and who, the film makes explicit, are heterosexual. They all delight in being cared for by Snow White and the kisses that she gives them on their way to work. Even in death, the dwarfs venerate Snow White in a glass coffin.

The newer films allude to homosexuality through the portrayal of certain male characters. In the film *Pocahontas,* Governor Ratcliff's lackey is depicted as the stereotypical gay male: he is a hairdresser, grooming both the dog and himself, he proposes giving the Native Americans fruit baskets wrapped in pink bows as a welcoming gift, and he is overly emotional and sensitive. While these stereotypical depictions are common in popular culture, nevertheless they are not typically images that the average gay male emulates. Through representations such as this, homosexuality is coded as deviant, violating dominant gender prescriptions for men. In this case, the viewer comes to associate the lackey with Governor Ratcliff, the villain in the story. The viewer also learns how to socially control such deviant behavior by seeing the other Englishmen ridicule and belittle Ratcliff's lackey and model "appropriate" masculinity as a contrast. This practice is examined and explained in Jeffery Weeks' article, "The Construction of Homosexuality," which details the ways in which homosexuals have historically been demonized and coded as evil or deviant in comparison to the general heterosexual population.

While the gay male is coded as deviant, lesbians remain absent in both the old and new generation of Disney films. This may stem from the fact that the stereotypical portrayal of lesbians is of the masculine female. Since the typical Disney plot hinges on limited notions of femininity and a gendered division of labor rooted in patriarchal belief systems, there is no room here for the masculine female. By leaving no room for the masculine female, Disney is, in effect, coding this form of gender and sexuality as deviant through its omission. These examples make clear the way heterosexuality functions as an organizing institution.

In light of the ways in which Disney portrays gays and lesbians, there is a tension that exists between this cultural coding and the actual practices of the Disney Corporation. The Walt Disney Company has been hailed as a "gay friendly" company. This categorization is the culmination of several factors. First, and foremost, Disney is one of the few corporations in the United States that offers benefits to same-sex domestic partners. Not only are they recognizing gay and lesbian relationships but the company is granting these unions the same benefits as married heterosexuals. In so doing, the company is challenging the effects of the very deviant label it so knowingly or unknowingly places upon those characters coded as homosexual in their animated films. However, the company only makes these same-sex partnership benefits available to full-time employees. Disney avoids paying out benefits to many—homosexual or heterosexual—by limiting the number of employees they hire as full time.

Second, Disney owns and operates the network, ABC, that aired the television situation comedy (sitcom) "Ellen." This was one of the first shows to deal directly with issues of gays or lesbians. However, shortly after the infamous "coming out episode," the show was cancelled and subsequently went off the air. Third and finally, the Walt Disney Company has special weeks at Walt Disney World that are set aside especially for gay and lesbian families to visit the theme park. In essence, the company is setting aside a certain time frame to celebrate this "special" group of guests. This effort represents a first among major corporations in honoring the lives of gay and lesbian families. Even so, this effort pales in comparison to the massive opportunities available to heterosexual couples and families the rest of the year at Disney World. This is perhaps most apparent in the prominence of the Cinderella Wedding Pavilion and the numerous heterosexual couples who choose Walt Disney World as their wedding and honeymoon destination.

The End ...

In closing this is only the beginning of the work that needs to be done to interrogate the institution of heterosexuality and its operation within the realm of the magical world called Disney. While Disney holds a prominent place within the ideologies and illusions surrounding heterosexuality, patriarchy, and capitalism, securing this place does not come without resistance. Increasingly, there are more "campy" readings of the films coming out of the gay and lesbian community. This is especially true in gay male culture as well as from reports of an increasingly homosexual subculture emerging among the employees of Walt Disney World.

The heterosexual imaginary—the illusion that institutionalized heterosexuality provides a sense of well-being—is very visible in the films of the Walt Disney Company and is perpetuated in Disney culture year after year. The production of the heterosexual imaginary is the core product of Disney films and the contradiction it seeks to mask in providing benefits to gay and lesbian consumers and employees. While the viewers identify with the characters and reap significant pleasure from the films and other Disney products, what they really identify with and subscribe to are the dominant discourses and ideologies of gender and heterosexuality. These discourses and ideologies instruct us on the culturally prescribed display and enactment of masculinity and femininity, as well as guide us in desiring and practicing the preferred heterosexual practice: marriage and its embedded class privilege. Most importantly, these animated fantasies perpetuate the illusion that romance represents true love and mask the ways heterosexuality and patriarchy are at work in our society today. In so doing, these films and the Disney Corporation secure the place of institutionalized and illusory heterosexuality in the ruling order.

References

Adorno, Theodor and Max Horkheimer. 1944. The culture industry: Enlightenment as mass deception, in Lawrence Grossberg, Cary Nelson and Paula Treichler (eds.) *Cultural studies.*

Bell, Elizabeth, Lynda Haas and Laura Sells. 1995. *From mouse to mermaid: The politics of film, gender, and culture.* Bloomington: Indiana University Press.

Bell, Elizabeth. 1995. 'Somatexts at the Disney shop: Constructing the pentimentos of women's animated bodies', in Elizabeth Bell, Lynda Haas and Laura Sells (eds.) *From mouse to mermaid: The politics of film, gender, and culture.* Bloomington: Indiana University Press.

Brewer, Rose M. 1993 (1997). Theorizing race, class, and gender, in Rosemary Hennessey and Chrys Ingraham (eds.) *Materialist feminism: A reader in class, difference, and women's lives,* New York: Routledge.

Brown, Rita Mae. 1976. *A plain brown rapper.* Diana Press.

Bunch, Charlotte. 1975. Not for lesbians only. *Quest: A feminist quarterly,* (Fall).

Fjellman, Stephen. 1992. *Vinyl leaves: Walt Disney World and America.* Boulder, CO: Westview Press.

Giroux, Henry. 1994. Animating youth: The disneyfication of children's culture. *Socialist review,* 24 (3): 23–55.

Hoerrner, Keisha. 1996. Gender roles in Disney films: Analyzing behaviors from Snow White to Samba. *Women's Studies in Communication,* 19 (2), 213–228.

Ingraham, Chrys. 1999. *White weddings: Romancing heterosexuality in popular culture.* New York: Routledge.

Ingraham, Chrys 1994. The heterosexual imaginary: Feminist sociology and theories of gender. *Sociological Theory,* 12 (2, July): 203–219.

Jackson, Stevi. 1993. Love and romance as objects of feminist knowledge, in M. Kennedy, C. Lubelska and V. Walsh (eds.) *Making connections: Women's studies, women's movements, women's lives.* London: Taylor and Francis.

Kuenz, Jane. 1993. It's a small world after all: Disney and the pleasures of identification. *South Atlantic quarterly,* 92 (1): 78.

Redstockings. 1975. *Feminist revolution.* New York: Random House Press.

Rich, Adrienne. 1980. Compulsory heterosexuality and lesbian existence. *Signs,* 5 (Summer), 631–660.

Smoodin, Eric. 1994. *Disney discourse: Producing the magic kingdom.* New York: Routledge.

VanEvery, Jo. 1996. Heterosexuality and domestic life, in Diane Richardson, (ed.) *Theorizing heterosexuality*, Buckingham: Open University Press.

Weeks, Jeffery. 1996. The construction of homosexuality. in Steven Sideman. (ed.) *Queer theory/sociology*, MA: Blackwell Publishers.

Wittig, Monique. 1992. *The straight mind.* Boston: Beacon Press.

Zipes, Jack. 1995. Breaking the Disney spell, in Elizabeth Bell, Lynda Haas and Laura Sells. *From mouse to mermaid: The politics of film, gender, and culture.* Bloomington: Indiana University Press.

Zavarzadeh, Mas'ud. 1991. *Seeing film politically.* Albany: SUNY Press.

Notes

1. *Disney First Quarter Report*, February 2000.
2. Giroux, 1994; Bell, Haas, Sells, 1995; Smoodin, 1994; Fjellman, 1992
3. Hoerrner, 1996: 214
4. Redstockings, 1975; Rita Mae Brown, 1976; Charlotte Bunch, 1975
5. Rich, 1980
6. Wittig, 1992
7. Ingraham, 1994
8. Brewer, 1993
9. Ingraham, 1999
10. I watched each film a minimum of three times. The first viewing was merely the pictures without the sound. This allowed me to observe the ways in which the images, by themselves, create messages with regard to heterosexuality as well as hierarchies of race, class, gender, and sexuality. In the second viewing, I watched the film with sound only and no picture. This allowed me to focus on the actual words that were being said by each of the characters. The final viewing consisted of watching it in its entirety with both picture and sound. This allowed me to see how the images and sounds work together to present a complete picture.
11. Zipes, 1995: 21
12. VanEvery: 1996
13. Jackson: 1993
14. Ingraham, 1999: 139
15. Bell, 1995: 116
16. Bell, 1995: 119
17. Zavarzadeh, 1991: 93
18. Jackson, 1993: 42
19. Kuenz: 1993
20. Adorno and Horkheimer, 1944: 37

CHAPTER 9

Out of Wedlock: Why Some Poor Women Reject Marriage

MARGARET WALSH[1]

The latest U.S. Census Bureau survey reports that 4 million American households are made up of unmarried couples, a major increase over the last generation. About half of single women under 30 have lived with a man outside marriage at some time during their young adulthood. More than half of the couples who marry today will divorce, and women spend more years of their lives unmarried than married. About one in three births are to single women. Women raising children alone are far more likely to know poverty compared to any other group. What do these widely reported trends in marriage, cohabitation, and childbearing tell us?

In the 1990s, I explored the changing pattern of heterosexual relationships by interviewing working-class and poor women in their twenties and thirties on the topic of marriage and childbearing. These 50 young mothers lived in rural communities in the northeastern United States. Although not a statistically representative group, I selected them to illustrate the varieties of ways in which single women with children are coping outside of traditional marriage. The welfare reforms of 1996 overtly encouraged marriage as a solution to poverty, but these women knew better. They had no illusions about the connection between marriage and money in their own lives. Some of them had been married for a time. These women's experiences show that marriage does not bring them the security, stability, and respectability touted by conservative politicians. Poor women who marry the poor men in their neighborhoods do not benefit from the economic privileges that middle- and upper-class marriages promise: steady income, health care benefits, child support. Those benefits are reserved for women and children connected to men with a steady income who share their resources. The decisions that poor women in my sample made to marry and divorce (or to avoid marriage altogether and look for other sources of help as they raise their families) offer insights about economics and gender relations, about the growing independence of women, and their shrinking expectations of men.

Marsha's Story

Twenty-nine-year-old Marsha was born in New Hampshire, but she and her siblings rarely stayed in the same school for more than a year or two. Her father's work in the military transported the family to Texas, Arkansas, Missouri, Arizona, and California before he retired in the late 1980s to northern New England. Her mother used to say Marsha had "an adventurous soul" because she would hunt, fish, and explore whatever her new surroundings had to offer.

> I didn't stay long enough to make those kind of close friends but we were very lucky, you know, because some of the things we've seen, other people don't get to see in a whole lifetime.

Surprising her family and friends, Marsha settled down early. At 19, she was impressed by a burly 26-year-old man she met at the state fair and they dated for four months. At the time he worked at a construction job in another state, but he drove home on weekends so they could spend time together. The relationship progressed quickly. "One day he just flat-out asked me to marry him, and I don't know if it was because I was so young or if I was stupid or I was just love-blind or whatever they call it. I said yes." Marsha became pregnant with their first child within two months, and stopped working. Even before their baby was born, she worried that the marriage was a mistake. Most of their early problems were financial.

> I never knew where the money was going. He made eight dollars an hour at the time, which wasn't bad. I got $30.00 a week for grocery money and to pay whatever other bills that need to be paid. We had our water, gas, electricity, turned off quite often and there were times where I had to beg them to leave it on for maybe a day or two, until I could pay it, and sometimes they would because I had a small child.

They fought over money and never seemed to have enough. Her husband's view was that he should be able to support them without her working. Yet, he could not earn enough to pay the bills. So he blamed her for their troubles, and insisted that she do more with less. Marsha decided to work to supplement their income but it was a struggle: "Every job I had was sabotaged. He didn't want me doing what I wanted to do. He wanted me to do what he wanted me to do." Despite her own early wanderings, she planned to raise her family in one place, and she refused to give up on the relationship.

> My ex-husband couldn't pay bills and I couldn't figure out why we were always moving and then, when I figured it out, I took the checkbook away from him, but that still didn't work, so we ended up moving quite a bit while we were married.

The couple had two more children over a period of six years, but both Marsha and her husband were miserable:

> I got to the point when I didn't care anymore. I didn't care about the house. I didn't care about nothing. I lived in a house which had a hole in the floor, you know, almost two foot wide in all directions. I had to put a piece of plywood over it, so I wouldn't fall through. I would ask him, 'Fix this.' The sink was falling in. You'd sit on the toilet, and you'd have to hold on for dear life. I lived in an absolute shack and a lot of people thought it was all my fault.

The final break in the marriage came when he moved out of their house and in with a new girlfriend. Marsha recalls that when she filed for divorce she realized it was the first time she ever actively stood up for herself in the marriage. She won full custody of the children with the support of her ex-mother-in-law who testified on her behalf in divorce court, and then helped Marsha find a decent job. "She pointed me in the right direction and it was something I really needed and still, to this day, she says I'm her daughter."

After the divorce, Marsha worked 75 hours a week as a deli manager, trying to make ends meet. She was proud to have stayed off welfare at first. But "it got to the point where my babysitter finally told me one day that my son just walked alone for the first time. Now I had seen my older two kids walk so that really upset me." Coincidentally, Marsha was fired from her job the very next day because she told a supervisor that her manager was stealing money from the store. The date was December 24.

> I felt like the weight of the world had lifted off my shoulders and I went home, cooked Christmas dinner and, after the kids were asleep, I sat down and decided what I was going to do. I didn't want to go on welfare, but I knew, if I didn't, I would not get the education

> I needed to provide for my kids, because my ex-husband was not doing a great job. I got eighty dollars a week, child support, for all three of them and not apiece either.

In the three years since her divorce, Marsha has achieved many of the things she thought she would have accomplished during her eight-year marriage.

> Just sitting at the table every night, eating supper together, talking about the day, we didn't have that until I got a divorce. There was no structure. I was always wondering what was going on with him and I was trying to get everything settled at home and it was one thing after another. Now we have a decent house to live in, clothes for my kids, and food. And once we get home, from about three o'clock until 8 o'clock at night is time for my kids. You know, I didn't have that until I got divorced.

Marsha wants to graduate from college and find a decent job in the computer field.

> I want to be able to pay for everything, without having welfare nosing around in my business. I just want to be stable in my own life. I don't want somebody else providing for me, so if they leave, I'm not depending on their money to take care of me and my kids.

Marsha does have a new boyfriend who she describes as mainly a friend. "We've been close. But, it's not where he is living with me or anything. I don't want that. I've got my own place. I pay my own bills and that's the way I want it. And it's the same with him."

Why Marriage? Why Not?

Although the details differ, the theme of Marsha's story was repeated again and again in the interviews I conducted with young women about their relationships with men and their views of marriage. These were women I met at community colleges, childcare centers, and family health clinics. Like Marsha, some of the women who are now divorced had married young, often in their teens, to gain independence from parents or to fill the space after leaving high school. They married their first sexual partner, sometimes only after discovering an unplanned pregnancy. Without the resources to invest in a marriage—good jobs with benefits, money for a house, a rainy day fund—their hopes and expectations for the relationship plummeted. Their experience of failure reflected their gendered understanding of the marital roles of wife and husband, which neither was able to fulfill. As teenagers, they embraced idealized versions of the domestic and work spheres. Their men had not won enough bread, and they, as women, had not adequately made a home.

Marrying the First Guy Who Comes Along

Television soap operas feature romanticized images of married couples with leisure time, material possessions, and few responsibilities. The availability of contraception, the expansion of higher education, and the extension of "youth" from the teens to the mid-twenties in the United States have increased the age at which people make many life decisions. However, research studies suggest that most pregnancies (regardless of the race, age, or class of the mother) are "unplanned" in the sense that they are unexpected or ill timed. For some women marriage is the only answer to a pregnancy when it occurs unexpectedly. No other alternatives are considered because no other options exist at the moment. As one woman facing pregnancy at age 17 described it,

> I got married because I got pregnant and I wasn't doing it by myself. I wasn't going to have a child by myself. And also because the father of the child was not sexually abusive, physically abusive, emotionally abusive. I figured, 'I made the bed, I'll lie in it?'

In this example, the problem of single motherhood was "solved" by marriage. One of the main factors women considered when deciding about marriage was how a future husband would behave based on evidence from their courtship. Finding a man who was not abusive was "good enough" and she married him. However, this man did not have a steady job, and he was not involved with baby care. The mother was punishing herself for being irresponsible, and she was afraid of living alone. Eventually the couple divorced, however, and she did raise her child on her own.

Money Changes Everything

Poverty strains relationships; yet, sometimes women "try out" marriage believing the popular notion that it is the one solution to their problem. Just as many couples are programmed to believe that having children requires marriage, couples also come to think of the marriage as a means to prosperity. In the interviews I conducted, this myth dissolved as soon as poor couples crossed the marital threshold. In the scenario described above, the wife described coming home from her winter wedding to a trailer that had snow literally coming inside from the leaking roof and piling blanket on top of blanket for warmth. "I remember thinking, 'Is this what love is?' 'Cause this sure isn't what marriage is supposed to be. I didn't have a clue." Trying to keep warm in an unheated trailer was less than romantic and posed serious danger to their health and to the baby. Before long, they moved in with her parents, and the fighting began as they lost privacy and struggled under their new responsibilities as new parents themselves. Their increased dependence on family for financial help after the first child came ran contrary to everything they expected from marriage. The relationship never recovered and they split five years later. Another important factor in women's orientation toward marriage is their assessment of their parents' relationship and economic standing.

Changing Attitudes about Marriage

The women I interviewed talked at length about their parents and siblings, often comparing their families of origin to the households they formed when they had their own boyfriends, husbands, and/or children. In the 1960s and 1970s, their own parents married to bring security to their relationships and worked in steady manufacturing jobs to provide resources for their children. They wanted to earn enough to be able to purchase a home, a trailer, or a camp for their families. They wanted their children to have a better life than they had themselves. Not all families achieved this goal, however. Some parents went through periods of unemployment and hard times, hoping that things would eventually get easier. Some mothers tried to hide family problems and "make it okay." Even when their marriages were in trouble, most of the couples decided to stay together at least until their children grew up, especially those from religious backgrounds.

In early adolescence, these young women began to form their own ideas about the kind of adult they hoped to be. They saw their options for the future by looking at their older siblings and friends, and they received messages from important people in their lives—parents, relatives, and teachers. The quality of these interactions strengthened or diminished their aspirations, opened or closed their opportunities for the future. As teenagers, these women's friendships and their romantic relationships with men also began to shape their future.

The single women in my study who viewed marriage favorably shared similar family histories. The majority were raised by two adults with steady incomes, putting them in the solid working-class or lower middle-class categories. They grew up in large families with relatives living nearby. Most women reported seeing their grandparents on a regular basis. Often, they remembered visiting with cousins and other members of their extended families on Sunday afternoons after Church to share dinner before beginning another week. The parents of the women in my study had four or more children spaced close together. The community institutions surrounding these couples as well as their friends and families supported and encouraged the success of their marriages.

Only a few of the women had college-educated parents, but some of the women's fathers had spent time in the military, learned new skills, and "saw the world" for a couple of years. They married in their twenties, and saved for a house. Some lived at home with their parents for a few years to save money or to help out with younger brothers and sisters. Some ran small family businesses; or, fathers worked in manufacturing jobs with benefits and earned enough so that mothers could take breaks from work when their children were young. After graduating from high school, mothers worked as secretaries in a local business or sometimes in one of the many factories. The wives and husbands had different responsibilities, but they talked over and agreed on aims and goals for their family. They had high expectations for educating their children, and they earned enough money to pay their bills and make ends meet. These couples had the financial resources to care for their children, and with two parents, they had the luxury of spending time together, talking and listening to one another, and enjoying each other's company. In some sense, then, they resembled those idealized images of prosperity displayed by married couples on television and movies at the time. These marriages held their economic value and their emotional worth for the family and community.

By contrast, the women in my study who held unfavorable views toward marriage also shared some characteristics. As a group, they had parents with unsteady work histories and long periods of unemployment. Most of their parents did not finish high school, and they married young with few other options. Because neither parent had valuable work skills, the families had no choice but to move when a job opportunity arose. Few families owned any property at all, and some of their marriages broke up from economic pressures that led to constant arguments. As children, these women were more likely to spend time in single parent families or in "blended" families—with stepparents and stepsiblings. When one of their parents remarried, they often moved again to another home, where they had to adjust to a different school environment and make new friends.

Many of these women recalled that they felt uncomfortable at school, and they had too many burdens at home to care about doing well in school. They did not play sports or receive any special recognition, and they did not receive "the right kind" of attention from teachers in the classroom. Their parents may have been supportive but stressed themselves, and the girls heard all of the family fights and knew exactly how tight money was for the month. They felt they were "not like the other kids" who had new clothes and spending money while their mothers shopped at the Salvation Army and used food stamps at the grocery store. These households were overwhelmingly poor and struggling. While the marital relationships they described may have begun with love, romance, and emotional connections, they did not (could not?) hold their economic value to the couple, the family, and community. These families were poorer.

Life as a Wife: The Dream and The Reality

When I asked women about their family plans when they were younger, almost everyone recalled stories of playing with dolls and acting out the roles of Bride and Mommy with their school friends. But the dream and the reality were in conflict. As one woman put it, "I thought I'd have the house with the garden, the husband and kids, the white picket fence. You know. It didn't work out that way, but the next best thing is what I have now. I still have a family."

After becoming pregnant, the women did not know what to expect from motherhood but compared to their male partners, they felt ready for the responsibility. Some of the women worked as nursing assistants and preschool teachers, making enough for themselves but not able to easily support families alone. Most often, they described their former boyfriends and husbands as immature, unfaithful, and unemployed. Before entering marriage, these women looked for any alternatives that would help them stay single and set up independent households. For those with resources, this meant relying on their parents and extended families. For others, this meant settling for the men or relying on welfare, since their own families were usually too burdened to help them and their new child out.

Some women compared their own relationships to their parents' marriages, and they wondered if they could do better. For others, their relationships reminded them of their parents failed marriages, and they worried that their attempts at marriage would be doomed from the beginning. Because my study consists only of divorced, separated, or never married women, I am not able to compare these single women's histories to other couples who remained married. I also do not know how the male partners would describe their own feelings about these failed relationships. However, it is fascinating to consider how these young women's attitudes about future relationships have changed since their dreamy childhood. With the hindsight of divorce or the present struggle of raising young children outside of marriage, many women firmly rejected the possibility of marriage (or re-marriage) for themselves. They felt ambivalent about starting new relationships, and others were saddened that the "institution of marriage" had failed them.

> I am not in a hurry to get married. I'm still young. If this one works, fine. If it doesn't, I'll move on.

> It's a piece of paper. I feel if you love somebody, you don't need a piece of paper. You don't need to change your name. You don't need to go through all of that. It's good for your income tax—when you make your annual claim.

> I don't know about marriage…it's a total commitment and we need to be ready. That's your life partner from the wedding until you die, and I just think people say that without thinking about what it actually means.

One could argue that children require a larger (more demanding) commitment than marriage; yet, none of these women expressed regrets about motherhood. One woman said that if she were not a mother, "I probably wouldn't even be here. I'd probably be in a different state living a whole different life." Instead, they found that having children kept them "grounded" and helped them to aspire to higher standards for themselves and the men in their lives. They quickly moved beyond their early romantic visions of marriage and made a more realistic assessment of whether the benefits of marriage outweighed its limitations. When deciding about marriage, the women weighed their options—sized up the relationship with the child's father, consulted with their own parents and friends—and most did not marry. Others divorced within a few years. The ability to choose a life that was different from their own mothers' experience depended on how much assistance family members could offer, their own work opportunities, and educational prospects. Women who chose to head families alone over marriage were more likely to have support systems in place at the time they became pregnant.

Policies that advise poor young mothers to marry only reinforce inequalities that exist in the social structure. In these types of discussions, marriage is wrongly used as a proxy for economic stability. Women need good jobs of their own, not merely an available man, so they can make good family decisions for themselves. Poor young mothers, regardless of marital status, need better paying work, help with caring for children, and greater financial assistance so that they can pursue their own education. Marriage may—or may not—come later.

Notes

1. This essay draws on Walsh's *Mothers' Helpers: The Resources of Female Headed Households in a Working Class Community,* Ph.D. Dissertation, University of New Hampshire, 1997.

CHAPTER 10

The Production of Heterosexuality at the High School Prom

AMY L. BEST

The popular 1999 teen film, *Never Been Kissed*, is a romantic comedy about a young woman's self-discovery through her return to high school ten years after she has graduated. Set at South Glen, a fictional high school in the sub-urbs of Chicago, this film offers its audience a slice of suburban middle-class high school life. We watch students as they shuffle to and from class, throw food at each other in the cafeteria, and run laps for gym class. Significantly, in one of the final scenes of the film, we watch the senior class attend their high school prom. Traditionally defined as the culmination of high school, the prom is a critical scene. The students of South Glen have selected as their prom theme *"Made for Each Other: Famous Couples in History."* At the prom, we catch a glimpse of different couples from both his-tory's past and present: Adam and Eve, Martha and George Washington, Sonny Martha and George and Cher, Joseph and a very pregnant Mary all drift across the screen as we are presented with snapshots of the prom. The female protagonist and her date bring to life Shakespeare's Rosalind and Orlando. Even Disco Barbie and Disco Ken and Malibu Barbie and Malibu Ken are among the cast of characters.

As one might expect, each of the couples is a heterosexual pair, no one is dressed in drag and notably few students seem to attend alone. Normative heterosexuality is actively reinscribed through the film's prom scene in two distinct, though interrelated ways. While erasing the fact of queerness from the historical landscape, this scene also works to naturalize heterosexuality.

Heterosexuality is presumed to be enduring and timeless. In this way, this film, like so many other popular cultural images targeting teen audiences, reproduces heterosexuality as a normative feature of American cultural life of both past and present, and at the same time embeds heterosexual ideology within American mainstream youth culture.

Of course, one cannot help but wonder what might have happened had Disco Ken and Malibu Ken abandoned their Barbies to attend together? Or in keeping with an accurate historical record what might have happened had Virginia Woolf and Ethel Smyth danced the night away? Would the presence of queerness subvert the tyranny of heterosexuality in this space? Not likely. In fact, the film does offer a gratuitous clip of a group of young men walking into the prom dressed as *The Village People*, an all-male 1970s disco group generally acknowledged also to be an all gay group. The image of *the Village People* is a fleeting one perhaps included to evoke a few cheap laughs from the audience. Queer presence symbolized in the image of *the Village People* seems to resecure the prom as a heterosexual event more than possibly subverting it. This is because the *Village People* remain on the margins of this cultural space and few other queer signifiers are visible.

That the high school prom (as both representation and event) privileges heterosexuality seems almost too prosaic a claim to make. But it is the assumed transparence of heterosexuality in this cultural space that is so significant. Normative heterosexuality precisely because it is so obvious, is routinely ignored, ritually obscured, and in general taken for granted. As a result, heterosexual practices are rarely made problematic and in most cases the institution of heterosexuality escapes critical analysis.[1] The question then is not whether the high school prom upholds heterosexuality as a social institution; of course it does (although it would be difficult to argue that the practices that normalize heterosexuality through the prom are seamless in their operation). The reproduction of heterosexuality as a social institution may been seen in the organizational practices adopted by local schools, the prom-lore that pervades American popular culture, and in the interactional and discursive fields through which kids prepare for, attend, talk about, and even remember their proms. Many schools, including one that I studied, still require students to attend their proms with dates of the "opposite" sex, dress codes intended to prevent gender bending are regularly enforced, young women are still presented with corsages by their escorts, and young couples often dance their last dance to a song that celebrates heterosexual love.[2] The crowning of the prom king and queen is perhaps the most coveted practice of all prom rituals and one steeped in heterosexual pomp and circumstance. And while a lesbian may be crowned prom king (although apparently not prom queen) as in the recent case of one high school, make no mistake heterosexuality, as a social institution is rarely dethroned.

Proms privilege heterosexuality largely through the ability to repeatedly link the prom with a range of romantic symbols and signifiers. The idea of dreamy romance (traces of which are certainly visible in the film discussed above) is one of the central organizing concepts upon which meanings of the prom hinge. The image of the prom as a site of romantic possibility, where the promise of sweet love and tender affections infuse to create a magical night, is an enduring one in mainstream culture, telegraphed in the pages of teen magazines and teen films and embedded in the stories young men and young women tell about their proms.

Through its celebration of dreamy romance, the prom serves to draw young women and young men into a set of discursive relations that are central to the ongoing institutional operation of heterosexual dominance and the reproduction of gender identities and inequalities. In her examination of weddings, Chrys Ingraham (1999) refers to this process as the heterosexual imaginary at work.

> The heterosexual imaginary is that way of thinking that conceals the operation of heterosexuality in structuring gender (across race, class and sexuality) and closes off any critical analysis of heterosexuality as an organizing institution. It is a belief system that relies on romantic and sacred notions of heterosexuality in order to create and maintain the illusion of well-being. At the same time this romantic view prevents us from seeing how institutionalized sexuality actually works to organize gender while preserving racial, class and sexual hierarchies as well.[3]

It is the repeated invocation of romance without an interrogation of its cultural and political foundations that works to obscure the normative dimensions of heterosexuality while also stabilizing them. Largely relegated to the realm of feeling, romance is thought to be private, intimate, and above all else, outside the contested terrain of politics; in this way, it conceals the very political workings of domination it serves. Romance carries tremendous ideological force; it naturalizes and normalizes heterosexual and gender controls and shapes and organizes modern constructions of self.[4] Consider, for example, the following narrative written by a young African-American man about his prom. His narrative reveals the deep embeddedness of romance as it is defined at the prom within the institution of heterosexuality.

> The girl I went to my prom with was just one of my friends. So I knew nothing sexual was going to happen and didn't expect it to either. Having already established that, I was able to concentrate on

just having a good time instead of trying to figure out how to get her to do other things. We danced together and had a really good time. When I got to her house she was ready and looked pretty…. During the prom and in the limo we took pictures together. We laughed and danced. It felt awkward spending so much time with a girl that wasn't my girlfriend but treating her like she was. I had to keep reminding myself that it was her night too and it didn't make it better if I was constantly running off to dance with other girls.

Romance (and/or sex) seems remote; yet, even in its absence, hetero-romantic codes continue to organize the meanings he uses to narrate his prom and to define himself within this scene as a heternormatively masculine subject (that is, given that heterosexual conquest is defined as a normative masculine practice).[5] "I was able to have a good time instead of trying to…get her to do other things," the young man reveals. He also suggests that his prom is a departure from the more conventional romance narrative, insofar as actual romance never materializes. Yet, his account demonstrates the extent to which our ability to recognize this cultural event as "the prom" and not something else is reliant upon a very calculated and coordinated presentation of heterosexuality. "It felt awkward spending so much time with a girl who wasn't my girlfriend but treating her like she was." The idea that the prom requires a highly scripted performance is a theme that also presents itself in a number of prom magazines. Consider one prom article entitled, "Five Ways to Make Your Prom More Romantic:"

> Treat him like a real date (even if he's only a pal). That means holding back your urge to challenge him to an arm wrestle on the buffet table or keeping quiet when you want to gush about how hot other guys look in their tuxes. You may not be into locking lips with your date, but you can make him feel special by acting psyched to be there with him.
>
> *YM special prom issue* (1996)

As the article suggests what remains important is the public performance of hetero-romance. While the couple may not be intimately tied, what matters is the appearance that they are. Gender ideology is also relevant here inasmuch as this heteromantic performance depends upon a willingness to participate in the normalizing practices that uphold an organization of gender (The girl must censor her own sexual desire, discipline her body, and focus her attention on fulfilling her date's needs over her own).[6] The taken-for-granted rules of prom dating (as they are identified here) sustain the link between the prom and romance and ultimately preserve a discursive and material arrangement in which heterosexuality is the privileged form.

The idea that proms are sites of romantic promise is deeply entrenched within American popular culture. A range of media has provided a host of images of the prom that repeatedly draw upon a narrative of heteroromance to tell the story of the prom. The theme of prom romance has presented itself through a range of television sitcoms and dramas including *Beverly Hills 90210, Roseanne, That Seventies Show, Buffy the Vampire Slayer, Dawson's Creek, Boy Meets World, Saved by the Bell,* and *Sabrina the Teenage Witch.* Teen prom magazines such as *Seventeen, Young and Modern,* and *Your Prom* (the last of which is interestingly published by *Modern Bride*) repeatedly feature in their tables of contents articles that advise their readers (most of whom are female) how to navigate the often-perilous waters of prom romance. In page after page, heterosexual and gender ideology serve as the basis through which the coordinates of romance are mapped.[7] The use of heteroromantic codes may also be seen in scores of teen prom films such as *Pretty In Pink, Valley Girl, Footloose, 10 Things I Hate About You, Trippin', Never Been Kissed,* and *She's all That.* Predictably, the popular construction of the prom as a moment filled with romantic promise is also a gendered one; this narrative is almost always told through the voice of a girl and primarily centers on her struggle to makes sense of romance as it relates to her self identity.[8] Significantly, even the most astute reader of popular culture would be hard pressed to find an image that does not re-secure the prom as a fundamentally heteroromantic event entrenched in a logic of gender. As a consequence, our ability as readers of culture to think beyond the perimeters of heterosexual and gender conformity as we define romance at the prom or beyond is limited as we are rarely presented with alternatives to a heteroromantic template.

As a modern romantic comedy about coming of age around the prom, the popular 1999 teen film, *She's All That,* makes use of heterosexual and gender ideologies to tell its tale. This film firmly establishes romance as a heterosexual construct through its character depictions and the use of both a conventional romantic narrative and a counter narrative. Early in the film we meet Laney Boggs (played by Rachel Leigh Cook), a slightly offbeat girl, disinterested in the daily banter of "popularity," disaffected from school and alienated from her peers. By Hollywood standards, she is not your "typical" girl. Rather than shopping endlessly and fixated on romance like other (Hollywood) girls, Laney spends much of her time alone in the basement of her father's house painting. The meager social life she maintains exists outside school. (Despite her apparent failings as a teen beauty queen, given that this is a romantic comedy her heterosexuality is largely assumed from the beginning of the film, as it is assumed with all other characters in the film).

Laney's life takes a sudden turn when Zack Syler (played by Freddie Prinze Jr.), the most popular boy in school (who recently had been "dumped" by his long-time girlfriend and horribly wicked prom queen expectant), accepts a bet proposed by his best friend that he can turn even the most pitiful wallflower into the prom queen. Laney, unequivocally recognized as the weirdest girl in school, is chosen for the bet. With a mere six weeks before the prom, Zack gets to work: he enlists his sister to make her over into a teen beauty queen, and takes Laney to parties attended exclusively by the popular clique.

Determined to win the bet, Zack relentlessly pursues her. Inevitably and predictably, both Zack and Laney begin to realize their emerging affections for one another. But eventually, Laney learns the truth—her newfound popularity had been a ruse and the mysterious but welcomed attentions of Zack Syler had been the result of a cruelly inspired bet between two boys. Defeated, she returns to her artist's perch in the basement and denounces teen romance for what it is, a sham. She is determined not to attend her prom, even though she has been nominated for prom queen. However, on the night of the prom, Laney does end up attending her prom though not with Zack but with his friend, Dean, the very one who had initiated the bet in the first place. Unbeknownst to her, Dean plans to lure Laney to a hotel room for a night of sex following the prom.[9] When Zack learns of Dean's duplicitous plan, he frantically searches for them, calling every hotel in town in the hopes of foiling Dean's efforts and saving Laney. After a fruitless search, Zack arrives at Laney's house and waits for her return to avail himself and declare his love. She is surprised to find him at her home when she finally returns. "How long have you been here?" she asks. Realizing he has waited quite sometime, she questions, "You missed your prom?" as though to imply the magnitude of such a sacrifice and perhaps even the depths of his love. After a few moments of silence he remarks, "You know I made that bet before I knew you" (he pauses adding), "before I knew me." In the scene to follow, Zack and Laney dance their first dance together beneath a blanket of stars. Presumably overcome by this serendipitous turn of events at one point, starry-eyed Laney remarks, "I feel just like Julia Roberts in *Pretty Woman*, you know except for the whole hooker thing." Their eyes lock and they at last kiss.

What is interesting about this film is the fact that it draws upon competing ideological frames to construct its story (perhaps this accounts for its success as a film). On the one hand, this film incorporates liberal feminist themes about female empowerment and self-determination (like many teen films today). Even early in the film it is made clear that Laney embraces a form of feminist individualism. Laney in many ways is her own woman. At the prom she is not elected prom queen yet she seems to care little about her defeat. When Laney returns home after the prom, we also learn that she did not need to be saved by her prince as one might expect in a conventional romantic film. In fact she saved herself from the snare of Dean's sexual ruse. This we realize as she remarks to Zack with a deliberate frankness, "sexual harassment is still a big issue these days" as she opens her small evening purse to reveal a foghorn, which we then understand she used to ward off Dean's unwanted advances.

Yet, this film fails to challenge the heterosexual foundations upon which gender inequalities rely. While *She's all That* rewrites romance with attention to feminine independence, this film also paradoxically draws upon the familiar trappings of a Cinderella tale of heteroromance. In this way, *She's All That* works to privilege romantic love in the lives of young women and in so doing, solidifies the connection between romance and the construction of feminine subjectivity. Romance is narrowly defined as a distinctly heterosexual construct. This film naturalizes heterosexuality and recuperates heteronormativity, even as it works to challenge traditional gender ideologies about feminine acquiescence to romance. What is especially interesting about this film then, is its use of a model of feminist resistance to dominant gender ideologies to both stabilize and obscure heteronormativity. In the end, its use of liberal feminist notions is precisely what works to obscure the ways this film's narrative upholds heterosexuality as the taken-for-granted norm.

Ideologies of heteroromantic love also organize the popular 1999 teen film *Never Been Kissed* (as briefly discussed in the introduction to this chapter). This story revolves around Josey Geller (Drew Barrymore) who, eight years after her high school prom, works as a copy editor for her hometown newspaper. Just as in high school, she is nothing special. She leads an almost invisible existence, one without love. The absence of romance in her life is made clear early in the film. In one scene we watch her sitting alone on her couch doing needlepoint. As she finishes the needlepoint pillow she proudly displays her finished work to her cat, and then adds the pillow to the accumulating mound of needlepoint pillows already on her bed.

Like Laney's in *She's all That*, Josey's life takes an unexpected turn. She is given the opportunity to return to high school as an undercover investigative reporter to find out about teens today. However, once there, her peers remind her of the daily torment she previously endured as a teen herself. Through a series of flashbacks, we gain a sense of Josey's former high school self—a wallflower who somehow is undeserving of romance. In one flashback, she learns she has been asked to the prom by the most popular boy in school on whom she has a secret crush. Not realizing she is being set up for disappointment and humiliation, she readies herself for the prom. The audiences watches as she twirls before the mirror to admire the image she sees before her—a lucky girl who is about to be whisked off to her prom by a dreamy boy. The phone rings: it is her date calling her outside. Filled with the promise of a wondrous night of fairy tale romance, she rushes out to her front stoop and awaits his arrival. Yet instead of being presented with a corsage, as she had hoped, she is assaulted by raw eggs by her date. Devastated by this unexpected turn of events, she drops to the ground in tears as her date drives off with another girl to the prom.

Harboring this memory, years later, she admits she never fully recovered. Yet, it is also made clear that she has yet to abandon the hope of romance's eventual emergence. As one might expect, it is her return to high school and attending her prom that finally enables romantic love to flourish. In fact, her second chance at attending her prom brings her not only the man of her dreams (significantly her English teacher) but popularity, a prized prom date, and the much-coveted honor—the throne. Unlike her former wallflower self, this time she finds herself the unexpected recipient of male attention. On prom night, we find her once again on her front stoop awaiting the arrival of her date. As he nears in the limo, she shudders as the painful memory of her past prom is momentarily relived. Unlike the last time, she is presented with the long awaited corsage, finally getting to attend the prom escorted by a dream date. As an adult returning to high school, Josey Geller is given the opportunity to renarrate her past and rewrite her present. As is obvious, romance is central to this identity project.

Both *She's all That* and *Never Been Kissed* use heterosexual romance as the basis through which the characters resolve their own moral dilemmas. Josey, Laney, and even Zack struggle to find themselves and the three undergo a significant transformation in self-understanding as each film unfolds. Importantly, it is romantic love that leads to self-discovery. As Zack's remarks reveal, "You know I made that bet before I knew you, before I knew me." In this way, heteroromanctic ideology is upheld as central to self-formation.

Interestingly, a number of contemporary films draw upon the narrative of prom romance as a way to explore a broad range of social issues relevant to their teen and adult audiences alike. For example, the 1984 popular teen film *Footloose* starring Kevin Bacon addresses intergenerational conflict and teen censorship through the romantic relationship that develops between small town pastor's daughter and wild child and the brooding, city kid Bacon. The popular 1986 John Hughes movie *Pretty in Pink* makes use of hetero-romance ideology to explore and ultimately bridge the enormous class divide that separates Blane (Andrew McCarthy), an upper-crust "richie" shrouded in unshackled privilege, and Andy (Molly Ringwald), a saintly but poor girl from the wrong side of the tracks. Heterosexual romance, as it unfolds around the prom, functions in this film to resolve the ongoing class tensions between the ruling-class richies and the disaffected underclass of freaks and geeks of the teen world.

While not a film specifically about the prom, the blockbuster hit *What Women Want* (released in 2000 starring box office hard-hitters Mel Gibson and Helen Hunt) uses the prom as a way to work through the relationship between father and daughter. This film revolves around Nick Marshall, an insensitive, pompous middle-aged Casanova and misogynist advertising executive who has little understanding of or interest in *what women want*, including his estranged fifteen-year-old daughter, Alex, a young woman in her own right. His relationship with his daughter is clearly strained as her anger toward him is regularly displayed in scenes in which the two are featured (she often glibly addresses him as "Uncle Dad" or plainly Nick). This all changes, however, on one fateful night when he is sent home by his new boss (Helen Hunt), for whom he demonstrates considerable disdain simply because she is a woman, with a box of feminine consumer products: antiwrinkle cream, a waxing kit, pantyhose, bath beads, and a padded bra. In an attempt to get inside women's heads, he uses each of the products as he downs a bottle of red wine. He is accidentally electrocuted and when he awakes the following morning, he realizes he is able to access the most private and intimate thoughts of women, including the secret thoughts of his own daughter. He realizes that his daughter largely considers him a pompous jerk and pathetic father. Through a series of comic scenes with different women, he learns what women really think about him: he is bad in bed, his cologne is too strong, and his jokes are sexist. As he peers at himself through the eyes of these women, he realizes he is not the man he thought he was. He also comes to develop a sense of empathy for women, a quality he sorely lacked. In listening to the most private thoughts of women, he begins to understand the difficulty of being "the modern woman" (defined through this film by the struggle to balance the often opposing demands of being a woman and a professional success) and the internal strife this produces.[10] Through his daughter, he learns about the struggles of *becoming* a woman. In one scene, Nick takes his daughter shopping for a prom dress where he learns she is a virgin but plans to have sex on prom night with her eighteen-year-old boyfriend, Cameron with whom she is falling in love. "I can't believe this is the dress I'll be wearing as my last night as a virgin," she excitedly utters to herself as she stands before the mirror. With these words, Nick falls out of his chair onto the floor of the department store dressing room.

But on the night of the prom Alex decides she is not ready to have sex. Her boyfriend is enraged by her decision and abandons her on the dance floor to make out with another girl. Her romantic hope shattered, Alex retreats to the bathroom and sobs in a bathroom stall for the remainder of the prom. Oddly enough, it is Nick who comes to her rescue offering these reassuring words as he parks himself in the bathroom stall next to hers,

> Oh honey, I'm so sorry but believe it or not I know what it's like to be a woman. It's not as easy as it looks. And you stood up for yourself. You know how ahead of the game you are. You are so much smarter than me. And look at you, that clown made out with a girl with a tongue ring over you. Honey, you look beautiful.

"Thanks Dad," she responds and the scene concludes as Nick gently tucks his daughter into bed.

While this is a film ultimately about a man's struggle to be a better man, it makes use of the "teen" dilemmas around romance (through the prom) to explore the nature of this struggle. Nick becomes a better man as he learns to listen to his daughter, to empathize with her struggles, and to identify with her reality as a young woman in search of love. But, in the process, this film upholds the notion that heteroromance (specifically as it emerges around the prom) is central to becoming a woman. This film repeatedly draws upon a familiar gender trope: men are cavalier pigs and women hopeless romantics. It is the pursuit of sex that blinds all men and it is the work of women to guide them on the path to moral goodness. The assumption at work here is that men and women are cut from a different cloth. In these ways, this film naturalizes ideologies of gender difference and upholds a gender order in which heterosexuality is the privileged ground where identity struggles are played out and ultimately resolved.

Given the repeated invocation of romance and the prom in a range of popular cultural sites, it is not surprising that many young women would also draw upon these discursive codes as they narrate their proms. The theme of heteroromantic love pervaded young women's accounts as they discussed their prom experiences. Consider the following narratives both offered by two young women:

> As a little girl, I always fantasized about this famous night where I would resemble Cinderella in my gown, with my best friends at my side as we all prepared for a night out at New York City.... My Romeo-type boyfriend that showers me with flowers and compliments me the whole night through. Nothing would go wrong on prom night and "perfect" would be the only word to describe it.
>
> Asian-American female

I remember commenting that night that I felt like a princess and that I wished I got this type of treatment all the time. It is only one of the nights where the guys actually seemed to care if you are having fun or not. Everyone should feel that special. Those nights are some of the only nights where girls are treated like ladies.

European-American female

As in cultural representations, romance is interpreted as a critically important part of the prom. Conjuring the familiar image of the princess at the ball, both young women narrate their prom within a fantasy of heterosexual romance and significantly, respect. For the second young woman writer, the prom signifies a momentary escape from her ongoing relations with boyfriends and other male peers that she implies is distinctly different from the usual night out.[11] Here, but not elsewhere, girls are treated with kindness and care. Significantly, girls' discussions of romance tended to center on their being the recipients of boys' "kind" treatment.[12] Consider another narrative written by a young white woman:

I remember I almost didn't have a date. I ended up asking and going with my ex-boyfriend. The actual event was really fun. He was being really nice to me and a perfect gentlemen. We ended up being picked as one of the best looking couples at the event.

While simply having a date enables girls to gain legitimate entry to the space of the prom, having a "good" date, one who showers you with kindness and respect, serves as a resource through which girls evaluate themselves along a continuum of heterosexual desirability. For many young women, having a "good" prom date was internalized as a means both to measure their feminine self-worth and solidify their heterosexual identities. Again, hetero-romance is central to girls' identity projects.

But these girls must read for romance; some found romantic meaning in the gestures their dates made toward them. One young woman wrote, "My prom experience was very typical. When he came to the door he gave me a kiss on the cheek and a single long stemmed rose." Another girl wrote, "Since it had gotten chilly, my date let me wear his jacket." As consumers of popular romance, these two girls were able to recognize these gestures as acts of chivalry through which romance can be experienced. Compare their accounts to those found in one prom magazine article titled, *Romance: Your Mushiest Prom Night Moments*: "He suddenly put his arms around my waist and pulled me in tight—it sent shivers up my spine!", "He took my hand in his and looked deep into my eyes and said that he loved me! I was so incredibly happy I started to cry." The similarities are striking.

In recognizing these gestures as important, these girls are able to locate their prom experience within a specific discourse of romance organized primarily around chivalry and sexual innocence. While drawing upon such symbols provides girls with neatly packaged meanings of what the prom is, offering them codes to define particular relations or utterances as romantic, the use of such symbols also secures young women's consent to heterosexual dominance. The promise of heterosexual romance in this space becomes a powerful ideological tool. The sheer delight and pleasure with which some girls spoke about these romantic interludes offers testimony of the productive power of the heterosexual imaginary. Heterosexual dominance is secured not through force but through pleasure. And girls actively participate in its reproduction.

Through the use of romance ideology, the prom works to secure girls' consent to prevailing feminine forms and reproduce the institution of heterosexuality. However, their investment in heterosexual romance, precisely because of its connection to their feminine identities, forces many to forfeit their claims for equality in this space. This can been seen most vividly in the tales in which girls' romantic hopes never materialize. Their stories of romance gone awry not only demonstrate the unequal power relations that are secured through a sexual order that both relies upon and upholds heterosexuality, but the ways in which romance ideology produces feminine subjects within gendered hierarchy.[13] Consider the following account by one white girl who went to the prom with her former boyfriend:

> Afterwards we went to a friend's house where everyone was getting together. I'll never forget that part. My date ended up with another girl at the party. They were in the dark room together all night. I was so devastated. Ironically quite a few girls also got dumped by their date that night! We all tried to make the best of the situation and ended up having fun overall.

This girl's reaction is revealing. Although upset with the outcome of the evening, she accepts her date's action, which admittedly may be easier for her to do as she suggests other young women found themselves in similar situations. What is most interesting here is her tone of resignation. It is partly through girls' resignation that power is concentrated in the hands of these young men and normalized as a fundamental feature of heterosexual dating.

Another narrative written by a white girl tells of a similar series of power struggles that led to romance unrealized.

> I went to the prom with my boyfriend of three and a half years. It was a nightmare. I was class president and had many responsibilities to

take care of during the night. However, my boyfriend became angry because he wanted me by his side all night. So after the prom a group of us rented a hotel room and after we got there, he and a few friends got back into the limo and left. He came back two hours later drunk. What a lovely night. Needless to say the $350.00 dress was a waste and all the hype of a romantic night was quickly diminished.

In this girl's narrative, contradictory readings of prom romance produce an irresolvable conflict between her and her date. For her, there is room for romance and friendship, sociability and school duties. His expectation of romance, according to her, is that she will be by his side throughout the night, and refuse all other commitments. Interference by others encroaches upon his vision of a romantic night, while her expectation of romance can be reconciled with her other responsibilities. Because she is unwilling to meet his demands, this seemingly retaliatory act (getting drunk after the prom) spoils the possibility for romance after the prom.

Although many girls carefully tried to manage these dating relations, often their efforts were unavailing. Another young white woman wrote:

I went to my junior prom with my boyfriend at the time and another couple that we were really good friends with. We had it planned out and thought it was going to be great but it ended up a disaster. The couple we went to the prom with were Harry and Michelle and my boyfriend's name was Bill. Harry had a yacht so before the prom we went to the yacht (all dressed for the prom) and took the yacht to a restaurant across the lake. This sounded like it was going to be so much fun but it turned out it was very windy that day. As we were going on the lake in the yacht that wind was messing up my hair and water was coming up onto the yacht because Harry's father was going too fast. So right off the bat I was in a bad mood because I had spent so much time doing my hair for the prom and it was a mess. We docked the boat and went into a beautiful restaurant on the water. Sounds nice but Harry didn't really want to be at the prom a long time so he tried to take his time eating and ordering more food to drag it out as long as possible. This made me nervous because I wanted to go to the prom. We got to the prom late. My boyfriend would hardly dance, took a limo back to the yacht to stay the night and got into a big fight.

While her story begins to clarify the extensive work girls do to create "the" perfect romantic night and its importance to the project of heteronormative femininity, more significantly, it sheds light on the ongoing operation of masculine power within the context of heterosexual dating, how it works, and is sustained through a series of minor events: Harry prolongs dinner, causing them to arrive late at the prom and, once there, her boyfriend was unwilling to dance.

What is not addressed in the narratives written by these young women is how romance works to gain young women's consent to the ongoing production of gender inequalities, while also normalizing heterosexuality. The discourse of romantic love, as it comes into being around the prom, restricts girls' claims for equality in heterosexual dating relationships. As feminist scholars have long argued, ideologies of heterosexual romance and girls' investments in romantic ideals work to uphold traditional conceptions of femininity and as a consequence diminish the sense of power young women may claim in their heterosexual relationships with young men.[14] As a result, girls rarely enter their relationships with their dates with the same level of power whether at the prom or beyond. The struggle for girls to claim equality in their dating relations often requires that they forfeit the promise of heteroromance. If girls challenge the power boys exercise over them at the prom, this often requires that they also construct alternative understandings of themselves as gendered subjects.

If romance is contingent upon the display of kindness and care by boys toward girls in this space as I suggested earlier, then, outward challenges to boys' insensitivity by girls would undermine their public performance as girls deserving of boys' kind treatment. Ultimately, their status as feminine girls depends upon the public management of boys' romantic gestures. This is central to the hetero-romantic performance of the prom. Being treated well by a date in front of an audience of their peers seems to matter most, and many girls are simply unwilling to undermine the public performance of romantic affection (or relinquish the hope for its eventual emergence) for greater equality.

But some girls do pursue dates for reasons other than romance, or reject them altogether. In doing so, they often struggle to rework the social and discursive practices that define romance. Many girls reject the promise of hetero-romance in favor of dates who would maximize their ability to socialize. In selecting dates, consideration of how their dates might navigate local school relations was important for two young women of color whom I interviewed:

> SJ: Bringing somebody that doesn't go to the school, it's also difficult because you're pretty much in a womb…. It's hard bringing somebody from [another] atmosphere into this one because then they don't know anybody so, now you want to get up and you want to dance and…
>
> KL: Socialize.

SJ: And you can't because he's there and he's like, "wait a minute you're leaving me by myself." I know some girl, she brought her boyfriend to the prom, he didn't dance with her one time.

> KL: He sat down the whole time.

SJ: He didn't dance with her the whole time and that, wait a minute you're going to her prom and you're not going to dance and she had to sit there with him…. And then you're stuck and he rains on your parade too.

These two young women approach the prom pragmatically, offering the story of another girl whose prom was ruined by her date's unwillingness to dance as confirmation that girls who privilege hetero-romance are usually disappointed. They are more concerned with having fun than with negotiating the burdens of heterosexual dating. Separating romantic success from prom success, they contradict the dominant construction of the prom as a romantic space.

Other girls also rejected the romantic meanings attached to the prom. As a young white woman explained during an interview,

> I think the nice thing about the prom is it's generally treated as something special but also sort of more casual. They [the school] don't play it up to be a big romantic night, maybe like they do at some dances. If it were built up as a very romantic thing I don't think I'd be very comfortable because I don't have romance (laughs). But I like that fact.

Another white girl wrote:

> I didn't go with my boyfriend of two years because he had already graduated and didn't want to go again. So I went with one of my best guy friends I had known since about second grade. I also went with my best friend and one of our close guy friends. Both the guys are hilarious. I swear they could be comedians. Anyway I remember having so much fun hanging out with those guys before we even got to the prom. They are so nice. No one was trying to impress anybody. Out of the two proms I went with my boyfriend trying to be romantic, I definitely had more fun with my friends who didn't care.

This young woman's narrative, which privileges friendship and sociability over romance, hints at how the expectations of romance and efforts to create hetero-romance at the prom is work that can be labor intensive. Indeed, as a number of feminist scholars have argued, romance ideology works to reproduce a gender division of labor. An Asian American young woman expressed a similar unwillingness to do the work of dating at the prom.

> I ended [up] going to the prom with a friend. I got asked out by a couple of guys I knew but I wasn't really interested. I thought that if I went with a date "date," it would mean that I would be "stuck" with that person the whole night.

Some girls forsake romance at the prom because of the difficult ground they must cover in managing their public sexual identities and their feminine identities as was the case with this young Latina,

> Sometimes it's just better to go with a friend because you know he dances, or meet there or something because you dance. Nobody's to say who's that? Why are you dancing that close to him?

While many young women express deep investments in the heteromantic codes organizing the prom, other young women refuse to read the prom as a romantic moment largely because romantic dating seemed too complicated and messy for them. Alluding to the work required to participate in a hetero-romance, one young woman wrote,

> I went to the prom solo. Everyone was talking about me behind my back and felt sorry for me. BLAH, BLAH, BLAH. I was excited. I had no worries of what corsage to get, how to act fake, and that social concept of what to wear.

Her narrative works to expose the performance the prom requires.

Proms are moments when ideologies of gender, romance, and heterosexuality intersect often in contradictory ways. Some girls reject romance at the prom to avoid these conflicts. Much is at stake for these girls. Girls must manage their sexual reputations and sexual identities in this highly public scene. Sometimes, it is easier to simply abandon romance. But there is also a sense that these girls are silencing their own desires in doing so. "My date was trying to get me to sleep with him but I was not in the mood for his 'bull.' I had no intention of sleeping with him at all, because I did not trust him." This young African-American woman did not have sex, not because she did not want to, but because she did not trust her prom date.

How young women's talk about romance, while varied, reflects their understandings of themselves as feminine within a culture in which heterosexuality, though conventionally understood as an expression of the "natural", is a profoundly social practice secured and upheld through a range of social processes, including but not limited to the prom.[15] Whether romance materializes or not, the high school prom is an important space where young women (and young men) as they make sense of gender and heterosexual cultural codes embed these codes within their everyday lives. While some young women rejected romance, their rejections should not be conflated with a disavowal of heterosexuality. Few girls outwardly challenged heterosexuality as the taken-for-granted norm, even though many of these young women were clearly limited by it.

The high school prom is an iconic event in American culture, one that is consistently drawn upon in contemporary media to show the triumphs and travails of youth. One need only take a cursory look at the profuse media images that depict the prom to gain a sense of this event's importance not only to lives of teens but also to American cultural life. The idea of dreamy romance is one of the key organizing concepts upon which meanings of the prom rest. Through an examination of various popular cultural sites, this chapter has examined how heterosexuality is privileged in this space through the repeated use of romantic symbols and signifiers. I have argued that these images not only depend upon our culture's willingness to accept heterosexuality as a "natural" given but also *confirm* and *reify* this reality. Proms have been made meaningful in the wider culture through a heteronormative lens.

In addition to identifying how the prom is linked to romance through popular cultural representations, this chapter also makes visible how heterosexuality is discursively produced and legitimized through girls' talk about the prom. Young women constructed and drew upon a range of meanings to make sense of their romantic relationships at the prom, and subsequently themselves as heterosexual and gendered. Many drew upon conventional romantic codes to make sense of this event, suggestive, I would argue, of their deep investment in the discursive forms that frame heterosexual romance in American culture. In doing so, they upheld the conception of the prom as a fundamentally heterosexual space. I have also suggested that as young women define the meaning of the space of the prom, they are also defining themselves within the cultural perimeters of femininity. This meaning-making process is central to the ongoing operation of heterosexual dominance. Young women's investments, I have argued, stem in part from their investment in a set of discursive codes through which femininity is made publicly meaningful. However, as a consequence of such investment girls must forfeit their claims to gender equality within the context of their heterosexual relationships. The lack of agency some of these girls exerted as they narrated their proms is revealing. It is suggestive, I would argue, of the feminine acquiescence embedded in the cultural narrative of heterosexual romance.

Perhaps, this explains why other young women rejected romance. For these girls, a discourse of romance worked to silence their expressions of self. Unwilling to be implicated in an organization of unequal power or navigate the messy field through which girls' sexuality gets defined, some girls abandoned a project of romance, although not heterosexuality itself. While not fully undermining the construction of the prom as a romantic space, their readings of this event force a space for cultural codes formed around gender could be debated and quite possibly reworked. However, it is also clear that their rejections of romance are not refusals of heterosexual complicity. These young women actively reinscribe normative heterosexuality inasmuch as the connection between romance ideology and heterosexual ideology is left unaddressed.

Lastly, this analysis also has implications for understanding the social practices that entrench heterosexual dominance within American institutions, specifically American high schools (although precisely how this works is beyond the scope of this chapter). It is difficult to argue that the ideology of heterosexual normativity as it takes shape through the prom is seamless in its scope. Certainly the idea that proms uphold heterosexuality as a social institution in uncontested ways has been complicated by the recent emergence of the "gay prom" and the struggles of queer students to attend their own school proms. While the prom normalizes and institutionalizes heterosexuality, this cultural event has been taken up by queer kids as a space to solidify their identities *as* queer kids and contest heterosexuality as a taken-for-granted cultural practice. While certainly not debunking the tyranny of heterosexuality, what may be drawn from the case of gay proms is that young men and young women do not passively accept sexual scripts formalized through the high school prom (or any other cultural event for that matter) with complete unanimity. The very practices that are intended to inculcate individuals to dominant culture are always negotiated and every once in a while give rise to resistance. Queer proms exemplify a political strategy to take a cultural resource belonging to heterosexual society and use it to expose and challenge its hegemony. What can be argued then is that an event like the prom, as it comes into being through the relations and talk of its participants, embeds normative meanings about heterosexuality and gender in school and the culture beyond. Young women (and young men) come to understand their experiences and identities in terms of these cultural meanings and in this way, sustain the culture of high school as a heterosexual one in which heterosexuality and gender inequality are normative features. Significantly, it becomes virtually impossible for young men and young women to narrate this school event and thus, their schooling and their identities without mention of gender and heterosexual codes. Even in the case of students who reject romance at the prom, they must still use hetero-romantic themes to narrate and interpret this school event and themselves as young men and young women.

Struggles to redefine romance continue to take shape within a larger set of institutional and ideological forces that may allow for some room, but also continue to secure, naturalize, and institutionalize romance as a mechanism of gender and heterosexual controls. Understanding how events like the prom legitimate specific ideological practices through its celebration of heterosexual romance is important to understanding how identities and cultural meanings are constructed and secured through day-to-day life in contemporary American institutions.

References

Best, Amy L. 2000. *Prom night: Youth, schools, and popular culture.* New York: Routledge.

Butler, Judith. 1990. *Gender trouble: Feminism and the subversion of identity.* New York: Routledge.

Cancian, Francesca. 1987. *Love in America: Gender and self-development.* Cambridge: Cambridge University Press.

Christian Smith, Linda. K. 1993. Voices of resistance: young women readers of romance fiction, in Michelle Fine and Lois Weis (eds.) *Beyond silenced voices: Class, race, and gender in United States schools.* Albany, NY: State University of New York Press.

Connell, R. W. 1995. *Masculinities.* Berkeley: University of California Press.

Durham, Meenakshi, Gigi. 1998. Dilemmas of desire: representations of adolescent sexuality in two teen magazines, *Youth and society,* 29(3): 369–389.

Eder, Donna, Evans Catherine Colleen and Stephen Parker. 1995. *School talk: Gender and adolescent culture.* New Jersey: Rutgers University Press.

Fine, Michelle. 1993. Sexuality, schooling and adolescent females: the missing discourse of desire, in Michelle Fine and Lois Weis (eds.) *Beyond silenced voices: Class, race and gender in United States Schools.* Albany, NY: State University of New York Press.

Fricke, Aaron. 1984. *Reflections of a rock lobster: A story about growing up gay.* Boston: Alyson.

Granello, Darcy Haag. 1997. Using Beverly Hills, 90210 to explore developmental issues in female adolescents, *Youth and society,* 29(1): 24–53.

Holland, Dorothy C. and Margaret A. Eisenhart. 1991. *Educated in romance: Women, achievement and college culture.* Chicago: University of Chicago Press.

Illouz, Eva. 1997. *Consuming the romantic utopia: Love and the cultural contradictions of capitalism.* Berekely: University of California Press.

Ingraham, Chrys. 1999. *White wedding: Romancing heterosexuality in popular culture.* New York: Routledge.

Krisman, Anne. 1987. Radiator girls: the opinions and experiences of working class girls in an East London comprehensive, *Cultural studies,* 1: 219–230.

Leahy, Terry. 1994. Taking up a position: discourse of femininity and adolescence in the context of man/girl relationships, *Gender and society,* 8(1): 48–72.

Lesko, Nancy. 1988. The curriculum of the body: lessons from a catholic high school, in Leslie G. Roman and Linda Christian-Smith (eds.) *Becoming feminine: The politics of popular culture.* London: The Falmer Press.

Mac An Ghaill, Mairtin. 1994. *The making of men: Masculinities, sexualities and schooling.* Buckingham: Open University Press.

McRobbie, Angela. 1991. *Feminism and youth culture: From Jackie to just seventeen.* Boston: Unwin Hyman.

McRobbie, Angela and Jenny Garber. 1981. Girls and subcultures, in Angela McRobbie (ed.) *Feminism and youth culture: From Jackie to just seventeen.* Boston: Unwin Hyman.

Orenstein, Peggy and the American Association of University Women. 1994. *School girls: Young women, self-esteem and the confidence gap.* New York: Doubleday.

Proweller, Amira. 1998. *Constructing female identities: Meaning making in an upper middle class youth culture.* Albany, NY: State University of New York Press.

Radway, Janice. 1984. *Reading the romance: Women, patriarchy and popular literature.* Chapel Hill: University of North Carolina Press.

Roman, Leslie G. and Linda Christian-Smith (eds.) 1988. *Becoming feminine: The politics of popular culture.* London: The Falmer Press.

Thomas, Calvin (eds.). 2000. *Straight with a twist: Queer theory and the subject of heterosexuality.* Urbana, IL: University of Illinois Press.

Thompson, Sharon. 1995. *Going all the way: Teenage girls' tales of sex, romance and pregnancy.* New York: Hill and Wang.

Tolman, Deborah L. 1994. Doing desire: adolescent girls' struggle for/with sexuality, *Gender and society,* 8(3): 324–342.

Walkerdine, Valerie. 1990. *Schoolgirl fictions.* London: Verso.

Notes

1. I say in most cases because the emergence of the gay prom in the mid-1990s, while a marginalized cultural event, presents challenges to the absolute power of heteronormativity as it is secured through the prom.
2. School mandates requiring compulsory heterosexuality at the prom were legally challenged in 1981 in the Rhode Island Supreme Court by Aaron Fricke, a gay student who sued his school to attend the prom with another gay young man. The courts protected Fricke's right to attend his prom as gay young man under the First Amendment's freedom of expression. See Fricke (1984).
3. Ingraham, 1999: 16
4. See, for example, Cancian (1987); Holland and Eisenhart (1991); Illouz (1997); Ingraham (1999); McRobbie and Garber (1981); Radway (1984); Thompson (1995).
5. I borrow the term "heteronormatively masculine subject" from Calvin Thomas (2000), which is a term he uses to talk about straight masculinity. See also Connell (1995) and MacAn Ghaill (1994) for an examination of masculinity as it intersects with heterosexuality.
6. For a more in-depth examination of the ways in which gender ideologies organize young women's conditions of existence, see Eder et al. (1995); Granello (1997); Krisman (1987); Proweller, (1998); Roman and Christian-Smith (1988); and Walkerdine (1990).
7. See Durham (1998) for a further examination of the ways in which sexual desire and romance are mapped through girls' fashion magazines. For a more general discussion of the social organization of girls' sexual desire, see Fine (1993); Lesko (1988); and Tolman (1994).
8. Proms are constructed as feminine sites where girls are expected to be especially invested. It is largely a consequence of this gendered organization that I have decided to focus this analysis on girls, the heterosexual organization of the prom, and the ideologies of romance. Analyses of prom ideology as it intersects with romance ideology sheds significant light on ways in which girls in particular are drawn into a set of social/discursive relations that maintain an order of gender and heterosexuality.
9. In popular cultural texts, the narrative of sex on prom night is also an important one. So fundamentally part of our cultural prom lore, this theme has appeared in countless TV shows such as *Roseanne, Beverly Hills 90210, That Seventies Show,* and *Boy Meets World,* and in a number of Hollywood films including: *She's All That, She's Out of Control,* and *Peggy Sue Got Married.* In the 1999 teen film, *American Pie,* the entire premise is based on the four male characters losing their virginity before prom night. In most of these TV shows and films, sex is set up in opposition to romance. The narrative of sex on prom night is often told through the voices of the male characters.
10. The class assumptions should not be overlooked here. This film, like so many others, narrowly defines the identity struggles of all women based upon a set of struggles that is largely specific to professional middle-class women. In this way, this film generalizes the experiences of all women, thereby overlooking the significant class, race, and sexual differences that shape the realities of American women in contemporary society.

11. Christian-Smith (1993) has argued in her research on romance readership among girls that many girls derive pleasure from reading romance novels precisely because they do *not* mirror their actual lives.

12. Rarely did girls raise the issue of sex or discuss their own sexual desire or sexual agency. For many of the girls in this study, romance is constructed in opposition to sex. As Leahy (1994) argues, tenderness and attention to girls' emotional desires instead of their sexual desire pattern ideal romantic moments (which are admittedly shaped by middle-class notions of love and courtship).

13. For an examination of the production of gender within hierarchical binary, see Butler (1990).

14. See, for example, Holland and Eisenhart (1991); Orenstein (1994).

15. This chapter is part of a larger study focusing on how the high school prom operates as a space where kids make sense of what it means to be young in culture today, negotiate the process of schooling, solidify their social identities, and struggle against forms of authority. See Best (2000), *Prom Night: Youth Schools and Popular Culture*. This study draws upon a range of materials for analysis, including observation, in-depth and informal interviewing, archival and contemporary documents, and narrative analysis, although for my purposes here I rely primarily on interview and narrative data gathered between 1995 and 1998. I collected seventy-three narratives written by college students, largely first-year students, about their memories of their high school proms in 1995 and 1996. Narratives were between one-half and one and one-half pages long. Of these narratives, European-American women wrote forty-two. I collected nine narratives written by African-American women, five by Asian-American women, and two narratives from Latinas. I collected fifteen narratives by young men: two Asian-American, ten European-American, two African-American young men, and one Latino. I asked students to write about their prom memories, leaving it open so that students could identify those issues most relevant to their own prom experience. Students constructed their narratives around a range of themes relating to proms: some focusing on their preparations for the prom, some writing about their school's social structure, and others centering their narratives on the post-prom events. Many young women wrote about the difficult process of choosing a dress, while others wrote about their romantic expectations of the prom.

I also conducted twenty-two in-depth interviews with (11) male and (11) female high school students, mostly seniors, before and after their prom. I interviewed one Latina and five African-American young women, one of whom is bi-racial but identifies herself as African American. Five interviews were conducted with European-American girls. Of the young men interviewed, four were African American, one Latino, one Asian American, and five were European Americans.

This chapter also draws from ethnographic research conducted at four different public high schools. While this analysis relies less on the ethnographic data I collected, some mention of the schools is important given that that most of the kids I interviewed attended one of the four schools studied. While similar in some ways, these schools differed by curriculum, setting, and the race and class composition of their students. Woodrow High School is located in a mid-sized city and is racially, ethnically, and class mixed. Hudson, situated in a large urban setting, is a racially and class integrated school. Rudolph, a suburban high school, is predominantly European American and upper-middle class. Stylone, recognized as one of the most academically rigorous public schools in the United States, is comprised of primarily Asian- and European-American students, most of whom are middle or upper-middle class. In addition to attending these schools' proms, I made several visits to the schools, talking with students before and after the prom and observing their preprom and postprom activities. Observing at these schools in their cafeterias, their hallways, and at their preprom events in the weeks before prom night, I had the opportunity to speak informally with scores of students about proms, school, dating, popularity, life after high school, prom dresses, being young, and life in their local communities.

CHAPTER **11**

Speak Now or Forever Hold Your Peace: The Filming of "Wedding Advice"

KAREN SOSNOSKI

Episode 1: Wedding Dreams and Fantasies

Carole wacey (age 33)
I can remember as a child you put the towel on your head and you
wrap it on and you walk down the aisle and you have a great time.
I think most young girls do that—You always have that sort of idea
it's way off in the future.

Mikah larsen (age 9)
This is Colleen [holds up a Barbie doll]. She looks like a horseback
rider, but she's really a reverend. She's the only one of my Barbies
that looks like a reverend. In the church, Barbie—I mean, Margaret
and Mark [looks up, giggles]—are going to get married and Colleen
is the minister.

Carole wacey
It's actually kind of interesting cuz it's the year 2000 and I can
remember thinking when I was a young girl: '2000, I'll be 33 and I'll
be married, I'll probably have children.' And I'm not and I don't and
it is what it is.

Mikah larsen
Barbie is wearing a wedding dress, a veil, and a ring, and the ring is
blue and it's borrowed and you have to have something borrowed

and something blue and the ring is both blue *and* borrowed. Her earrings are old and her dress and her veil are new. This is the only stuff I have for Ken, so...[Performs ceremony]. Then they'd run out of the church and go into the limousine. [Confidential.] (I've seen that in the movies.)

Sarah blustain (age 31)
If you ask women, they *do* say they've dressed up their Barbie dolls and they had a Ken doll—maybe you had a Ken doll?—do the proposing; I never did that—I don't know—I can not tell you—Maybe there's some lurking pathology—why I never responded that way.
I think most women look at [weddings] and say 'this is coming to me, this is *my* day, to dress up, to be the center of attention, to be a virgin.' It didn't matter how many boyfriends you had, or if you had been a heroin addict, on that day you were a blushing bride.

Ana levenson (age 42)
I wanted someone who wanted to have a family the way I wanted to have—who had family values and somebody who let me love him as much as I could and somebody with whom I could feel here was a balance—a balance and an equilibrium—like a non-complicated thing—like "yes, we'll be together for the rest of our lives and that's the way it will be and that's perfect." I was asking for a lot and I found it.

For many people, women in particular, wedding fantasies blossom in seasons of transition. This is the case in Carson McCullers' coming of age novel, *The Member of the Wedding.* Twelve-year-old Frankie's curious wedding fantasy opens doors for her—as surely as any wedding usher opens doors for the traditional bride into the church or temple:

Frankie sat at the table with her eyes half closed, and she thought about a wedding. She saw a silent church, a strange snow slanting down against the colored windows. The groom in this wedding was her brother and there was a brightness where his face should be. The bride was there in a long, white train, and the bride was also faceless. There was something about this wedding that gave Frankie a feeling she could not name.[1]

Frankie, ready for a change, imagines that as a "member of the wedding," she will be able to start afresh in Winter Hill, far away from her hometown in which she is stigmatized as a freak who "smells bad." In her fantasy, Frankie's name becomes Jasmine, so that it matches the J. names of her brother, John, and her sister-in-law, Jarvis. Post wedding, Frankie presumably will not have to suffer the potential loneliness or lesser status of being a solitary stranger in a strange land. Her fantasy, however, does not lack adventure. Given that Frankie is from the hot South, the imagery of her daydream, the "strange white snow," bespeaks her longing for virgin territory to explore. *Strange* white snow suggests that this is the territory of her inner world as well as her outer one. What better way to mark the need for a new identity, a new situation, perhaps a new community, than with the "strangeness" of a ceremony, an event set apart from the lives or the selves we are trying to leave?

Unlike the traditional wedding, Frankie's fantasy opens doors and then leaves them open. There is "brightness" where her brother's face should be; her sister-in-law remains "faceless."

As a member of the wedding, Frankie can fill the groom's position, the bride's position, or neither. The *snow* is virginal, Frankie does not have to be. The first letter of Frankie's new first name matches those of her partners, however, it is still her name alone, and she alone chooses it. No one proposes marriage to Frankie—she proposes it to herself. As a member of the wedding, Frankie gains security and excitement, shelter and possibility, social acceptance as a woman, and social freedom as a woman. If this is what weddings and marriage were about, who would not want to be married?

Episode 2: The Proposal

Helen sosnoski (92)
He told me that he loved me very much and all and that he'd like me to be a wife to him and a mother to his children and he'd like to make me happy the best he could.

Karen sosnoski
Do you remember what you said?

Helen sosnoski
[Laughing.] That I don't remember.

Ana levenson
So I put all the time I needed and I read more than 200 plus profiles and I liked only one from all of them—I liked only, absolutely one, and that was my husband, my now husband, Howie.
[But I was] going back to my old habit of being contacted by a guy. I got five or six messages a day—I got very, very busy, meeting people, answering people, ten or twelve of them. What happened, the very first day we could see it wasn't going to work out. It takes, oh, ugh, five seconds, or less. Remember you know so much about the guys already—you even know how much he's making...all the

basics you know—then you go for the chemistry—that sparkle—you hope to have that the first time you see. You go there and you say 'Oh my Gosh,' you have to spend fifteen minutes or two hours to have coffee with this guy who I *knew* I don't want to spend my life with him.

Sarah blustain

The first thing we did was like he gave me that ring and it was like 'I got you this ring' [a peach candy ring] and it was so unlike a regular proposal that I was really happy and I reacted in this weird intellectual way like I normally would and I went to the OED and looked up the word 'wife' and in hindsight, I ask 'What was I thinking?' you know, because as cynical as I may be or not interested in…like the first response to run to the dictionary seems a bit crazy to me you know but we looked up 'wife' and it was like, 'alewife,' and 'fishwife' and I don't know, I didn't like 'wife' so much.

Ana levenson

For the first time in my life I decided to contact a guy and take the initiative for the first time in my life…to follow my instincts because before I'd had them but I'd never listen to them. I went right for it, I said [to Howie], 'let's have our cup of coffee.' And we didn't even talk on the phone. So we met on November 23rd at 8:00 am. in Santa Monica and that was it! That was it! We got married on October 16th 1998 with very few friends in L.A. and last year our families came and we got married again with a rabbi and here we are. [Proud.]

Sarah blustain

I started noticing how many couples there are who have been together for years like you two have and she wanted to get married but she wouldn't ask. What we do is we wait and we wait and we wait until the man—sorry to be so gender specific here—until *he* does the asking …. I don't necessarily buy this thing that men don't want to get married. If these men are getting down on their knees, then they've got to want it to some extent.

Patrick mcgann (age 45)

I was never a kind of romantic type I guess, at least not in that [down on the knees proposal] type of way, but I didn't have a good alternative, so I just. I don't know.

In the summer of 1999, like an older version of Carson McCullers' Frankie, I was beginning to feel in need of a new start and a ceremony to mark it. I had just finished my doctoral dissertation and come off of a year of an extra heavy teaching load. Tired of seeing my identity based, for better or worse, on what I had accomplished or failed to accomplish, I vowed to enter a new, more relationship-oriented phase of my life. I was 34, and my partner of eighteen (then) years, Fred, and I were considering whether or not to start a family. I had begun reconnecting with family members and old friends. While I had always resisted marriage on feminist grounds, I began to reconsider my views. Why not get married and celebrate something, a relationship, that in the long run was more important to me than my dissertation or any other achievement? I bought Fred a ring, wrote him a poem, and awkwardly but purposefully, got down on my knee. Fred was embarrassed to see me acting like a stranger. He asked me how much the ring cost, entreated me to stand up, wondered how I could have forgotten to chill the champagne. He joked about needing a manicure; but then, as if he too were following a script, he accepted.

I knew that Fred was already a "we of me" if not necessarily *the* "we of me," but as in the case of Frankie, the wedding ceremony and its implications for my future identity, both as an individual and as a partner with Fred, remained fuzzy and strange. At first, I liked it this way and so did Fred. We had always prided ourselves on being different from our friends, set apart by our serious relationship at a young age (17) when no one else was serious, and by our casual, easy relationship (at 34), while most of the other couples we knew seemed driven to climb relationship "steps." We did not realize how difficult it might be for us to maintain our sense of difference or how likely it was that this sense of difference itself might be illusory.

Episode 3: 'Singles' Count their Blessings

Charlie wiss (age 42)
I think when I was a teenager and early twenties and mid twenties, the thought of marriage never really occurred to me. I mean I knew it was something that people did and I'm pretty sure my parents did it, so you know the concept was like right in front of me all the time but it never really occurred to me as something I was going to do in that present incarnation of Charlie.

Margaret waldock (age 32)
There's this kind of Cinderella story that's fed to you as a little kid…. I think my parents tried not to foster that—but it comes from every direction in our culture this whole you get through childhood and adolescence and then when you become an adult woman, one of your goals should be to find a husband and then that part of your life starts.

Charlie wiss
I'd had a string of girlfriends and several of them were very interested in getting married to me but I just wasn't in that mindset and usually

we hit the nine month mark or so and they'd kind of want to up the commitment level and it was usually about then that I would flake.

Margaret waldock
I've definitely been in some long term relationships where you've been in the honeymoon period in the beginning and you sort of toy with that idea, 'oh wouldn't it be great to get married.'

Charlie wiss
So then I went through a period of kind of thinking 'oh, I bypassed all of these chances And maybe now I'm too old or something and I shouldn't have put it off for so long and maybe now I'll never find anybody.'

Margaret waldock
I definitely feel a lot of pressure. I've never gotten to the point where I've actually wanted to do it.

Charlie wiss
Now more recently things have taken another interesting turn in that that feeling has completely gone away and I've started to think maybe I really don't want to get married. It seems more of the marriages I am in close contact with are unhappy rather than happy, sorry to say, so I in some ways count my blessings.

Margaret waldock
The best things about being single? If you value being alone, you definitely have time for that.

Charlie wiss
I do things in a certain way and a certain order and certainly I would have to change some of that or a lot of that if I got married.

Margaret waldock
If you have an idea of how you want to progress through life you can do that, and there's no body else making demands on you.

Charlie wiss
I'd have to give up the thrill of being with somebody new, the nervousness of wondering if they like me, the excitement of finding out that they do like me, the thrill of kind of touching and being close with somebody for the first time. I think that's what you give up when you get married.

When Fred and I announced our engagement, our level of creative control over our relationship and related dreams changed—immediately. The bride and groom took on faces: our own, and others could see those faces even if we could not. Strangers pawed us at Fred's brothers' weddings (two that summer), badgering us to give them a date. Per standard wedding book advice, Fred and I began looking a year in advance for a wedding site. Unfortunately, the most appropriate wedding sites for a big wedding in VA are former slave plantations—how would we feel, we wondered, pledging everlasting love on a site of former slavery? We also found ourselves put off by the expectations of wedding site planners and caterers; every single one of them addressed their sales pitches at me, the "lucky bride," even though Fred plans the parties in our relationship. It became clear that a casual outdoor wedding could cost us over $20,000. Tension mounted as we imagined my modest, reserved, puritanical family and his larger than life, extroverted, wealthy family helping to facilitate our plans.

One night, in the middle of a fight about a wedding we had not even planned yet, Fred suggested: "enough." We agreed that if I cried or he swore once more, the wedding was off. To make a short engagement story shorter: I cried, he swore, and after a month of life on Fred's finger, the $900 engagement ring was put away as a reminder of how easy it is to turn a living relationship into a mediocre drama.

Fred and I grew confused that "engagement summer" as our usual patterns of relating to each other and to the idea of "being a couple" were stretched and warped into a new form by outside and inner pressure to marry "right." In response to perceived pressure, we began to throw out vague disclaimers.

—Fred, at a family member's wedding in Newport: "We're going to get married on a mountain top alone."

—Fred's mother: "That's what you think. I'm going to hire a personal trainer and climb with you—or parachute down, one way or another I'll be there."

I saw no point in getting married if not to have a ceremony that included loved ones, and while I took Fred's mother at her word, I could not see my shy parents making a spectacle of themselves by descending on our private ritual in parachutes. I suggested to Fred that we take a trip around the country visiting family and old friends—that we could consider this as our communion with them before doing the equivalent of walking down an aisle. Instead of walking down the aisle, however, I thought, we could climb a mountain. This would be a symbol of the journey we wanted to continue to take together. I was unclear where a wedding fit in or what the end goal of all this symbolism was. In our lack of clarity was hope. In the middle of the August heat that had begun to close around us like a wedding dress and suit, a daydream of strange snow slanting against colored windows returned to cool us.

Episode 4: Second Thoughts

Jeff drake (age 37)
I think the ideal there would be to have a partner for life and a complete—someone who's completely supportive of me and someone I'm completely supportive of.

Sharon hanscomb (age 33)
I had romantic notions about falling in love and getting married and having some kind of perfect husband that was going to take care of me. My mother always, I think she tended to encourage that in both my sister and I.

Jeff drake
I'm thirty-seven years old and I'm single.

Sharon hanscomb
I was twenty-two years old when I got married.

Jeff drake
I imagine that it's just a joyous thing to know that that person's going to be there for you for the rest of your life.

Sharon hanscomb
I found it very appealing to be with somebody who would always take care of me.

Jeff drake
I hesitate to speak for all men on many issues, but I think I can on this one. We don't plan weddings, at least not until we've got an engagement ring or someone we know we want to have an engagement ring for.

Sharon hanscomb
For women it's validation, it's like 'I've got a ring, I'm engaged,' and then the thing that people want to know, 'well what's the size of it?' 'How big is the diamond?' So you either have pride in the size of the diamond that the man has bought you, or you feel humiliated that it is small.

Jeff drake
What the ceremony's going to look like would probably not be something I'd have a really strong opinion about.

Sharon hanscomb
I think I got caught up in the planning of the wedding and the excitement and the people feeling very happy for me. Here I am

marrying somebody who is handsome, he's smart, he's college educated, he has a good job, he makes money. And a lot of money's being put into the wedding itself, people are flying in all over the place to attend.

Jeff drake
Sometimes that question pops up in my head, like 'am I able to live with someone else and be happy?' And what I say to myself is, 'yes, it's just a matter of finding that person that I really want to be with all the time.'

Sharon hanscomb
And it wasn't until I got back from this very elaborate honeymoon that I thought, 'oh my god, I don't know what I've done, I don't know what I've done to my life.'

Fred jumped on my idea of the nonwedding. He thought it could be a film, and so, we conceived our idea to create a documentary, "Wedding Advice." Were we alone in our ambivalence about weddings and marriage? We figured our documentary would answer this question or if not would at least help put it in a larger social context.

To these ends, we put our "wedding budget" toward the buying of film equipment and channeled my need for socializing into scheduling interviews with family, friends, and "experts"—of varied ages, races, religions, sexual orientations, and with varied relationships with marriage as an institution. We filmed over 100 interviews with people who directly or indirectly have influenced our thinking about marriage. Each interview concludes with my summarizing Fred's and my story and asking the interviewee for advice. "Is there any reason why Fred and I should wed?" Implied is the traditional rejoinder: "speak now or forever hold your peace."

Our interviewees, even friends who know us well, often ask if *we* think there is a reason not to wed. One problem that both of us have with "marriage" is that it is an exclusionary institution. For Fred, this means that marriage excludes our gay, lesbian, and also single heterosexual friends and that it glorifies the wealth of those (including us) that can afford the perfect wedding. I agree these are problems, but for me the issue feels more personal. Despite the fact that from the outside looking in, Fred's and my relationship is "normal," neither of us feels comfortable with normative ways of talking about marriage as "the next step," or as a coup for the woman, a chaining of the man. Neither of us wants to "settle down"—ever. In these respects, we are similar to the people Michael Warner imagines in *The Trouble with Normal*, people of very unremarkable gender identity, object choice, *and* sexual practice [who] might still passionately identify with and associate with queer people. Subjectively, they feel nothing of the normalcy that might be attributed to them.[2]

Warner perceptively points out that even an expanded catalog of identities can remain blind to the ways people suffer, often indiscriminately, from gendered norms, object-orientation norms, norms of sexual practice, and norms of subjective identification…it is possible to have a concrete sense of being in the same boat with people who may not share your sexual tastes at all—people who have had to survive the penalties of dissent from the norms of straight culture, for reasons that may be as various as the people themselves.[3]

Warner critiques marriage as a normative institution and suggests that to expand the institution to include gays and lesbians will not necessarily make it more freeing. With less of a social emphasis and more of a psychological emphasis, Dalma Heyn (1997) argues in *Marriage Shock* that women, in particular, may feel compelled to give up their identities in marriage in order to fit their own internalized images of "good wives." Although Warner argues against marriage, while Heyn seeks to reinterpret it, both authors' arguments allowed me, a heterosexual woman with extreme discomfort about the institution, to better understand my feelings. Additionally, the interviewing process led me to see firsthand that many apparently "normative" people resent or fear the rigid gender and sexual roles assigned to them, particularly when they marry. This fear and resentment do not necessarily make them "commitment-phobes."

Episode 5: Marriage Scripts

Jason katsapetses (age 33)
Funny thing, I grew up on a construction site, all my summers as a kid, I mean construction workers have their own language, their own coffee break discussions, their own lunch break discussions about, you know, 'Oh my old Lady' they'd call their wife and they'd always look at me as you know, you know, my father's boy, the son on the construction site, 'you're so lucky, you're single, you've got your whole life ahead of you.'

Matt klam (age 36)
I felt when I was going to other people's weddings that it was a certain kind of victim hood that I was made a part of. Then as we got closer, I felt like in writing about it or dredging up notes about it I was kind of staving off what was about to happen, and—you know—I think a lot of my writing was a hysterical defense, you

know, it was an hysterical *reaction*—'I don't want to be some plastic guy on a wedding cake' and 'I want to be me. Not some corny archetype of a groom.'

Abby wilkerson (age 43)
Being apparently heterosexual—whatever context I'm in, people tend to make assumptions about me. Like if they know Pat is my partner. Part of me is always being wiped out of the picture. And in some contexts, people perceive me as lesbian, and then they find out I'm married and they're like, 'what's she trying to pull?'

Jason katsapetses
So I portrayed [sic] marriage as not the greatest thing in the world, as this boring life that these *men* would always complain about and a beautiful realtor would go by and they'd all be whistling and it's stereotypical but it happens and I'm like 'geez, you know, maybe marriage gets *stale*—eventually you *do* find this young lady and you have *fun* and you go out and you party and you drink and you ...but once the kids come and once the burden of bills come and everything else.'

Helen sosnoski (age 92)
My mother wouldn't let me [work after marriage,] my father wouldn't let me. They said, my 'place was in the home.' Even Dad, before I wanted to go to work, before Edward was born, he said, 'No!' [she shouts this,] he says, 'Stay home.' That's why I cried so much in sixth grade [when she was pulled out of school] because I wanted to go to school instead of staying home. I wanted to be a teacher or a nurse! I couldn't. [Crosses her arms, humphs.] I wasn't the boss. My Dad was the boss.

Matt klam
I think one of the unfortunate things is you don't always do that, you know, what you need to do to keep yourself together ...instead, you sit down at the dinner table with a *can* of something and you say 'what happened to you today?' and all of the sudden you find yourself in some script.

Alice tracey (age 60)
By the time the wedding day arrived, my mother and her sisters had things pretty well organized and it was almost as if one were a character in a play. And you just sort of follow your role and my role was to be the bride and so that's what you do.

Helen sosnoski
I was told not to have any more children. I had toximia and I went into convulsions, you know, when I went into labor, they thought

I was going to be gone after that [lowers her eyes.] And my mother says, she says, 'don't have any more children if you can help it.' Well I didn't know nothing about trying to avoid not having any more children! [Looks up, indignant.] I didn't know about these things, nobody told me about, my parents didn't talk about things like that. [She had two more children after her first.]

Matt klam
I think we're dealing with the heart of the issue here [which] is people losing themselves, in something larger, some societal thing, which is big and takes you away from yourself. I don't think anybody enjoys that.
I mean I think the *first* time a man is asked to take the, um, flipper for the barbecue and walk over there to watch the burgers, you start to feel this strange wiring, you know, all the sudden it gets to be this very serious business. Or you feel your father or your grandfather or their ghosts standing over you saying, 'You're cooking it too much!' You know you have to do this to make sure it doesn't stick.

Abby wilkerson
Marriage is not a limitation in terms of how I live my life, but I've had problems with being mis-recognized and that's really frustrating.

Alice tracey
I think that's one thing about the world today that's better that more couples do have a more realistic idea of what they're doing rather than this happily ever after.

Like many *married* couples, Fred and I promise to work together as partners. We have well-earned confidence that we can keep this promise for the rest of our lives. The terms of our partnership, however, are less stable. He is not always my first emotional or financial or social responsibility—or visce versa. By the same token, we have chosen to stay in a monogamous relationship for many, many years, but this does not mean that we stopped growing or learning or expanding our sexual horizons in our teens, when we met. Neither of us encompasses the entirety of the other's sexuality, fantasy, or related sensuality and affection. For better and worse, as many of our interviewees assert, there can be no "happy ending" to the stories or relationships of people who are still alive and growing and in this sense, marriage, which promises to close a chapter on one's "single" life, is misleading. Marriage legitimizes some forms of sexuality and gender identity over others. This can create self-division and conflict where otherwise there is multiplicity and possibility. If Fred and I are to wed, our emotional and financial partnership will be recognized, yes, but the law and society at large will more easily ignore the competing demands on our duty, imagination, and emotion. These demands make our lives complicated, at times confusing, but certainly rich.

While we found ourselves frustrated and floundering in our early efforts to create a wedding, Fred and I have felt doors opening in the process of interviewing for "Wedding Advice." The interviews themselves reflect the richness, complexity, complication, and depth that we value in others. In creating our film, we have begun to create a community of witnesses to and models for our relationship, people (or at least aspects of people) each of us might consider, to borrow Frankie's term, "the we of me." This community results from our personal and professional partnership but is not exclusive—either of "others" or of those "other" parts of ourselves and our relationship that do not fit the gender, sexual, or social norms we associate with marriage.

Episode 6: The Ceremony

> Pat mcgann
> Getting married is just weird anyway. The wedding, marriage, it's all weird.

> Abby wilkerson
> Yeah, I don't think we sorted out how to make it ours and what to do to make the marriage ours, and it just affected our relationship for a while, like maybe a year or so. It made everything weird getting married...

> Karen sosnoski
> What made it weird?

> Pat mcgann/Abby wilkerson
> Everything!

> Pat mcgann
> Just about everything.
> What *didn't* [make it weird]? The way I was dressed, well, uh, I had some sort of pinstripe suit which I never wore again after I got married.

> Abby wilkerson
> You wore it to a funeral, somebody's funeral—you wore it once.

> Pat mcgann
> Maybe, I mean I bought it solely for the wedding [shrugs] and it was just, you know, jut what I thought I was supposed to do. [Resigned, disappointed in himself, even momentarily sad.]

So I did it. [Looks at Abby.]
And the ring! By the time we went and bought the ring—I'd never
worn rings before, I'd never worn any sort of jewelry before, so that
was kind of weird and, I don't know, it felt like this sort of bizarre
kind of 'Now I'm a husband'—what the hell was that? You know and
the ring was sort of a symbol of that and not only *that* but I'd lost so
much weight by then? That, you know, from the diabetes, that it did-
n't fit? [Begins to wave his wand around to demonstrate.] It would
jangle around on my finger all the time to make me even more conscious of it, there was that and there were other things, I don't know.
[Looks at Abby.] You can talk about your weirdness. [They laugh.]

Abby wilkerson
Thanks.
Well, I was wearing my mother's dress and um and this was not my
mother's idea, it was my idea and I think maybe what I was trying to
do was somehow get her approval and, or something if I wore her
dress then she would buy into the whole thing or something and it
didn't particularly work—and it was weird wearing that dress, every
thing was weird and it was just like suddenly we were these. [stops,
can't think of the word.]

Pat mcgann
Pod People.

Abby wilkerson
Pod People!

Pat mcgann
I don't remember anything about the vows.

Abby wilkerson
I *do* remember that we got him *not* to introduce us as Mr. and Mrs.
Pat McGann since I wasn't taking Pat's name. He'd never done that
before. He was perfectly willing but he didn't *quite* know what to do
instead.

Our interviewing process for "Wedding Advice" feels ceremonial. There
is the twenty minutes to half an hour (sometimes longer) of nervous flut-
tering as Fred sets up the camera equipment. There is the sharing of old stories, the advice. There are the meals or drinks or simple conversations that
we enjoy with our interviewees post interview. More than that, however, and
more than I think I could gain from a traditional marriage, there is a sense of
peace that comes from taking the time to truly listen to other people explain
their life choices and lack of choice, their loves and disappointments. Mid

interview, a shift usually occurs as my mind clears and I am in the moment. Correspondingly, I often see the interviewees' faces soften, become younger and truer as they realize they can answer my questions, that they know themselves. Fred and I leave these interview sessions feeling tremendously grateful, a feeling that resonates in our day-to-day relationship with each other in a way that the stress of "one perfect day," one day of perfect self-consciousness, probably would not.

After months of filming, with our film itself in progress, we still are not sure whether we will marry. Regardless of my doubts about the value of the institution, I do not judge heterosexual people for marrying or gay and lesbian people for fighting to marry. As many of our interviewees point out, marriage offers real benefits (medical, social, and financial). While I do not see why these benefits should be limited to people who choose to live as twosomes, it is possible that I will marry, selfishly, to shore up these privileges for myself and my children. I will not do so without recognizing the cost to me and to others.

Fred and I will not have a white wedding ceremony. For us, interviews with friends, family, and "experts" have been our ceremony, one that reflects our need for the sacred and the set apart in every day of our lives, not just one day. Our interviewees have been tremendously honest and self-aware in revealing the fault lines, inconsistencies, and vulnerabilities in this legal and social system, marriage. It would be possible for one to respond to these fault lines with fear, "recovering from them" or even sealing them over to keep "others" out. Those who care to, however—and many men and women we have interviewed do care to—may hack away at these weak spots, creating space for doors, windows, and alliances.

Episode 7: Excerpted Wedding Advice

Matt klam
Right before my grandfather died, I went to visit him, two weeks before, and I'm Jewish, and I was worried—Lara's not Jewish, in fact her Uncles fought for the Nazis, her mom's from Dresden, they had to fight—and I'm sitting there feeling guilty because I'm not doing this *thing*, you know I'm not *forcing my fiance to convert*, I'm not suggesting it, I'm not looking for a Jewish woman—
And I said something to my grandfather, after—she had just called and we were talking for a minute and—I got off the phone, and I said, 'but she's not Jewish.' And he said, 'Do you see what you're doing? You're putting a division where there isn't any'—and he just meant you got two people, don't try to throw something into the mix that doesn't belong there.

So maybe you two guys don't need that? Maybe you got married when you were seventeen? Maybe it all seems redundant to you.

Abby wilkerson
I wouldn't presume to tell you or anybody else what you should do.

Pat mcgann
We could, I guess, speak in terms of ourselves more easily.
I'd say make sure that you're going to enjoy it. If you're going to start off, if you have a ceremony like that it's always a start—I think it's really important to make it yours.

With us, I don't think anybody really—but I don't think we had a concept or felt the need to do that.

Don't let the ceremony kind of get in the way of what you've already got. A ceremony should be a ceremony of what you already have.

Ana levenson
The very first thing, because of my experience, is don't lie to yourself, don't lie to yourself, whatever you feel don't hide from yourself, listen to what you know and what you need.

Carole wacey
You should ask your friends to help you out anyway. I love you both. I think this could be a great journey for you instead of spending the next year going from wedding mill to wedding mill wondering if the correct shade of sea shell pink is just so …whatever you decide, I'll go with you to pick out the big white wedding dress—if you decide not to get married—whatever you guys want. I'm here for you.

Kim zeytoonjian (Jason's fiance)
My question back to you would be: 'why not?' If you're saying you're committed, what's the issue in not getting married?

Jason katsepesis
We're trying to downplay the whole thing and have a big party.

Kim zeytoonjian
It doesn't mean that you love anybody more or less. It could be very superficial. We went looking for a wedding band, the guy said, 'this doesn't matter'—it's not about the rings, it's about you two …

I'm actually maybe a little embarrassed to say that it's really fun trying on the wedding dresses. Once you put on the dress and your mother starts crying. It makes me feel really good. And I know that my father would have really liked to see it. I never clipped a picture before, now I've got a whole notebook. I go on the internet: 'What color should my veil be?' It's actually a little sick! But it's fun. People should do what ever they want to do. There's a lot of people involved—how much it means to your parents and everybody else?

Sarah blustain
I think that I would say it to you because you've been together even longer [than her friends] that you stayed 'single'—single in the public way, or in the policy way (I don't know, here we are in Washington) for all this time for a reason and if you get married you'll also get married for a reason and it has nothing to do with your 'track record' as you know, that you decided just to be partners for life and not get married. [She says to do what's easiest for us and our future kids, whether that means staying unmarried or marrying.]

Helen sosnoski
Yeah, I know, [you've been together] almost ten years.

Karen sosnoski
Eighteen years.

Helen sosnoski
Well, all right, almost nineteen years, I'm wrong, but I thought ten, at least in my memory. To me I think you're foolish for waiting that long because in case you are married and you intend to have children—or maybe you don't—but if God blesses you with one, you wouldn't throw it away would you? [She explains why waiting so long to have children is not a good thing.]

I figure it's not my life, it's her life and his life. I don't interfere in anybody's life. It's like Edward [their oldest son] got converted without our knowledge. Afterward, we found the thing on the desk under the typewriter, after he was married already. Dad says, 'See what he did?' 'Well, I said, what can I do? I can't undo it now.' [Laughs, hides her face.] So I says, 'so…. God is everywhere,' I told Dad. [Laughs, shrugs, pleased with herself.] Well I had to do the best explanation to him the best I could!

References

Heyn, Dalma. 1997. *Marriage shock: The transformation of women into wives.* New York: Dell Publishing.
McCullers, Carson. 1947; reprinted 1987. The member of the wedding, in *Collected stories of Carson McCullers*, pp. 255–392. Boston: Houghton Mifflin Company.

Warner, Michael. 1999. *The trouble with normal sex, politics, and the ethics of queer life.* New York: The Free Press.

Notes

1. McCullers 1947: 258
2. 1999: 37
3. 1999: 37

Steven Seidman Essay

Film	Year	Box Office Gross
1. Advise and Consent	1962	45th Top Money-Maker of 1962 ($2,000,000)
2. The Children's Hour	1961	48th Top Money-Maker of 1962 ($1,800,000)
3. The Group	1966	37th Top Money-Maker of 1966 ($3,000,000)
4. Midnight Cowboy	1969	16th Top Money-Maker of 1970 ($4,036,491)
5. Pawnbroker	1965	42nd Top Money-Maker of 1965 ($2,500,000)
6. All That Jazz	1979	16th Top Money-Maker of 1980 ($20,000,000)
7. Anderson Tapes	1971	17th Top Money-Maker of 1971 ($5,000,000)
8. Blazing Saddles	1973	6th Top Money-Maker of 1974 ($16,500,000)
9. Boys in the Band	1970	25th Top Money-Maker of 1970 ($3,216,380)
10. Car Wash	1976	49th Top Money-Maker of 1976 ($4,190,000)
11. Dog Day Afternoon	1975	7th Top Money-Maker of 1976 ($19,800,000)
12. Five Easy Pieces	1970	31th Top Money-Maker of 1970 ($2,637,000)
13. Julia	1977	Box office Bomb ($1,000,000)

Film	Year	Box Office Gross
14. Looking For Mr. Goodbar	1977	31th Top Money-Maker of 1977 ($9,087,240)
15. Manhattan	1979	19th Top Money-Maker of 1979 ($16,908,439)
16. Next Stop, Greenwich Village	1976	109th Top Money-Maker of 1976 ($1,061,000)
17. Ode to Billy Joe	1976	15th Top Money-Maker of 1976 ($10,400,00)
18. American Gigolo	1980	28th Top Money-Maker of 1980 ($11,500,000)
19. Cruising	1980	49th Top Money-Maker of 1980 ($6,990,890)
20. Desert Hearts	1985	145th Top Money-Maker of 1986 ($1,233,637)
21. Making Love	1982	53rd Top Money-Maker of 1982 ($6,100,000)
22. Personal Best	1982	102nd Top Money-Maker of 1982 ($3,000,000)
23. Silkwood	1983	23rd Top Money-Maker of 1984 ($17,800,000)
24. St. Elmo's Fire	1985	24th Top Money-Maker of 1985 ($16,343,197)
25. Sudden Impact	1983	10th Top Money-Maker of 1984 ($34,600,000)
26. Torch Song Trilogy	1988	111th Top Money-Maker of 1989 ($2,500,000)
27. Ace Ventura: Pet Detective	1994	15th Top Money-Maker of 1994 ($72,217,396)
28. Basic Instinct	1992	8th Top Money-Maker of 1992 ($53,000,000)
29. Billy Bathgate	1991	84th Top Money-Maker of 1991 ($7,000,000)
30. Boys On The Side	1994	76th Top Money-Maker of 1995 ($23,440,188)
31. Chasing Amy	1997	121th Top Money-Maker of 1997 ($12,027,147)
32. Falling Down	1993	35th Top Money-Maker of 1993 ($40,903,593)
33. Father of the Bride	1991	30th Top Money-Maker of 1991 ($19,000,000)
34. Go Fish	1994	180th Top Money-Maker of 1994 ($2,408,311)

Film	Year	Box Office Gross
35. Higher Learning	1995	39th Top Money-Maker of 1995 ($38,290,723)
36. In and Out	1997	9th Top Money-Maker of 1998 ($63,826,569) [Preliminary gross]
37. Jeffrey	1995	184th Top Money-Maker of 1995 ($3,487,767)
38. Kiss Me Guido	1998	(No Numbers)
39. Longtime Companion	1990	131th Top Money-Maker of 1990 ($2,200,000)
40. Mo' Money	1992	39th Top Money-Maker of 1992 ($19,200,000)
41. My Best Friend's Wedding	1997	6th Top Money-Maker of 1997 ($126,713,608)
42. My Own Private Idaho	1991	137th Top Money-Maker of 1991 ($2,550,000)
43. Object of My Affection	1998	(No Numbers)
44. Philadelphia	1993	14th Top Money-Maker of 1994 ($76,878,958)
45. Set It Off	1996	44th Top Money-Maker of 1996 ($34,325,720)
46. The Incredibly True Adventure of Two Girls in Love	1995	213th Top Money-Maker of 1995 ($1,977,544)
47. Threesome	1994	100th top Money-Maker of 1994 ($14,815,317)

About the Contributors

Amy L. Best is Assistant Professor of Sociology at San Jose State University. Associate Professor of Sociology at George Mason University. Her research focuses on youth identity formation and popular culture. She is author of *Prom night: youth, schools and popular culture,* which was selected for the *2002 American Educational Studies Association Critics' Choice Award.* She is currently completing a second book on kids and cars (NYU Press).

Chris Brickell is a lecturer in the Gender and Women's Studies Programme at the University of Otago in Dunedin, New Zealand, and his research interests include gender, sexuality, and consumer culture as well as sociologies and histories of representation. His writing has appeared in several edited collections and a number of journals, including *Gender, Place and Culture, Sexualities, Journal of Consumer Culture,* and *Journal of Design History.*

Carrie L. Cokely is Assistant Professor of Sociology at Meredith College in Raleigh, North Carolina, specializing in social inequality and cultural studies.

Laurie Essig has contributed to *Legal Affairs,* NPR's "All Things Considered," and *Salon.com.* She is the author of *Queer in Russia* (Duke) and teaches sociology at the University of Vermount.

Robert Heasley is Associate Professor of Sociology at Indiana University of Pennsylvania where he teaches courses on sexuality, and men and masculinity. He has worked extensively with men on issues of intimacy, relationships, sexuality and violence. His publications include *Sexual lives: A reader on the theories and realities of human sexualities* (co-edited with Betsy Crane).

Chrys Ingraham is Associate Professor of Sociology at Russell Sage College in Troy, NY where she specializes in gender, sexuality, race, and class, social responsibility, women's studies, and theory. She is also Director of Women's Studies and coordinates The Helen M. Upton Center. An international expert in critical heterosexual studies, her publications include *White Weddings: Romancing Heterosexuality in Popular Culture* (Routledge 1999) and *Materialist Feminism: A Reader in Class, Difference and Women's Lives* (with Rosemary Hennessy) (Routledge 1997) and book chapters in *The Handbook of Gender and Women's Studies* (Sage), *The Handbook of Lesbian and Gay Studies* (Sage), *Sexualities* (McGraw-Hill), and *Queer Theory/Sociology* (Blackwell).

Stevi Jackson is Professor of Sociology and Director of the Centre for Women's Studies at the University of York, U.K. and is an international expert on heterosexuality, gender, feminist theory, and the sociology of childhood. Her many books include *Childhood and sexuality, Women's studies: A reader* (co-edited); *Christine Delphy, feminism and sexuality* (co-edited with Sue Scott), *Contemporary feminist theories* (co-edited with Jackie Jones), and *Concerning heterosexuality*.

Diane Richardson is Professor of sociology and social policy and Director of the Centre for Gender and Women's Studies at the University of Newcastle upon Tyne, U.K. and is an international authority in the area of the sociology of sexuality, with many related publications. Her books include *Rethinking sexuality, Theorising heterosexuality*, and The handbook of lesbian and gay studies (co-edited with Steven Seidman). She has recently co-edited a special issue of the journal Sexualities and is currently working on Intersections between Feminist and Queer Theory (co-edited with Mark Casey and Janice McLaughlin).

Steven Seidman is Professor of sociology at the State University of New York at Albany, and a national and international expert on sexuality and social theory. His many books include *Beyond the closet: The transformation of gay and lesbian life, Embattled eros: Sexual politics and ethics in contemporary America, Romantic longings: Love in America, 1830–1980*, and *The handbook of lesbian and gay studies* (co-edited with Diane Richardson).

Karen Sosnoski is a freelance writer and filmmaker whose many accomplishments include the award-winning film "Wedding Advice: Speak Now or Forever Hold Your Peace" (with Fred Zeytoonjian) along with many articles, fiction, and poetry. She is completing her first novel Dreaming in the Sleepless Complex and is working on a film about Vasectomies.

Mason Stokes is Associate Professor of English at Skidmore College in Saratoga Springs, New York. He is the author of *The color of sex: Whiteness, heterosexuality, and the fictions of white supremacy*, as well as essays in *American Quarterly, Transition, Callaloo*, and *American Literary History*.

Margaret Walsh is Associate Professor of sociology and women's studies at Keene State College in New Hampshire. She specializes in stratification, families, and qualitative methods and has published a variety of articles and book chapters on rural poverty in the South, New England, and upstate New York. Her forthcoming book is titled *Taking sociology to work.*

Index

Suffix "n" attached to the page numbers refers to Notes section.